ENCYCLOPEDIA

OF

Technology and Applied Sciences

8

Plastics – Sailing

Marshall Cavendish
New York • London • Toronto • Sydney

England
Research
Fellow, Department of Materials Science and Metallurgy, University of
Cambridge, Cambridge, England

Martin Campbell-Kelly, Department of Computer Science, University of
Warwick, Coventry, England

Mark S. Coyne, Associate Professor, Department of Agronomy,
University of Kentucky, Lexington, Kentucky

R. Cengiz Ertekin, Professor, Department of Ocean Engineering,
University of Hawaii at Manoa, Honolulu, Hawaii

Donald R. Franceschetti, Ph.D., Distinguished Service Professor,
Departments of Physics and Chemistry, The University of Memphis,
Memphis, Tennessee

Colin Harding, Curator of Photographic Technology, National Museum of
Photography, Film, and Television, Bradford, England

Lee E. Harris, Ph.D., P.E., Associate Professor, Division of Marine and
Environmental Systems, Florida Institute of Technology,
Melbourne, Florida

Deborah Korenstein, Instructor in Medicine, Mount Sinai School of
Medicine, New York, New York

John Liffen, Associate Curator, The Science Museum, London, England

Robert C. Mebane, Ph.D., Professor, Department of Chemistry
University of Tennessee at Chattanooga, Chattanooga, Tennessee

Peter R. Morris, Visiting Fellow, Bath University, Bath, England

Christopher M. Pastore, Director of Research, Philadelphia College of
Textiles and Science, Philadelphia, Pennsylvania

Sunday Popo-Ola, Ph.D., Department of Civil Engineering, Imperial
College, London, England

Marc D. Rayman, Ph.D., Principal Engineer, National Aeronautics and
Space Administration (NASA) Jet Propulsion Laboratory at the
California Institute of Technology, Pasadena, California

John M. Ritz, Ph.D., Professor, Department of Occupational and
Technical Studies, Old Dominion University, Norfolk, Virginia

John Robinson, Former Curator, The Science Museum, London, England

Thomas R. Rybolt, Professor, Department of Chemistry, University
of Tennessee at Chattanooga, Chattanooga, Tennessee

Mark E. Sanders, Associate Professor, Department of Technology
Education, College of Human Resources and Education, Virginia Tech,
Blacksburg, Virginia

Anthony E. Schwaller, Ph.D., Professor, Department of Environmental
and Technological Studies, College of Science and Engineering,
St. Cloud State University, St. Cloud, Minnesota

J. Derek Smith, Ph.D., Department of Engineering, University of
Cambridge, Cambridge, England

Colin Uttley, Programmes Manager, The Science Museum, London,
England

Phil Whitfield, Professor, School of Life, Basic Medical, and Health
Sciences, King's College London, London, England

Marshall Cavendish Corporation
99 White Plains Road
Tarrytown, New York 10591-9001

© 2000 Marshall Cavendish Corporation

Created by **Brown Partworks Ltd.**

Library of Congress Cataloging-in-Publication Data

Encyclopedia of technology and applied sciences.
      p.   cm.
      Includes bibliographical references.
      Contents: 1. Abacus–Beverages—2. Bicycle–Codes and ciphers—3. Color–Engine—
4. Engineering–Gyroscope—5. Hand tools–Leather—6. Light and optics–Military communications
and control—7. Military vehicles–Plant hormone—8. Plastics–Sailing—9. Satellite–Tank—10.
Technology in ancient civilizations–Wood and woodworking—11. Indexes.
      ISBN 0-7614-7116-2 (set)
      1. Technology Encyclopedias, Juvenile. [1. Technology Encyclopedias.]
T48.E52   2000
603—dc21

                                          99-14520
                                        CIP

      ISBN 0-7614-7116-2 (set)
      ISBN 0-7614-7124-3 (vol. 8)
Printed in Malaysia
Bound in U.S.A.
      06 05 04 03 02 01 00 54321

PHOTOGRAPHIC CREDITS

The Bettmann Archive: *1123*
Canon U.K.: *1059*
Corbis: *1015:* Marc Garanger/Corbis; *1016:* Michael S. Yamashita/Corbis; *1020:* Bob Krist/Corbis;
1021: Richard Hamilton Smith/Corbis; *1023:* Philip James Corwin/Corbis; *1025:* Chinch Gryniewicz,
Ecoscene/Corbis; *1028:* The Purcell Team/Corbis; *1029:* Lowell Georgia/Corbis; *1031:* Jacqui Hurst/Corbis;
1032: Keren Su/Corbis; *1033:* Robert Estall/Corbis; *1034:* Dave G. Houser/Corbis; *1035:* Tim
Thompson/Corbis; *1037:* Neil Rabinowitz/Corbis; *1038:* Lowell Georgia/Corbis; *1040:* Corbis–Bettmann;
1042: Tim Wright/Corbis; *1044:* Yann Arthus-Bertrand/Corbis; *1045:* Corbis–Bettmann; *1046:* Buddy
Mays/Corbis; *1047:* Richard A. Cooke/Corbis; *1048:* Pierre Colombel/Corbis; *1049:* Gianni Dagli Orti/Corbis;
1050: Paul Seheult, Eye Ubiquitous/Corbis; *1053:* Jacqui Hurst/Corbis; *1055:* Corbis–Bettmann;
1057: Wolfgang Kaehler/Corbis; *1058 (top):* Science Pictures Ltd./Corbis; *1061:* Jim Sugar Photography/Corbis;
1062: Corbis; *1063:* David Lees/Corbis; *1066:* Gary Braasch/Corbis; *1071:* Charles E. Rotkin/Corbis;
1072: Paul Almasy/Corbis; *1073:* Neil Rabinowitz/Corbis; *1074:* Nik Wheeler/Corbis; *1076:* George
Hall/Corbis; *1080:* Jim Sugar Photography/Corbis; *1082:* Paul Almasy/Corbis; *1083:* Dave Bartruff/Corbis;
1084 & 1087: Colin Garratt, Milepost 92½/Corbis; *1089:* Josef Scaylea/Corbis; *1090:* Michael Maslan Historic
Photography/Corbis; *1092:* Charles E. Rotkin/Corbis; *1093:* Colin Garratt, Milepost 92½/Corbis;
1096: Jonathan Blair/Corbis; *1104:* Hulton–Deutsch/Corbis; *1105:* Amos Nachoum/Corbis; *1112:* Roger
Wood/Corbis; *1113:* Michael S. Yamashita/Corbis; *1115:* Kevin Fleming/Corbis; *1116:* Jeffry W.
Myers/Corbis; *1117 & 1118:* Joseph Sohm, ChromoSohmn Inc./Corbis; *1119:* Richard Hamilton Smith/Corbis;
1120: Yann Arthus-Bertrand/Corbis; *1121:* Bennett Dean, Eye Ubiquitous/Corbis; *1133:* Corbis–Bettmann;
1134: Hulton–Deutsch /Corbis; *1137:* Robert Landau/Corbis; *1139:* Hulton–Deutsch/Corbis; *1140:* Michael
Freeman/Corbis; *1143:* Richard Hamilton Smith/Corbis; *1145:* Bob Krist/Corbis; *1147:* Neil Rabinowitz/Corbis
Hulton Getty: *1017; 1030; 1070; 1081; 1141*
Image Bank: *1013:* Chris Close/Image Bank; *1052:* Bernard Roussel/Image Bank; *1068:* Gabriel M.
Covian/Image Bank; *1111:* Ulf E. Wallin/Image Bank; *1125:* Jon Love/Image Bank; *1142:* Gary Cralle/Image
Bank; *1144:* Stephen Marks/Image Bank; *1149:* Pete Turner/Image Bank
Image Select: *1085:* Image Select; *1086, 1091, 1100, 1122:* Ann Ronan at Image Select
Mary Evans Picture Library: *1088; 1101; 1124; 1132; 1150*
Rex Features: *1098:* Jorgensen/Rex Features
Science Photo Library: *1019:* Maximillian Stock Ltd./SPL; *1026:* Vanessa Vick/SPL; *1039:* Martin Bond/SPL;
1041: Bill Longchore/SPL; *1058 (bottom):* John Howard/SPL; *1060:* Maximilian Stock Ltd./SPL;
1064: C. S. Langlois/Publiphoto Division/SPL; *1075:* Keith Kent/SPL; *1078:* Novosti/SPL; *1094:* Takeshi
Takahara/SPL; *1097:* Dick Luria/SPL; *1107:* Adam Hart Davis/SPL; *1110:* Paul Shambroom/SPL; *1127:* Hank
Morgan/SPL; *1128:* NASA/SPL; *1129:* David Parker for ESA/SPL; *1131:* David Ducros for ESA/SPL;
1136: Seth Joel/SPL
TRH Pictures: *1027:* Eurolist/TRH Pictures; *1065:* Ford/TRH Pictures; *1067:* Rolls Royce/TRH Pictures;
1095: TRH Pictures, *1099:* SCNF/TRH Pictures; *1102, 1135, 1146:* TRH Pictures

ILLUSTRATION CREDITS
© **Marshall Cavendish Picture Library:** *1018, 1054, 1106*

Cover illustration: illustration of a communications satellite
Title page illustration: this innovative piece of architecture beneath La
Grande Arche, Paris, France, was designed by Peter Rice. It was made
using steel, glass lenses, and PTFE (Teflon). Marc Garanger/Corbis

CONTENTS

USEFUL INFORMATION

Use this table to convert the English system (or the imperial system), the system of units common in the United States (e.g., inches, miles, quarts), to the metric system (e.g., meters, kilometers, liters) or to convert the metric system to the English system. You can convert one measurement into another by multiplying. For example, to convert centimeters into inches, multiply the number of centimeters by 0.3937. To convert inches into centimeters, multiply the number of inches by 2.54.

To convert	into	multiply by
Acres	Square feet	43,560
	Square yards	4840
	Square miles	0.00156
	Square meters	4046.856
	Hectares	0.40468
Celsius	Fahrenheit	First multiply by 1.8 then add 32
Centimeters	Inches	0.3937
	Feet	0.0328
Cubic cm	Cubic inches	0.06102
Cubic feet	Cubic inches	1728
	Cubic yards	0.037037
	Gallons	7.48
	Cubic meters	0.028317
	Liters	28.32
Cubic inches	Fluid ounces	0.554113
	Cups	0.069264
	Quarts	0.017316
	Gallons	0.004329
	Liters	0.016387
	Milliliters	16.387064
Cubic meters	Cubic feet	35.3145
	Cubic yards	1.30795
Cubic yards	Cubic feet	27
	Cubic meters	0.76456
Cups, fluid	Quarts	0.25
	Pints	0.5
	Ounces	8
	Milliliters	237
	Tablespoons	16
	Teaspoons	48
Fahrenheit	Celsius	First subtract 32 then divide by 1.8
Feet	Centimeters	30.48
	Meters	0.3048
	Kilometers	0.0003
	Inches	12
	Yards	0.3333
	Miles	0.00019
Gallons	Quarts	4
	Pints	8
	Cups	16
	Ounces	128
	Liters	3.785
	Milliliters	3785
	Cubic inches	231
	Cubic feet	0.1337
	Cubic yards	0.00495
	Cubic meters	0.00379
	British gallons	0.8327
Grams	Ounces	0.03527
	Pounds	0.0022
Hectares	Square meters	10,000
	Acres	2.471
Horsepower	Foot-pounds per minute	33,000
	British thermal units (Btu) per minute	42.42
	British thermal units (Btu) per hour	2546
	Kilowatts	0.7457
	Metric horsepower	1.014
Inches	Feet	0.08333
Inches (continued)	Yards	0.02778
	Centimeters	2.54
	Meters	0.0254
Kilograms	Grams	1000
	Ounces	35.274
	Pounds	2.2046
	Short tons	0.0011
	Long tons	0.00098
	Metric tons (tonnes)	0.001
Kilometers	Meters	1000
	Miles	0.62137
	Yards	1093.6
	Feet	3280.8
Kilowatts	British thermal units (Btu) per minute	56.9
	Horsepower	1.341
	Metric horsepower	1.397
Kilowatt-hours	British thermal units (Btu)	3413
Knots	Statute miles per hour	1.1508
Leagues	Miles	3
Liters	Milliliters	1000
	Fluid ounces	33.814
	Quarts	1.05669
	British gallons	0.21998
	Cubic inches	61.02374
	Cubic feet	0.13531
Meters	Inches	39.37
	Feet	3.28083
	Yards	1.09361
	Miles	0.000621
	Kilometers	0.001
	Centimeters	100
	Millimeters	1000
Miles	Inches	63,360
	Feet	5280
	Yards	1760
	Meters	1609.34
	Kilometers	1.60934
	Nautical miles	0.8684
Miles nautical, U.S. and International	Statute miles	1.1508
	Feet	6076.115
	Meters	1852
Miles per minute	Feet per second	88
	Knots	52.104
Milliliters	Fluid ounces	0.0338
	Cubic inches	0.061
	Liters	0.001
Millimeters	Centimeters	0.1
	Meters	0.001
	Inches	0.03937
Ounces, avoirdupois	Pounds	0.0625
	Grams	28.34952
	Kilograms	0.0283495
Ounces, fluid	Pints	0.0625
	Quarts	0.03125
	Cubic inches	1.80469
	Cubic feet	0.00104
	Milliliters	29.57353
	Liters	0.02957
Pints, fluid	Ounces, fluid	16
	Quarts, fluid	0.5
Pints, fluid (continued)	Cubic inches	28.8745
	Cubic feet	0.01671
	Milliliters	473.17647
	Liters	0.473176
Pounds	Ounces	16
	Grams	453.59237
	Kilograms	0.45359
	Tons	0.0005
	Tons, long	0.000446
	Metric tons (tonnes)	0.0004536
Quarts, fluid	Ounces, fluid	32
	Pints, fluid	2
	Gallons	0.25
	Cubic inches	57.749
	Cubic feet	0.033421
	Liters	0.946358
	Milliliters	946.358
Square centimeters	Square inches	0.155
Square feet	Square inches	144
	Square meters	0.093
	Square yards	0.111
Square inches	Square centimeters	6.452
	Square feet	0.0069
Square kilometers	Hectares	100
	Square meters	1,000,000
	Square miles	0.3861
Square meters	Square feet	10.758
	Square yards	1.196
Square miles	Acres	640
	Square kilometers	2.59
Square yards	Square feet	9
	Square inches	1296
	Square meters	0.836
Tablespoons	Ounces, fluid	0.5
	Teaspoons	3
	Milliliters	14.7868
Teaspoons	Ounces, fluid	0.16667
	Tablespoons	0.3333
	Milliliters	4.9289
Tons, Long	Pounds	2240
	Kilograms	1016.047
	Short tons	1.12
	Metric tons (tonnes)	1.016
Tons, short	Pounds	2000
	Kilograms	907.185
	Long tons	0.89286
	Metric tonnes	0.907
Tons, Metric (tonnes)	Pounds	2204.62
	Kilograms	1000
	Long tons	0.984206
	Short tons	1.10231
Watts	British thermal units (Btu) per hour	3.415
	Horsepower	0.00134
Yards	Inches	36
	Feet	3
	Miles	0.0005681
	Centimeters	91.44
	Meters	0.9144

PLASTICS

Plastics are organic, polymeric materials that can be easily shaped under heat or pressure

Plastics are used in a wide variety of applications that ranges from food containers and packaging to ropes, pipes, and building materials. Since the 1950s, plastics have come to be used in place of many natural materials such as paper, wood, and metals. Plastics are so versatile because they are light, corrosion-resistant, nontoxic, and durable, as well as being good electrical and thermal insulators. Plastic objects can be produced in a multitude of forms by heating and molding, which adds to their versatility (see BUILDING TECHNIQUES, MODERN; INSULATION; METALS; METALWORKING; PACKAGING INDUSTRY).

Although most plastics are synthetic, the term *plastic*, which means "capable of being molded," also covers a few natural substances such as shellac, which is used in varnish. The starting materials for most plastics are petroleum derivatives. The increasing importance of plastics in everyday life has accompanied the growth of the petroleum industry since the 1940s. World production of plastics in 1997 was 143 million tons (130 million tonnes).

THE CHEMISTRY OF PLASTICS

Plastics belong to a broader class of materials called polymers, which are large molecules made up of many thousands of simple repeated chemical units called monomers. A polymer molecule can be thought of as being like a chain whose links are the monomers. Polymers are widespread in nature: cellulose and starch (the building materials from which plants are made and the most abundant polymers on Earth) are made up of glucose monomers. Proteins are polymers, and so is the genetic material DNA (deoxyribonucleic acid). There are also some semi-natural polymers, such as cellulose acetate, which are made by chemically modifying a natural polymer.

Polymerization

There are two principal types of polymerization reactions: addition and condensation.

Addition polymerization. Addition polymerization is used to produce the simplest synthetic polymer, polyethylene. This polymer, also called polyethene, is made by causing molecules of ethylene (ethene, $CH_2=CH_2$) to react together and form chains. The

A roll of low-density polyethylene film.

ethylene molecule is characterized by the double bond between its two carbon atoms. One of these bonds can easily break open, whereupon each carbon atom becomes free to bond with an atom outside the ethylene molecule in a process called addition. If this bonding takes place with carbon atoms from other ethylene molecules, a chain starts to build up of the form $-CH_2-CH_2-CH_2-CH_2-$.

Addition polymerization can also be used to make polymers from propylene (propene, $CH_2=CH-CH_3$), styrene (phenylethene, $CH_2=CH-C_6H_5$), acrylonitrile (propenonitrile, $CH_2=CH-CN$), and many other molecules that contain double bonds.

Condensation polymerization. Condensation polymerization produces polymers by joining together two different types of reactive chemical groups, with the simultaneous loss of simple molecules such as water. The following two reactions are examples of this process:

CONNECTIONS

- The raw materials that make plastics are products of **OIL REFINING** and the organic **CHEMICAL INDUSTRY**.

- **RUBBER** is another type of polymeric material.

A MODEL OF A POLYETHYLENE POLYMER

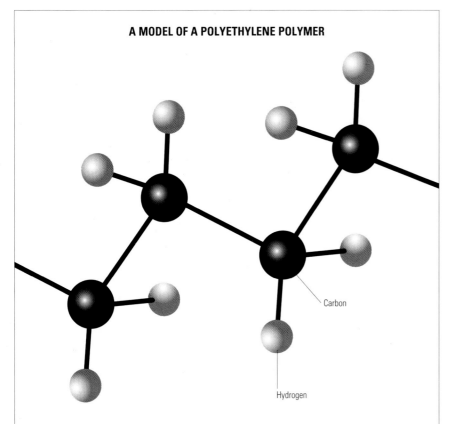

Carbon

Hydrogen

This model represents a section of the chain of a polyethylene molecule. Each sphere represents an atom. The black rods represent the bonds between the atoms.

$$-CO_2H + HO- \rightarrow -CO_2- + H_2O$$
acid + alcohol $\rightarrow$ ester + water

$$-CO_2H + H_2N- \rightarrow -CO-HN- + H_2O$$
acid + amine $\rightarrow$ amide + water

If the starting materials contain two or more reactive groups, such as the ones above, in each molecule, successive condensation reactions lead to the formation of chains and three-dimensional networks known as condensation polymers. Condensation polymers include polyesters; polyamides, such as nylon; melamine-formaldehyde resins; and phenol-formaldehyde resins, such as Bakelite. Epoxy resins are produced from epichlorohydrin and bisphenol-A (a compound with two hydroxy groups): epichlorohydrin has an epoxy group, to which a hydroxy group can be added, and a chlorine atom that can be displaced by a hydroxy in a condensation reaction.

TYPES OF PLASTICS

There are two main types of plastics: thermoplastics and thermosets. Thermoplastic materials consist of polymer molecules that are not linked together and can therefore slide over one another very easily. This means that they are easily formed into different shapes. When heated, they soften and eventually melt. Polyethylene and polyvinyl chloride (PVC) are examples of thermoplastics. Even some of the harder polymers, such as polymethyl methacrylate (PMMA, or plexiglass), are classified as thermoplastic because they become softer when heated.

Thermosets behave in a completely different way. In their original form, they contain some chemical groups that can react together when heated. As a consequence, warming a thermoset might soften it slightly until the temperature is reached where the reaction between groups starts to occur. Further heating will start to create more links between chains so that what starts off as a loosely bound net becomes a rigid, three-dimensional network.

Thermosets are useful where the hardness of the finished material is important. The polymer can be poured into a mold and then heated to encourage the formation of further links between polymers. The result is a hard object in the shape of the mold.

The properties of a plastic are also affected by a structural property called branching. In the polymerization of ethylene, for example, most of the molecules join together in straight chains. Occasionally, however, an ethylene molecule will attach itself at a point along a chain that has already been formed, starting a new chain, or branch. Branching results in T-shaped or comb-shaped polymer molecules rather than straight, or linear, chains.

Polymers that are mainly linear, such as high-density polyethylene, tend to be harder than those with branched chains, such as low-density polyethylene. This is because linear molecules tend to line up alongside each other and form solid, crystalline regions, which make the material harder and denser. Branches obstruct this type of packing, and the result is a material that is softer and less dense than a linear polymer. It is often possible to influence the extent of branching by controlling the conditions of the polymerization reaction. In this way, the properties of the final polymer can be influenced.

Polyethylene and polypropylene

Introduced in the 1930s, polyethylene is still one of the most useful plastics. It is made in two forms: low-density polyethylene (LDPE) and high-density polyethylene (HDPE). The type depends on the extent of branching of the polymer chains that occurs during the addition-polymerization reaction. LDPE is highly branched. It is a clear, flexible material but is relatively weak. It is used to make grocery bags, trash bags, and packaging, as well as to insulate electrical cables. HDPE is much less branched than LDPE. This makes it stiffer, harder, and stronger than LDPE. HDPE is mainly used to make articles such as food crates, pipes, buckets, and bowls.

Polypropylene has the same basic chain, or backbone, as polyethylene, but with a methyl ($-CH_3$) group attached in place of a hydrogen atom on every second carbon atom in the chain:

$$-[CH_2-CH_2]_x- \qquad -[CH_2-CH(CH_3)]_x-$$
polyethylene $\qquad$ polypropylene

Polypropylene is tougher than polyethylene, and is used to make a wide range of objects that exploit this property. These include margarine tubs, stacking chairs, carpets, and disposable syringes.

Polystyrene

Although polystyrene was discovered as long ago as 1839, it was not produced commercially until 1937. Polystyrene is an addition polymer with the same backbone as polyethylene, but with a phenyl (C_6H_5) group attached to every second carbon atom. It is a very hard, brittle material that is rarely used in its pure form. Most polystyrene is produced as solid beads that contain pentane (C_5H_{12}), an inert hydrocarbon that boils at 97°F (36°C). These beads are sold to processors, who use them to produce molded objects. The beads are heated to 212°F (100°C) using steam, which softens the polymer and makes the pentane boil, forming tiny bubbles inside the polymer. The beads, expanded to over 40 times their original size, are then heated again inside a mold. They expand further and fuse together to form the finished object. In time, the gas inside the bubbles diffuses out and is replaced by air.

The foamy structure of expanded polystyrene gives it three important properties. First, because the trapped air is an excellent insulator, it can be used to make insulating packaging for food and drinks and insulating panels for refrigerators and freezers (see REFRIGERATION). Secondly, it absorbs shock well, which makes it useful as protective packaging. Third, the foam is very light, which minimizes transportation costs for foam-packaged articles.

Polyvinyl chloride

Polyvinyl chloride (PVC, $-[CH_2-CHCl]_x-$) was the first thermoplastic to go into production in the 1920s. PVC has the same backbone chain as polyethylene, but with a chlorine atom attached in place of a hydrogen atom on every second carbon atom. In its pure form, PVC is hard, stiff, and very tough, which makes it ideal for many heavy-duty applications such as pipes, gutters, window frames, and shoe soles. It can be made more flexible by the addition of substances called plasticizers. These are solvents with very high boiling points. The plasticizers occupy the spaces between polymer chains. Their presence helps the polymers to slip over one another, which increases the flexibility of the plastic. Plasticized PVC has been used to make flexible films, such as those that are used for wrapping food.

Polymethyl methacrylate

Also known by the trade names Plexiglas and Lucite, polymethyl methacrylate (PMMA, or acrylic) was first produced commercially in 1934. The main characteristic of PMMA is its transparency. It is also stiff, hard, shatterproof, and very durable. It is often used as a substitute for glass in windows and in car lights. Shortly after its discovery, it was in great demand for making shatterproof windshields for aircraft and other military vehicles during World War II (1939–1945). However, its application as a glass substitute is limited by the fact that it scratches easily. PMMA is widely used in illuminated signs, where its transparency allows the easy transmission of light through the sign, which ensures a bright display.

Polytetrafluoroethylene

Polytetrafluoroethylene (PTFE, $-[CF_2-CF_2]_x-$) is known by a number of trade names, one of which is Teflon. It is highly valued for its nonstick, low-friction properties and chemical inertness. The use of PTFE linings for cooking utensils such as pans and baking trays has made dishwashing far less of a chore; nonstick cookware is easier to clean because food residues cannot adhere to the PTFE linings. PTFE is

SUBSTITUTES FOR NATURAL POLYMERS

Kayaks need to be strong and light. Originally they were made from wood and animal skins but are now made from fiberglass or, as in the photograph above, molded from various plastics.

Humans have always made use of the natural polymers in materials such as cotton, silk, ivory, and horn. Ornaments have been made from horn for centuries. In the United States, shellac (an extract from an insect) was mixed with wood flour to make photograph frames in the mid-19th century. The demand for such objects grew with the growth of the population and the spread of manufacturing industries that could make them. However, supplies of these natural materials were unreliable, and some were even becoming scarce: at the height of ivory's popularity, the tusks from 100,000 elephants were being used each year for ivory combs, piano keys, buttons, cutlery handles, and billiard balls.

There was increasing pressure for chemists to develop artificial substitutes. The founding father of the polymer industry was probably the English chemist Alexander Parkes (1813–1890), who synthesized cellulose nitrate in 1855. He made it by chemically modifying cellulose (a natural polymer found in plants), and it went on display at the Great Exhibition in London in 1862. In the United States, John Wesley Hyatt (1837–1920) made cellulose nitrate especially for billiard balls. Unfortunately, the new

ivory substitute was rather hazardous: the billiard balls would often burst into flame when they came near a lighted cigar. Hyatt modified his process and produced a related plastic that became known as celluloid. In 1872, he founded the Celluloid Company of Newark, New Jersey, to produce a wide range of household goods, including false teeth. These were to find a ready market over the next 75 years or so, until synthetic plastics superseded them.

Meanwhile, demand for silk began to outstrip supply and the first substitute was made in France in 1891. This artificial silk was cellulose acetate, another semisynthetic polymer. It could also be used to stiffen the fabric wings and fuselages of early airplanes (see AIRCRAFT DESIGN AND CONSTRUCTION).

Another early substitute for natural molded polymers was casein-formaldehyde, which was invented at the beginning of the 20th century and was made from curdled milk. The curds were dried, processed, and colored, and then extruded into rods and sheets. Treatment with formaldehyde hardened them so that they could be machined. Buttons, buckles, knitting needles, and fountain pens were all made from casein plastics.

A CLOSER LOOK

also used medically as a coating for joint replacements, because it is resistant to the frictional forces that would produce wear and tear on the joint.

Condensation polymers

The most important of the condensation polymers is nylon, which was discovered in the 1930s by U.S. chemist Wallace Carothers (1896–1937). Nylon can

be spun to form fibers for use in textiles and for making ropes and cables (see FIBERS AND YARNS; TEXTILES AND THEIR MANUFACTURE). Hard nylons are used to make machine parts such as gears and bearings.

Polyesters form another important class of condensation polymers. In a similar way to nylon, they can be spun to form fibers. One type of polyester, polyethylene terephthalate (PET), is produced in

THE HISTORY OF SYNTHETIC PLASTICS

The first synthetic plastic was invented in 1907 and went on sale in 1910. It was named Bakelite for its inventor, Belgian-born U.S. chemist Leo Baekeland (1863–1944). Bakelite is a hard, phenol-formaldehyde thermoset that is an excellent electrical insulator: it was used for years to make insulating casings and electric plugs and sockets, which were formed by heating Bakelite in molds. The uses of Bakelite were limited by its dark brown color and brittle nature.

Polyethylene was discovered by accident at British chemical company ICI over a weekend in March 1933. Researchers had left ethylene under pressure in a sealed reaction vessel on a Friday evening. When they returned on Monday, they discovered a curious, white, waxy solid in the reaction vessel. Further experiments showed the material had properties we now associate with plastics: it was easy to melt and mold. However, this polyethylene produced in early experiments was also explosive, and ICI could not go into full-scale production until the safety problems were solved.

The 1930s were truly the years when plastics development took off. PVC, polystyrene, nylon, PMMA, the silicones, the polyesters, and the epoxy resins were all discovered around this time. Polyethylene was used to insulate electrical cable as early as 1939. Polyethylene basins went on sale to the public in 1948. Polyethylene shopping bags, flexible bottles, and sandwich bags soon followed. Unfortunately, the quality of early polyethylene was poorer than modern polyethylene, and polyethylene goods acquired a reputation for being cheap and lacking in durability.

However, the quality of plastics improved as chemists came to understand polymers better. The production of addition polymers was helped by the development of catalysts by German Karl Ziegler (1898–1973) and Italian Giulio Natta (1903–1979) during the 1950s. They were awarded the Nobel prize for chemistry in 1963.

Recently developed plastics include polyetheretherketone (PEEK), which can withstand very high temperatures and is used for plastic kettles and the nose cones of aircraft; polycarbonates, which are tough polymers that are used for protective helmets; and

The case of this 1934 Modernity radio is molded Bakelite.

aramids, which are related chemically to nylon and can be formed into very tough fibers for making textiles.

An area that is currently of interest for researchers is the development of polymers that can conduct electricity. It has been shown that polyacetylenes (with the formula $-[CH=CH]_x-$) can conduct at least as well as copper. Current work is focusing on producing these polymers reliably and in useful quantities.

HISTORY OF TECHNOLOGY

granule form and can be made into a tough film with excellent tear and fatigue resistance. PET is used widely in food packaging; typical applications include bottles for beverages and trays for oven-ready meals.

Another major group of condensation polymers is the aramids. Developed since the 1960s, the aramids can be made into fibers that are exceptionally strong, tough, and resistant to impact. They are most often used in composite materials, and typical applications include ropes, tires, and linings for car brakes and clutches. The best known aramid is Kevlar, which is used to make the fabric for bulletproof vests (see COMPOSITE).

Thermosetting plastics

Many thermosetting plastics are made from the condensation of formaldehyde (methanal) with other simple molecules such as phenol, urea, or melamine. The three types of plastics that result are all hard, strong, and resistant to attack by chemicals. They also have good electrical insulation properties. The initial polymer chains are made to cross-link (form chemical bonds) with one another in a heating process called curing. This process forms a giant, three-dimensional network. This gives the thermosetting plastics their characteristic properties.

One of the first synthetic plastics was Bakelite (see the box above), made from phenol-formaldehyde (or phenolic) resin. Bakelite is stiff, hard, and strong, but it is also brittle and dark in color. It was once widely used for electrical fittings, telephones, and other domestic appliances. However, it has now been superseded by thermosets with superior properties. Urea-formaldehyde (UF) plastics are similar to Bakelite but are less brittle and more easy to form into shapes. Also, the light color of UF plastics allows them to be made into objects in a range of colors. They are widely used in electrical fittings and in parts of domestic appliances such as knobs.

The third group of formaldehyde products are the melamine-formaldehyde (MF) plastics. They are scratch and stain resistant, so they are often used to make kitchen work surfaces and tables that are easy to wipe clean. They are also used in lightweight eating utensils and plates for picnics and to bond wood layers into plywood.

FORMING PROCESSES

Compression molding

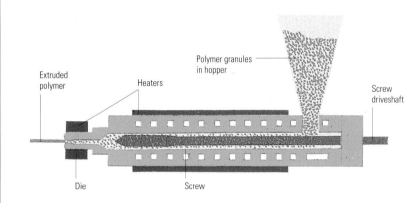

- Mold plunger
- Guide pin
- Thermosetting polymer in mold cavity
- Hydraulic plunger

In compression molding, a plunger pushes the melted thermosetting polymer into the desired shape (in this example, a bucket). Further heating sets the plastic.

Extrusion

- Extruded polymer
- Heaters
- Polymer granules in hopper
- Screw driveshaft
- Die
- Screw

Rods and strips of plastic can be formed by extrusion. Polymer pellets are pushed through a heating chamber by a screw and through an opening of the required shape.

Other important plastics

The polyurethanes are polymers that can be produced as foams. This is because the reaction by which the polymer chains build up also releases carbon dioxide gas. As the chains grow longer and the mixture gets thicker, the gas starts to become trapped as tiny bubbles. Polyurethane foams are used in furniture cushions and to provide a thermal insulation layer between the inner and outer shell of refrigerators. Polyurethanes are also used in surface coatings: the components that make the polymer are dissolved in solvent and then baked after application to the object to be coated. The heat makes the solvent evaporate and starts the polymerization reaction.

Acrylonitrile butadiene styrene (ABS) is an addition copolymer—it is produced from a blend of monomers, each of which contributes to the properties of the plastic. ABS is a thermoplastic with very high impact strength and toughness. It is also scratch resistant, light, and durable. It is widely used in kitchenware such as food processors and in cases for delicate equipment such as cameras. A vast number of plastics with a wide range of properties can be made by reacting different mixtures of monomers.

THE MANUFACTURE OF PLASTICS

The details of how a particular type of plastic is manufactured depend upon the nature of the monomer that is used. Many processes use a catalyst to ensure that the monomer molecules join together under economical conditions of temperature and pressure (see CATALYST, INDUSTRIAL). For instance, when polyethylene was first made in the 1930s, the conditions for manufacture were extreme: ethylene had to be heated to around 390°F (200°C) at a pressure of 1200 atmospheres for the polymerization to occur.

In the 1950s, Ziegler and Natta developed mixtures of titanium tetrachloride and aluminum triethyl to catalyze the reaction and allow it to proceed at a much milder 140°F (60°C) and at atmospheric pressure. Now chemists control the amount of both branching and cross-linking in polymer molecules by the use of specialty catalysts. In this way, they can obtain polymers with specific properties.

The properties of polymers are also modified by the use of a number of different additives. Fillers are added to increase strength, toughness, and stability to heat. These are usually simple materials such as chalk, sand, or talc, which can all be added as powders. Because fillers are relatively cheap, they also bring down the cost.

Many polymers start to decompose when exposed to ultraviolet light and oxygen. Stabilizers can inhibit these chemical reactions and so improve the durability of the plastic. The addition of dyes or pigments to plastics can be used to modify their color and transparency. Stabilizers are also necessary in many cases to prevent the color of the plastic from changing (see DYES AND DYEING).

Most polymers are flammable. For this reason, flame-retardant agents are essential additives in polymers that will be used in toys, furniture, and other domestic applications.

PLASTIC-FORMING TECHNIQUES

There are several different techniques used for forming plastics into the required shape; all use heat or pressure. The nature of the polymer and the size and shape of the finished product determine which forming technique is most appropriate.

Compression molding

The most widely used forming technique is molding, in which pellets or granules of the polymer are heated in a cavity and formed into the desired shape by the application of high pressure. For thermosetting polymers, compression molding is the most common forming technique (see the diagram at left). A cavity of the same shape as the finished item is filled with a mixture of polymer and any additives required. Under the influence of heat and pressure, the plastic first melts and then sets solid within the cavity as the polymer cures. The mixture is then cooled and the item is ejected from the mold. Typical products made by compression molding are knobs, hair dryers, and knife handles.

Injection molding

The most commonly used molding technique for thermoplastics, such as polyethylene and PVC, is injection molding. Preweighed amounts of polymer in pellet form are fed into a hopper. From there they are pushed forward into a heating chamber, where they melt. The molten polymer is injected through a nozzle into the mold. Setting is usually immediate. Injection molding is fully automated and very fast: typically a cycle takes between 10 and 30 seconds. Injection molding is used in the manufacture of items such as buckets, flowerpots, and supermarket crates.

Extrusion

Extrusion is similar to injection molding. A rotating screw is used to push polymer pellets through a heating chamber to form a continuous stream of molten polymer (see the diagram on page 1018). This is then pushed through a die—a plate that has an opening with the same shape as the cross section of the intended product. As the polymer emerges from the die, it is rapidly cooled by an air blower or a jet of water. Then it passes on to a conveyor belt. Extrusion is used to make anything with a constant cross section such as rods, tubes, gutters, and filaments. If a die in the form of a slit is used, plastic film and sheeting can be produced.

Calendering

Plastic sheeting can be made by calendering as well as by extrusion. In the calendering process a continuous flow of heated plastic is fed through a set of heated rollers, which squeeze it to a consistent thickness. A further set of rollers is used to cool the material and compress it further so that it emerges with the desired thickness.

Blow molding

Hollow plastic articles are usually made by blow molding a thermoplastic. The principle of blow molding comes from glassblowing (see GLASS AND GLASS MAKING). A piece of softened thermoplastic is put inside a mold that has an inlet for compressed air. When the air is blown through the inlet, the plastic is forced into contact with the contours of the mold, forming the desired shape. Blow molding is used in the manufacture of plastic bottles.

Vacuum forming

Vacuum forming is a technique related to blow molding. A sheet of softened thermoplastic is stretched above a mold, then a vacuum pump removes the air from below the sheet so that the pressure above it forces the sheet onto the mold. Vacuum forming is used for making detailed shapes such as chocolate-box liners, trays, and dishes.

Rotational molding

Rotational molding is an alternative process to blow molding and vacuum forming that developed recently. It has proved extremely useful for the manufacture of large, complex plastic objects such as

This machine uses injection molding to form blank compact discs. The discs produced must be completely smooth so that data can later be etched onto them as a series of fine depressions.

PLASTICS AND THE ENVIRONMENT

These colored plastic pellets will be used to make plastic bags.

The qualities that make plastics useful—lightness and chemical inertness—create problems when it comes to their disposal. Being light, plastics take up a disproportionate amount of space: plastics contribute only around 10 percent of the weight of household waste but occupy around 25 percent of its volume. The chemical inertness of plastics means they are not broken down easily by microbes in soil and water, as are natural materials such as paper and wood. Currently, most plastics are disposed of in landfills. However, the large volume and long life of plastic waste means that the volume of waste is constantly increasing and the scope for landfill disposal is diminishing. Four approaches are being adopted to reduce this problem.

Reduced volume. Manufacturers are now taking some responsibility for how their products are disposed of. There is a move to reduce plastics waste at the source by decreasing the amount of plastic packaging used and by providing the option of refillable plastic containers.

Biodegradable plastics. There are now several biodegradable plastics that have a shorter lifetime in the environment. Polyhydroxybutyrate (PHB), is a natural polyester made by certain species of bacteria. Unlike regular plastic, it can be degraded to carbon dioxide and water by soil bacteria. PHB is currently used in some shampoo bottles, but it is 15 times more expensive than polyethylene. Photodegradable polyethylene, which is used in the rings that bind packs of beverage cans together, absorbs light; this energy breaks the chemical bonds within the plastic. Once broken into smaller fragments, the plastic is easily degradable by soil bacteria.

There is also a plastic that dissolves in water, which can be used for hospital laundry. The bag goes into the washing machine with the clothes, so that members of the medical staff never have to touch items that are potentially infectious. Another approach is to make polyethylene with integrated starch granules. When dumped, the plastic is degraded into a powder by the action of soil bacteria that consume the starch. This powder is relatively easy to degrade compared to regular plastic.

Incineration. It is possible to recover energy from plastic waste by burning it and using the heat to generate electricity. The main concern with incineration is that burning plastics can release toxic substances, especially when the plastic is a substance such as PVC that contains chlorine. While the emissions can be controlled, it makes the incineration process expensive to operate to a safe standard.

Recycling. Many plastics can be recycled. However, there are many kinds of plastics in everyday use, and they need to be separated prior to recycling. Manufacturers now label many products to indicate the composition of the packaging and make the plastic easier to separate. Recycled plastic is of lower quality than new plastic and cannot be used in applications such as food packaging. Where appearance is important, bottles made from recycled plastic can be coated with new plastic.

WIDER IMPACT

storage tanks for oil, fuel, and water; lawn furniture; safety barriers; canoes; surfboards; and buoys. Plastic powder or paste is heated inside a closed mold that is slowly rotated in vertical and horizontal directions. This makes the plastic form a coating all over the inner surface of the mold. It is then cooled, and the mold opens to release the finished product. The process does not require the application of pressure, which makes it cheaper than other techniques. It can also be used, economically, to make relatively small numbers of products. Currently, 90 percent of rotational molding is done on polyethylene. However, it is also being tried with other plastics.

S. ALDRIDGE

See also: CASTING; CATALYST, INDUSTRIAL; CHEMICAL ENGINEERING; HOUSEHOLD APPLIANCES; MACHINE TOOL; MATERIALS SCIENCE; POLLUTION AND ITS CONTROL; WASTE DISPOSAL, RECYCLING, AND COMPOSTING.

Further reading:
Birley, A., and Haworth, B. *Physics of Plastics: Processing, Properties, and Materials Engineering.* New York: Hanser, 1992.
Brydson, J. *Plastics Materials.* Boston: Butterworth-Heinemann, 1995.
Fenichell, S. *Plastic: The Making of a Synthetic Century.* New York: HarperBusiness, 1996.

PLOW

The plow is one of the most significant agricultural implements ever invented. Used all over the world to prepare land for planting, it works by cutting and turning slices of land, thereby forming furrows in the soil.

Plowing is usually the first stage in the establishment of a seedbed (the ground prepared for growing seed) before sowing or planting. Plowing cuts and inverts the top soil layer, which aerates the soil and breaks up large lumps. Existing vegetation (including weeds) and crop residues are broken up and incorporated into the soil. Similarly, plowing can be used to introduce manure or fertilizer into the soil.

Although plowing is an extremely important agricultural task, it is not beneficial in every case. Repeated plowing of a piece of land can damage the structure of the soil and make it more prone to erosion. Compacted layers in the subsurface soil called plow pans can develop from repeatedly plowing wet soil. Some farmers have therefore adopted minimal tillage systems, where plowing and other cultivation is reduced. Periodically resting the soil from cultivation also helps avoid the problems of over-plowing.

The moldboard plow

The moldboard plow is the most widely used plow configuration, and this basic design has been used for centuries (see the box on page 1022). There are many types, but all have the same basic features and mode of operation. There are three crucial components: coulter, share, and moldboard. A vertical slot is cut by the coulter, which is a blade or sharp-edged disk mounted at the front of the plow. A blade called the share then makes a sideways cut at the base of the vertical slot. The slice of soil thus defined is then lifted and turned over by the moldboard, which is a long curved plate attached behind the share.

The share-moldboard unit is referred to as a plow bottom, body, or base. There are many different types of plow bottoms, designed for various soil conditions and for creating various kinds of furrows. For instance, clay soils are best worked by a deep share and a long, gently curved moldboard. Most bottoms are also fitted with a landside, which is a plate on the back of the moldboard that absorbs the sideways

This disc harrow is being pulled across a field of wheat stubble to break up the ground.

thrust exerted by the plow bottom as it moves through the soil. Modern plows typically have between two and eight bottoms.

The disk plow

Plows with a disk instead of separate coulter, share, and moldboard are common in many parts of the world. The disk plow (not to be confused with the disc harrow used to break up plowed ground) consists of a series of large, concave metal disks, each with a sharp or serrated edge. These are pulled through the soil at an angle so that a slice of soil is cut, undercut, and turned aside; a single disk thus fulfills the function of all three components of a moldboard plow. The rolling action of the disk plow generates less friction than the slicing action of the moldboard, which makes disk plows better suited to plowing heavy or sticky soils.

Plowing a field

The modern plow is connected directly to the back of a tractor, which supports the plow's weight (see TRACTOR). Hydraulic arms, powered by the tractor's engine, keep the plow level and control the depth of plowing (see HYDRAULICS AND PNEUMATICS). It may be fully mounted on the tractor, or there may be wheels at the back of the plow to support some of its weight.

One of the problems of operating a plow is that adjacent furrows must always be turned in the same direction; in other words, the moldboard must throw newly plowed soil away from the previous furrow. This can be achieved by plowing every furrow in the same direction. However, this requires careful planning. With one common method, a central ridge is first formed by plowing a pair of furrows, turning the soil into the middle. The tractor then travels around this ridge, plowing a furrow in toward the

CORE FACTS

- The plow is very important in arable farming and has been used for thousands of years.
- Plows cut the soil with horizontal and vertical blades, and then turn it over to one side with a curved plate called a moldboard. Some plows use disks to do these three tasks instead.
- Modern plows are powerful tractor-drawn implements that can be accurately controlled.

CONNECTIONS

● Most modern plows are pulled by **TRACTORS**.

● Once fields have been plowed and crops planted, many farmers use **CROP SPRAYING AND PROTECTION** to maximize the harvest. **HARVESTING MACHINERY** is brought in to cut, gather, and sort crops.

DEVELOPMENT OF PLOWS

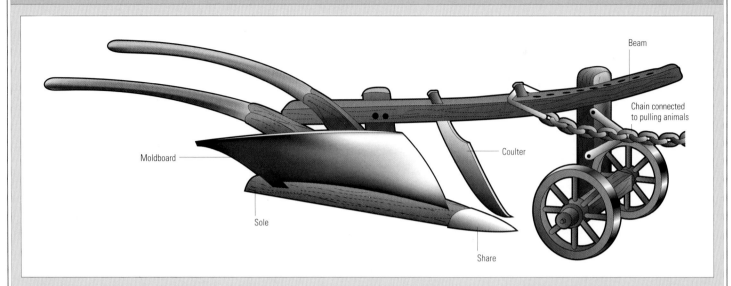

Beam

Chain connected to pulling animals

Coulter

Moldboard

Sole

Share

This simple moldboard plow was used in the 16th century.

The development of the plow has mirrored the general development of arable farming (see AGRICULTURE, HISTORY OF). The earliest plows were probably simple wooden poles, equipped with handles for pushing or pulling through the soil at an angle, and perhaps also with a basic share made of stone or bone. These would have been powered by humans and would have gouged a thin furrow in the soil but would not have turned it over. To achieve reasonable soil movement, a field would need to have been cross-plowed (plowed first in one direction, and then plowed again at right angles), with furrows spaced as closely as possible. The most convenient field shape was therefore a square. Draft animals such as oxen were used later to pull heavier plows.

In about the first century B.C.E., the Romans introduced the iron plowshare, which made the plow more suitable for the heavy soils that they encountered in northern Europe, especially since it allowed

a sharp coulter to be added to the plow. The addition of an iron moldboard in the 18th century was a crucial improvement because it allowed the successful cultivation of even heavier soils. This further expanded the potential area on which crops could be grown. This early design is still the basis of the modern moldboard plow, although improvements have been continuous, especially in recent centuries. For example, U.S. blacksmith John Deere (1804–1886) pioneered the integral cast-steel share-and-moldboard unit in the 19th century. His design was more rugged than plows made with separately cast parts, which made it particularly effective for the heavy soil of the Great Plains of North America.

Plows had to be pulled by cattle or horses until the invention of the steam plow in the 19th century. However, animals remained important until the introduction of the tractor in the first half of the 20th century, which made plowing much quicker and more efficient.

HISTORY OF TECHNOLOGY

center each time. Thus, all the furrows on one side will be made in one direction, and all those on the other in the opposite direction. As the tractor works outward, it has to travel farther on each pass.

Reversible plows allow a simpler approach. These have two sets of plow bottoms, which turn soil in opposite directions. At the end of a furrow, the plow is flipped over on its frame, usually by hydraulic power. It can then be run directly adjacent to the previous furrow, now plowing with the second set of bottoms. Another plow design that allows adjacent furrows to be plowed consecutively has a pair of moldboards joined at the front. This double bottom turns soil both ways simultaneously from the middle of the furrow. These plows generally create wider furrows than conventional plow bottoms.

Specialist plows

There are several plow-type implements with specialized functions. The chisel plow consists of a frame with a number of strong curved spikes that rip

through the soil as the plow is pulled. It is similar in design and effect to a heavy-duty harrow. Chisel plowing is sometimes used as an alternative to conventional plowing but is usually done to break up hard compacted soil.

The subsoiler also breaks up compacted soil but operates at greater depth. It has sturdy metal legs with a pointed foot; the subsoiler is pulled through the soil at a depth of 1–3 ft (0.3–1 m) by a powerful tractor. The mole plow is a deep-working implement used to create simple drainage channels.

T. ALLMAN

See also: AGRICULTURAL TRANSPORT AND MAINTENANCE MACHINERY; ARABLE FARMING; IRRIGATION AND LAND DRAINAGE; SOIL SCIENCE.

Further reading:
Hurt, D. R. *Agricultural Technology in the Twentieth Century.* Manhattan, Kansas: Sunflower University Press, 1991.

POLLUTION AND ITS CONTROL

Pollution is the contamination of the environment by the waste products of human activities

Windmills are used to generate power without burning fossil fuels and polluting the atmosphere.

About 10,000 years ago, a great number of human societies made the transition from being nomadic hunters to living in agricultural settlements. For the first time, men and women were able to transform the environment on a large scale by clearing land and herding animals. Farming was required to support not only the farmers themselves but also those filling other roles in increasingly complex and more populous civilizations, so higher-yield techniques were developed. Societies had to produce or starve, and environmental impact was rarely considered. Large areas of forest were destroyed, and soils were often depleted of their natural nutrients.

Still, there were factors that limited the effects that agricultural communities had on their environments. The materials used in farming and the products were all biodegradable (able to be broken down harmlessly in soils). Impacts were generally local, and the necessity of having large open fields limited population density. The Industrial Revolution of the 18th and 19th centuries changed all that. Suddenly many more products were being manufactured from materials that lasted a long time, even if the products themselves broke or were discarded. Factories dumped chemical waste into rivers and belched it into the air through smokestacks, allowing the pollution to travel far from its source.

Decades after astronauts on their way to the Moon first saw Earth hanging in space, people have come to understand that human activities have global effects on climate, plant and animal habitats, and their own health. Air pollution from factories on one continent causes acid rain on another. Chemicals in the soil and water make their way up the food chain and wind up on dinner plates. Communities struggling to find a place to throw away their garbage discover that it is not easy to dispose of.

The immediacy of the pollution problem has brought it into public consciousness. No longer is environmentalism only of interest to small groups of activists. Governments are increasingly becoming involved by legislating environmental protection measures and by funding environmental research. Recycling, organic gardening (without chemicals), water-saving plumbing fixtures, and automobile emissions control have become part of everyday life. The requirement for polluters to bear more of the costs of dealing with their waste has created a market for cleaner technologies that might previously have been dismissed on economic grounds.

CORE FACTS

- Air pollution has created holes in the ozone layer of the upper atmosphere, acid rain, smog, and respiratory problems and may be responsible for global warming.
- Sewage and industrial waste dumped into the ocean destroy marine habitats and imperil many important sources of food from the sea.
- Pollutants leaching through the soil and into the groundwater from landfills and other sources can contaminate drinking water supplies.
- Legislation, cleaner industrial processes and technologies, better cleanup methods, and changes in individual behavior are all important in pollution control.

CONNECTIONS

- Many **PESTICIDES AND HERBICIDES** and other chemicals used for **CROP SPRAYING AND PROTECTION** do not break down quickly and are harmful pollutants.

- **WIND POWER** and **SOLAR POWER** generate power without polluting the atmosphere.

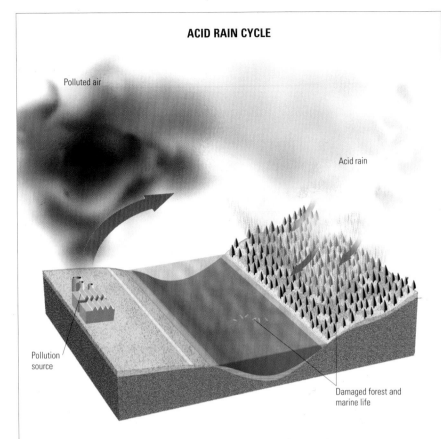

ACID RAIN CYCLE

Polluted air

Acid rain

Pollution source

Damaged forest and marine life

Gaseous sulfur dioxide, produced by the burning of fossil fuels, rises into the air with particles of ash or soot. The gas interacts with sunlight and water vapor in the upper atmosphere to form acid rain—droplets of sulfuric acid. Acid rain damages trees, marine life, and buildings and monuments—often far from the source of pollution.

Air pollution

Most air pollution is caused by the burning of fossil fuels such as gas, oil, and coal. Fossil fuels contain compounds of hydrogen and carbon called hydrocarbons. When these are burned, they combine with oxygen to form carbon dioxide and water. Carbon dioxide is not hazardous to health in normal atmospheric quantities: it is a product of respiration and is necessary for photosynthesis in plants. The presence of atmospheric carbon dioxide is responsible for the greenhouse effect, which is Earth's retention of heat from the Sun. Without the greenhouse effect, Earth would be too cold for humans to survive.

As one of the normal components of the atmosphere, carbon dioxide is absorbed in the oceans and used by plants to produce the oxygen people breathe. But the increase in atmospheric carbon dioxide caused by the burning of fossil fuels, almost 30 percent since preindustrial days, is disrupting the overall balance of atmospheric gases. Most scientists believe that by increasing the greenhouse effect, excess atmospheric carbon dioxide is causing a trend toward global warming. It takes only a few degrees' difference in average temperature to change the vegetation and weather patterns on which the human agricultural system and settlement patterns are based, causing regional famines and other disruptions. Increased melting of polar ice causes a rise in sea level and the flooding of coastal areas. Other air

pollutants such as refrigerant gases also act as greenhouse gases. In order to control the overall emissions from burning fossil fuels, the energy efficiency of factories, vehicles, and appliances must be increased and alternate power sources such as hydroelectricity and solar and wind power must be used.

Few fossil fuels are pure hydrocarbons: coal is mixed with inorganic impurities that form ash, both coal and oil can produce soot (fine carbon dust) if they are not completely burned, and some fossil fuels—notably coal—contain sulfur. When sulfur-containing fuels are burned, their sulfur content is converted to sulfur dioxide, which can form acid rain if it escapes to the atmosphere (see diagram at left). Acid rain eats away at natural and synthetic objects alike: the ancient Egyptian obelisk called Cleopatra's Needle has deteriorated more in the 120 years since it was brought to New York's Central Park than in the previous three millenia of natural weathering. Sulfur dioxide also causes respiratory illnesses by paralyzing the cilia (tiny hairs) that sweep irritants out of the respiratory tract. Emissions from power plants have been reduced by the use of flue-gas cleaning plants (see the box on page 1025), and coal with less sulfur naturally produces less sulfur dioxide when burned.

Motor vehicles are big contributors to air pollution. Incomplete combustion of gasoline, which consists of hydrocarbons and additives, results in the emission of carbon monoxide, nitrogen oxides, and organic compounds. Sunlight triggers chemical reactions between these and naturally occurring atmospheric gases to produce ozone. Together, these air pollutants are called smog. Breathing ozone causes irritation of the lungs and a reduced ability to fight infections. Carbon monoxide reduces the capacity of blood to carry oxygen and is lethal if it accumulates in a confined space. Many of the organic compounds present in exhaust fumes are carcinogens (cancer-causing agents). Beginning in the 1970s, increasingly strict emissions-control measures were required in automobiles. Catalytic converters were installed in exhaust systems in order to help meet these stricter requirements. The catalytic converter is a chamber containing pellets coated with metals that act as catalysts (triggers) for carbon monoxide or hydrocarbons to combine with oxygen and finish burning. Lead additives in gasoline were also eliminated to reduce the amount of lead in the air and because they would plug up and destroy the catalytic converters. Emissions controls have significantly reduced these air pollutants, but they have not addressed the increasing amounts of carbon dioxide, which is an inevitable product of burning fossil fuels.

Electric cars and trains are potentially nonpolluting: if hydroelectricity or wind power were used to provide their power, these modes of transport would indeed cause no pollution. At present, however, most electricity is generated from fossil fuels. Nevertheless, power stations use the energy content of fossil fuels more efficiently and produce less pollution than internal combustion engines.

Refrigerants such as chlorofluorocarbons (CFCs) are air pollutants that decompose extremely slowly and accumulate in the atmosphere. CFCs have also been used as propellants in aerosol cans, and CFCs that escape into the upper atmosphere participate in chemical reactions that destroy the ozone there. While ozone at ground level causes problems, in the stratosphere (upper atmosphere) it plays the vital role of screening out dangerous ultraviolet radiation from the Sun. The movement of CFCs in atmospheric currents results in increasingly large seasonal holes in the ozone layer above the poles. Ozone destruction means more ultraviolet radiation gets through, causing increased rates of skin cancer all over the world. The United States banned CFCs in aerosols in 1978, prompting the development of alternative propellants and an increased use of pump hairsprays and cleaners, and stick or roll-on deodorants. CFCs are being phased out in favor of more benign refrigerants, such as hydrofluorocarbons (HFCs), which decompose more readily than CFCs (see REFRIGERATION). Today, all new vehicles made in the United States use HFCs rather that CFCs in the manufacture of their air-conditioning systems.

Water pollution

Historically, oceans were generally considered to be so huge that they had an infinite capacity to absorb anything dumped into them. The oceans and the rivers that ran into them became convenient places in which to dispose of sewage and industrial waste. Pollution of marine ecosystems has depleted fish and shellfish populations and has made some catches unfit for human consumption. This endangers an important segment of the world food supply and affects the livelihood of many communities in coastal regions. Some beaches are too polluted to allow swimming. Destruction of coral reefs means the loss of an important barrier to beach erosion and storm damage, as well as one of Earth's richest habitats.

Accidental oil spills cause obvious local problems (see the box on page 1026), but routine marine operations, such as flushing out oil tanks, feed a constant stream of oil and other pollutants into the oceans. However, 80 percent of ocean pollution comes from sources on land. Most bays and harbors near population centers are badly polluted with municipal sewage. While modern sewage treatment plants have improved the situation through advanced technology, in many areas sewage treatment is inadequate, and in many developing countries it is almost nonexistent (see SEWAGE TREATMENT).

About 5 trillion gallons of industrial waste go directly into the oceans each year in the United States alone. Other pollutants, such as polychlorinated biphenyls (PCBs), are primarily deposited into the oceans from the atmosphere. These chemicals harm the reproduction of sea mammals and may lead to their extinctions. Industrial effluent (waste) is being addressed through legislation such as the Clean Water Act in the United States and the encouragement of cleaner technologies.

A drainpipe from an open sewer in Lamu, Kenya, discharges domestic waste directly into the Indian Ocean.

Marine and inland waters are also contaminated by runoff from fertilizers and pesticides from farms and lawns, and from highway and construction sites. Other pollutants are oil, paint, and any other toxic materials that might find their way down storm drains. Like sewage, fertilizers contain nitrogen and phosphorous that can cause excessive algal growth called red tides, which deplete the oxygen in the water, block sunlight, and generate toxins that kill other species. These types of pollution can only be controlled through public education and by banning particularly dangerous materials and practices.

The safety of drinking water is at risk from water pollution. Many municipalities get their water from polluted rivers and other bodies of water (see WATER SUPPLY AND TREATMENT). Anything that gets into the soil can pollute the groundwater, potentially poisoning wells that supply water for drinking.

CLEANING FLUE GASES

Every year, coal-burning power plants generate millions of tons of combustion gases—carbon dioxide with some sulfur dioxide—and particulate matter called fly ash, which comes from the inorganic (mineral) content of the coal.

Fly ash—otherwise known as pulverized-fuel ash—can be removed from the stream of flue gases in machines called electrostatic precipitators. The gases first pass through a metal grid to which a high voltage is applied. The voltage imparts an electric charge to the dust particles, which are then attracted to metal collecting surfaces that are grounded with discharge electrodes (electrical terminals). Fly ash is a nonhazardous waste and much of it is used to make breeze blocks (hollow blocks used in construction).

Sulfur dioxide may be removed in flue-gas desulfurization (FGD) plants. In these plants the flue gases are brought into contact with lime (calcium oxide, CaO) or limestone (calcium carbonate, $CaCO_3$), sometimes mixed with water. The sulfur dioxide in the flue gases reacts with these substances to form a mixture of gypsum (calcium sulfate, $CaSO_4$) and unreacted lime or limestone. This material can be used to make portland cement (see CEMENT AND CONCRETE) or it can be used to neutralize excessive soil acidity.

A CLOSER LOOK

CLEANING UP AFTER *EXXON VALDEZ*

Workers use high-pressure hoses to clean spilled oil from the Alaskan shore.

In 1989, the tanker *Exxon Valdez* spilled more than 10 million gallons (c.40 million liters) of oil in Alaska's Prince William Sound. Spread by a storm, the escaped oil was deposited along 1367 miles (2200 km) of coastline, killing 730 sea otters and tens of thousands of birds.

Exxon was charged $900 million in a court settlement, and a large number of paid and volunteer workers descended upon the area to help with the cleanup. Despite this, it was simply not feasible to reach all the oil by conventional means, particularly that which had seeped down into the sand and under rocks.

Under an agreement between Exxon and the U.S. Environmental Protection Agency, a bioremediation effort was attempted. The plan was to bring in oil-digesting microorganisms, until it was realized that there were already such organisms on Alaska's beaches. Being indigenous, they were already adapted to the cold and other local conditions. Nitrogen and phosphorus fertilizers were applied to help speed up the process.

The bioremediation was considered a success at the time; studies indicated that the oil degraded three to eight times faster than it would have normally. However, more recent studies of Prince William Sound have concluded that oil residues, in concentrations as low as 1 part per billion (ppb), continue to have an effect on the species there.

The *Exxon Valdez* spill proved that prompt action is important not only for marine life in the immediate vicinity but also because it prevents the oil from spreading to uncontaminated areas. In response to the accident, the U.S. Congress passed the Oil Pollution Control Act of 1990 to expand prevention and preparedness activities and response capabilities, and to foster research and development. It also established a trust for liability payments, funded by oil companies and shippers and administered by the Coast Guard.

A CLOSER LOOK

Pollution from solid wastes

Industrial societies dispose of as much as 4 lb (2 kg) of garbage per person every day, about 20 percent of which is incinerated; the rest winds up in landfills. However, increasingly stringent environmental legislation has made it more difficult to find locations for new landfills and the number of landfills has been decreasing as existing landfills are filling up and closing faster than new sites can be made available.

Solid wastes and hazardous chemicals dumped in landfills and elsewhere have the potential to pollute the soil upon which they lie as well as the groundwater below. Rainwater that falls on a landfill picks up water-soluble material as it percolates down through layers of trash—some of which may be toxic—and forms a solution called leachate.

Modern landfills are designed to protect the groundwater by containing the leachate. The landfill is lined with an impermeable material, such as heavy-duty plastic sheeting, and layers of low-permeability clay and sand. The leachate collects at the bottom of the landfill and is then pumped to a storage tank, where it is tested. Depending on the chemical contents of the leachate, it is sent to an ordinary sewage treatment plant or to a special processing plant. Methane produced by rotting garbage can also be used to fuel electrical generators.

Taking responsibility

Legislation, better technologies, and improved cleanup methods are all part of pollution control. But changes in behavior and society's expectations must also play a part. Even if fossil fuels burn cleanly, they still produce carbon dioxide that increases the greenhouse effect. Even if landfills do not allow pollutants to escape, Earth is running out of places to put them. In order to reduce pollution, people will have to consume less, discard less, and recycle more.

Such a recommendation is difficult to implement in a society in which continuous economic growth and ever-increasing standards of living are expected. Still, some changes have been put in place, such as widespread community and office recycling programs and carpooling incentives that involve reserved highway lanes and parking spaces for high-occupancy vehicles. Cleanup costs are beginning to be assigned back to polluters, and more people are questioning the values of the throwaway society.

S. CALVO

See also: ACCIDENTS AND DISASTERS; ENERGY RESOURCES; ENVIRONMENTAL ENGINEERING; HAZARDOUS WASTE; SEWAGE TREATMENT; WASTE DISPOSAL, RECYCLING, AND COMPOSTING.

Further reading:
Davies, J. and Mazurek, J. *Pollution Control in the United States.* Washington D.C.: Resources for the Future, 1998.
Theodore, M. and Theodore, L. *Major Environmental Issues Facing the 21st Century.* Upper Saddle River, NJ: Prentice Hall, 1996.

PORT AND HARBOR FACILITIES

Ports and harbors handle passengers and cargo, maintain safe channels, and guide ships to their moorings

An increasing number of nations must import food, manufactured goods, and raw materials, and to do so they need ships (see MERCHANT SHIPS). Although passenger travel has declined since the mid-20th century, cruise liners still provide income from tourism to many nations. These facts make harbors, and the ports built in them to receive ships, busy places that are crucial to national economies. But even the largest ports often have fewer spaces than the number of arriving ships. When ships float idle while awaiting a berth or take a long time at dockside, ship owners lose money and goods are delayed. Accordingly, marine civil engineers have steadily improved the efficiency and safety of port facilities and have introduced new methods of servicing ships that are too large for conventional ports or whose cargoes are hazardous. The United States government alone spent about $20 billion between 1950 and 2000 for harbor improvements.

Berths and berthing

When a ship comes into harbor, it may drop its anchor away from the shore and convey cargo or passengers to land in boats. Most often, however, ships stop alongside artificial structures built up on the shore. There are many sizes and types to accommodate the great variety of cargo and passenger vessels.

In the United States, *dock* is the most general common term for the place where a ship is moored, or tied up (see DOCK AND HARBOR CONSTRUCTION). In the United Kingdom, however, a dock is an artificially enclosed body of water, often with locks to maintain a steady surface level, inside which ships are moored. Locks are not used in the United States other than in large canals. In Canada, they are used in the St. Lawrence Seaway connecting the Great Lakes to the Atlantic Ocean (see CANAL AND INLAND WATERWAY; LOCK) and in special repair facilities. A wharf, pier, jetty, or quay (the terms are often used interchangeably) is a structure of that extends from the shore and can serve as a dock. A slip is the space between two piers that holds a single ship, much like a car in a parking space. A ship's location along a dock is its berth.

CORE FACTS

- The primary goal of port facilities is to transfer cargo as quickly as is safe because delays can reduce profits for the owners of both the cargo and the ship.
- In port, a ship berths at a dock, where there are facilities for loading, unloading, and storing cargo or for embarking or disembarking passengers.
- Cranes are the usual machinery for loading and unloading cargo, although some special ships require ramps, hoses, or conveyor belts instead.
- Ships rely upon a variety of outside equipment to make sure they dock safely, including tugs, buoys, radar, radio communications, fireboats, and police boats.

CONNECTIONS

- **ORE EXTRACTION AND PROCESSING** and **OIL REFINING** operations are often located near ports to reduce the costs of transporting raw materials.

The Queen Elizabeth II *docks in Victoria Harbour in Hong Kong. Oceangoing passenger vessels like this vast liner are used for leisure purposes rather than for transport.*

To get maximum use from shoreline space, many ports in wide harbors berth ships at piers that jut straight out from the shore like fingers. Ports on rivers, such as Vancouver, Washington, on the Columbia River, berth ships parallel to the banks.

Loading and unloading

A dock offers the means to load and unload a ship. At its most primitive, a dock is merely a place where stevedores (people who load and unload ships) can deposit cargo carried down a gangplank from the ship. To speed up the job, docks have cranes to lift general cargo out of a ship's hold. Fixed to the pier or on tracks, truck beds, or barges, these towering machines can hoist hundreds of tons at a time and

swing them onto waiting trucks or trains. The cargo may also be moved by special tractors, flatbed haulers, or forklifts to storage areas. A major portion of a port's space is occupied by staging areas and warehouses that keep goods until they can be distributed inland (see MECHANICAL HANDLING).

During the 1950s, specialized ships began to dominate cargo-carrying trade, particularly container ships and tankers. Container ships haul long rectangular steel boxes that are designed to fit directly onto truck beds or the flatbed cars of trains. To move the containers, dock workers use container cranes and straddle carriers, which look like long-legged mechanical insects on wheels. For ships that carry dry bulk cargo, such as ores, grains, or fertilizers, docks use systems of conveyor belts and hoses to move the cargo to silos (see CONVEYOR).

Liquid bulk cargoes such as oil require cautious treatment because they are sometimes combustible and dangerous to the environment. Moreover, the tankers and supertankers that carry them may be too large to enter a harbor. Floating docks or large buoys offshore receive the liquid cargo and pipe it to storage tanks ashore (see OIL TANKER AND BULK CARRIER).

Manufacturers export cars and other vehicles on ships equipped with large hatches, usually at the stern or on the sides. The hatches open to join onto adjustable ramps on the docks. Vehicles can then be rolled on or off directly through the hatches. These so-called ro-ro (roll-on-roll-off) facilities may include adjustable bridges, called link spans, to counteract the rise and fall of a ship because of tides and swells. Large parking lots hold the vehicles until they can be delivered to retailers.

Facilities at naval bases are more complex. There are barracks to house ships' crews while ashore and military police to guard the warships. A base also

BUOYS: HARBOR ROAD SIGNS

The most dangerous part of any voyage is entering and leaving the harbor. Waves and currents at the harbor entrance are particularly dangerous to navigation. Below the calm surface may lurk reefs, spires of rock, sandbars, and even wrecks—all invisible—that could damage or even sink a ship.

Since 1767 all U.S. harbors have had special floats called buoys anchored to the harbor bottom. These have helped ship captains steer clear of these dangers. Buoys come in a variety of shapes: cans, cones, spheres, pillars, spars (or spindles), and barrels. Every number, light, bell, whistle, radar reflector, color, and shape has a meaning and warns of a hazard or outlines a path.

When a ship enters a channel from the sea, buoys on the starboard (right side) are red with red lights on top and have even numbers in sequence. On the port (left side), buoys are green with green lights and have odd numbers in sequence. Buoys marking junctions or obstructions have horizontal bands; the color of the top band tells which side is the best passage for approaching vessels (red for right and green for left).

A CLOSER LOOK

has warehouses, cranes, and haulers specifically designed for munitions, including torpedoes and missiles with nuclear warheads, and means to load naval and army units, vehicles, and airplanes. From small patrol boats to gigantic aircraft carriers carrying thousands of sailors, naval vessels require versatile docks and an extensive supply and repair system (see WARSHIP).

Passenger ships and ferries

After 1950, airplanes gradually took away intercontinental passenger traffic from ocean liners. Vast, ornate, and luxurious ships, such as the *Mauretania* and *Queen Mary*, carried as many as 2000 people and berthed at bustling terminals in major port cities, most notably New York. The terminals were buildings sometimes the size of an entire city block where travelers could buy tickets, check their luggage, and await their departure in lounges or restaurants; terminals also held the offices of shipping lines or agents who supplied provisions for the ships.

By 1980 ocean liners no longer had regular schedules. Those still in operation became cruise ships for tourists, such as the *Queen Elizabeth II*. Many cruise ships are too large to dock at all of their ports of call, especially at islands and small cities in developing nations. Instead, they moor offshore and convey passengers ashore by motorboat.

Ferries are the last type of vessel to serve regularly scheduled passenger traffic (see FERRY). Some carry only passengers a short distance across a bay or river. However, most ferries accept both cars and passengers. They usually sail among islands with year-round residents, such as those off the New England coasts or in the Northwest's Puget Sound, or between nations separated by narrow waterways, such as the Scandinavian countries.

Although hovercraft and ferries conveying cars need specially designed berthing facilities, most ferry landings have common features (see HOVERCRAFT). A toll gate, where drivers pay the fare, opens to a staging area where cars wait in line until the ferry arrives. When it does, it discharges arriving vehicles down a ramp usually from the bow or stern onto a pier and to a road that goes around the staging area; departing cars then drive up the same ramp. Some ferry landing areas have lounges and snack bars for passenger comfort and fuel pumps and repair equipment for the ferries.

Harbor safety

Harbors are refuges from the perils of the open sea, as well as places for transferring cargo, yet most harbors are nonetheless dangerous to ships. The water is often shallow, and the approaches can be narrow and include such obstacles as sandbars and rocks. Port authorities must also prevent illegal imports; protect ships, their crews, and their freight from crime; and provide backup for firefighting.

To guide a ship, harbors contain several types of communication or sensing equipment. The buoy system is the oldest. Buoys are floats that have colors,

TUGS—THE PUSHIEST BOATS AROUND

A tugboat guides a freighter into harbor.

Modern cargo ships and tankers are immense; some are more than 1000 ft (300 m) long. They are built to plow through the open ocean. In port they are often out of their element, and they usually need help to ease up to a dock.

Tugs are small ships built for power and maneuverability. They are about 80–120 ft (24–36 m) long and have heavily reinforced bows, sterns, and deck fittings. Engines of up to 6000 horsepower, driving one or two propellers, give them immense power for their size. Many tugs have not only a main rudder but also rudders forward of the propellers on either side of the hull, or even propellers that pivot (see PROPELLER; RUDDER). They can practically turn in circles.

While the ship itself provides the main forward propulsion, tugs—working alone or in groups—use nudges and pulls to help the ship turn, move sideways, stop, or swing around. All this is directed from the ship's bridge by a harbor pilot (an employee of the harbor trained to guide ships into and out of dock).

A CLOSER LOOK

ANCIENT WONDERS

An engraving of the great Pharos (lighthouse) of Alexandria .

In the days of the ancient Greeks and Romans, harbor facilities sometimes reached monumental proportions. Two of them, in fact, were numbered among the Seven Wonders of the World.

The Colossus of Rhodes was a titanic bronze statue of a god wearing a crown of sun rays. Built beside the Greek island's harbor in 280 B.C.E., it was about 105 ft (32 m) high on a large marble base and faced out to sea. It was a thanksgiving to Helios, the sun god worshiped locally, and a landmark for mariners.

About the same time, Ptolemy I completed a lighthouse 400 ft (122 m) high on Pharos, an island in the harbor of Alexandria, Egypt. At the top of the rectangular tower, attendants burned wood and oil. A mirror designed by Archimedes projected the firelight as far as 30 miles (50 km) out to sea.

HISTORY OF TECHNOLOGY

lights, sound-makers, and symbols that direct ships into and out of a harbor and mark areas to be avoided (see navigation). U.S. harbors use the International Association of Lighthouse Authorities Maritime Buoyage System; some nations follow other systems, although there is a trend toward uniformity worldwide. Harbors with long approaches may also provide lighthouses, either on shore or on floating platforms, to guide ships when visibility is poor (see lighthouse and lightship).

Modern ports also maintain radio contact with ships to convey information about weather and dockside conditions (see MARITIME COMMUNICATION). Shore-based radar helps ships determine their location in bad weather, as do shipboard radar and the Global Positioning System, which fixes a ship's exact position with information from a network of satellites (see RADAR; SATELLITE).

In the restricted space of a harbor, big ships have difficulty maneuvering, so small and powerful tugboats provide the final escort to a dock. In case of emergency, ports have fireboats that can spray water onto a burning ship and boat ambulances or helicopters to carry the injured to hospitals ashore (see AMBULANCE AND EMERGENCY MEDICAL TREATMENT; FIREFIGHTING AND FIRE PROTECTION). Port authorities also supply physicians and inspectors to ensure that arriving crew, passengers, and agricultural goods are free of disease. If a contagion is onboard, a ship may be turned away or placed in quarantine (isolated from other ships and the shore for days or weeks).

Security is important to shipping companies in order to prevent injury and theft. Ports often have privately hired security police to keep out unauthorized persons; large shipping companies are likely to have security personnel of their own and fenced-in lots. Additionally, the city or state in charge of a port may assign police to harbor duty. In some harbors, such as the one at Rio de Janeiro in Brazil, piracy is a growing problem, and police boats patrol to discourage pirates on speedboats from attacking freighters and ferries.

Repair and construction

Ports have equipment to repair and construct docks, stabilize the shore, and keep channels clear. Barge-mounted digging equipment, such as power shovels and suction hoses, dredges up silt or sand washed in from streams or the ocean so that the harbor does not become too shallow for seagoing ships (see DREDGING). Barges may also carry cranes and equipment for divers in order to salvage materials lost overboard from ships or to clear away wrecked vessels.

Large ports set aside docks for construction and repair of ships and other vessels. Usually, ships' hulls are built near the shore and launched down ramps. The superstructures are then built on the floating hull, although small craft may be assembled entirely on shore and hoisted into the water. Ships receive repairs to their hulls and extensive overhauls in dry docks: a gate closes behind the ship, and the water inside the dock is pumped out so that shipbuilders have access to the outer hull (see BOATBUILDING AND SHIPBUILDING; SHIP AND BOAT).

R. SMITH

See also: BARGE; CRANE; HYDROFOIL; MARINE ENGINEERING; PACKAGING INDUSTRY; PROPELLER; SAFETY SYSTEMS; SEAPLANE AND FLYING BOAT; SHIP AND BOAT; SHIP AND BOAT, HISTORY OF.

Further reading:
European Docklands: Past, Present and Future. Edited by S. Al Naib. London, England: Northeast London Polytechnic, 1991.
Lloyd's Ports of the World. Colchester, England: Lloyds of London Press, Annual.
Fisher, B. *Urban Waterfronts.* New York: Van Nostrand Reinhold, 1998.
Gaythwaite, J. *Design of Marine Facilities for the Berthing, Mooring, and Repair of Vessels.* New York: Van Nostrand Reinhold, 1990.
Leigh, J. *Seaport: Waterfront at Work.* Charleston, South Carolina: Wyrick, 1996.

POTTERY

Pottery is any useful or decorative object produced by shaping clay and subjecting it to high temperatures

A potter pulls up the sides of a large pot.

Until the development of plastics in the 20th century, pottery, wood, glass, and pewter were the main materials used to make containers and utensils for food and other substances. Even today, with the development of a range of hard, long-lasting, and almost unbreakable plastics such as melamine, from which articles can be molded easily, pottery is still very popular, and cups, dishes, plates, and other household wares are still being manufactured from clay in enormous quantities.

In the past, bowls and platters have been made from wood, but this material is difficult to keep clean and is liable to absorb fats and oils from food. In addition, some kinds of woods are liable to split,

especially if they are repeatedly soaked in water and dried. Glass has also been used, but it is very fragile and prone to breakage, and its surface is easily scratched, so over time its transparency is lost. Pewter is easily worked into domestic utensils, but it is expensive and heavy.

Although it has never lost its popularity, pottery also has some disadvantages. For example, if it is dropped onto a hard surface, it is liable to shatter. In addition, most pottery is very heavy, and large stacks of it are unwieldy and awkward. When transported, it must be carefully packed and protected, and it should be handled with care to avoid chipping or cracking it: cracked pottery retains dirt and may become a hygiene hazard.

The popularity of pottery as a domestic material is not simply a matter of tradition. Much of it has an attractive shape and design, and it may be decorated by hand or machine. Tableware has a tough, impermeable glaze, which may be glossy or matte and is extremely durable. Most importantly, it can withstand repeated washing. Ware of the very best quality commands high prices, and some old tableware sets are kept as precious family heirlooms. Many vases and bowls are not actually used but are treated as objects of art, and some of them are considered almost priceless. In fact, pottery is not limited to domestic dishes and utensils. A tradition of pottery sculpture and the production of other pieces of artistic value dates back to ancient times. Many of the earliest known statues were fashioned from clay and then baked to produce earthenware.

CORE FACTS

- Pottery making has been a feature of human activity from the earliest times: archaeologists have found pottery dating back to the late Stone Age.
- A wide variety of clays can be used for pottery. In general, the higher the temperature used for firing, the harder and more durable the resulting object.
- Pottery may be hardened by a single firing, which leaves it porous and capable of absorbing water. This is called unglazed pottery.
- Pottery can be glazed by a second firing. Glazing is a hard, long-lasting, almost impermeable, and often decorative surface that is fused onto the pottery.
- Pottery is valued for both its usefulness and beauty. At its best, it is regarded as an art form.

CONNECTIONS

- **CERAMICS** are objects that are made at high temperatures from nonmetallic minerals such as clays. Examples of ceramics industries include pottery making and **BRICK MAKING**.

- **MATERIALS SCIENCE** is the study of the structure and properties of materials that make them useful in manufacturing and construction industries.

More than 6000 life-sized terra-cotta warriors, which were made between 221 and 206 B.C.E., now guard the imperial mausoleum at the foot of Mount Lushan in Xi'an, China.

was fired. These specimens show that some degree of sophistication and an interest in decoration were already features of early pottery production. It is entirely possible that pottery existed even earlier in human social evolution, but, as yet, there have been no earlier pottery pieces recovered as evidence.

Pottery was a flourishing industry in the Middle East and Far East as early as 6000 years ago. In these regions, kilns (large ovens in which pottery is fired) were in wide use. These early kilns consisted of a vertical chimney-like structure made of bricks, with a hot wood fire at the bottom. A perforated floor, through which the flames could pass, was placed above the fire to support the ware. Suitable ventilation and wind or fans ensured a constant updraft and adequate heat, and the top of the chimney was often partly closed. Egyptian tomb paintings show that crude potter's wheels, turned by hand, were in use as early as c.5000 years ago. The more modern, continuously turning version of the potter's wheel did not appear, however, until much later—probably not before the seventh century B.C.E.

Pottery was especially popular in China, Japan, and Korea. The Chinese were producing hand-painted and decorated ware over 4500 years ago. The evolution of Chinese pottery continued for thousands of years through many dynasties, and the heights to which it aspired were illustrated with the discovery, in 1974, of a buried army of 6000 life-sized figures of soldiers and horses made in a type of pottery called terra-cotta during the Qin dynasty (221–206 B.C.E.). Other high points of Chinese pottery came later, during the T'ang dynasty (618–906 C.E.) and Sung Dynasty (960–1279 C.E.), when delicate and elegantly decorated fine white porcelain bowls and vases, with clear, bluish, or greenish glazes, were produced. Most pottery connoisseurs would agree, however, that the peak of excellence in Chinese pottery was reached during the Ming dynasty (1368–1644 C.E.), which is famous for its production of priceless porcelain.

The indigenous populations of the Americas also produced pottery: the Pueblo populations of the region that is now Arizona and New Mexico are known to have made earthenware pottery as early as 600 C.E.; even earlier examples of pottery for practical and ceremonial uses—sometimes with ornate decorations—have been found near Chavín de Huantar, Peru, (dating from 800–400 B.C.E.), in the Valley of Mexico (dating from 1500–1000 B.C.E.), and in Ecuador (dating from c.3200 B.C.E.).

Until the 18th century, nearly all of the finest ware was imported to the United States from the Far East. However, today in the United States, the standard of pottery production and technology now rivals that of anywhere in the world. There is a facility in the Tennessee Valley devoted entirely to experimental research into pottery. The aesthetic aspects of U.S. pottery have also received substantial local and federal governmental encouragement, and the making of fine pottery is now widely sponsored as an art form.

History of pottery

Pottery is one of the earliest technologies of humankind. Its origins date from the time that fire became an important element in human social life. It is easy to see how readily early humans would have recognized the hardening effect of fire on clay, and how it would quickly have become apparent that useful items could be made by modeling them in clay and then heating them in a fire to produce a durable object. The earliest known collections of pottery were found in Japan, and it is widely considered that pottery production began there.

In 1960, pieces of brown pottery were found during excavations in a cave in Nagasaki, Japan. These were decorated with cuts and ridges and when fitted together were found to be parts of a round-bottomed container. Radiocarbon dating showed that they were made c.12,500 years ago, in the late Stone Age (Neolithic) period, when polished stone and flint tools and weapons were in use. This prehistoric period in Japan is known as the beginning of the Jomon period, from a term for the cord marks that were pressed into the clay of this pottery before it

CLAY

A China clay mine in Cornwall, England.

The term *clay* refers to almost any inorganic material of very small particle size—less than $^{16}/_{100,000}$ inch (4 µm, or $^{4}/_{1000}$ mm). Clays are generally formed by sedimentation of these tiny particles in water and may consist of materials as diverse as quartz, feldspar, zeolites, and iron hydroxides. Most clays, however, are phyllosilicates, which are complex crystal structures made of silicon oxide and aluminum, or magnesium oxides, arranged in sheets that are also known as mica sheets. The properties of clays depend on their crystalline structure. Some clays swell in water, others do not.

Not all clays are formed by sedimentation in oceans and lakes. Some of them form in poorly drained soil and others in environments subject to strong leaching (removal by seeping water). Clay minerals are found almost everywhere in Earth's upper crust, but high-grade commercial clays suitable for pottery are of limited distribution. In the United States, some of the best white kaolin clays, known as China clays, are found in large quantity only in Georgia and South Carolina. Other good commercial clays occur in Arizona, California, Florida, Mississippi, New Mexico, South Dakota, Texas, and Wyoming.

A CLOSER LOOK

Types of pottery

The many different types of pottery arise from differences in the clays used and in the temperatures at which these clays are fired. In general, the higher the temperature used to fire a piece, the better the quality of the pottery.

Earthenware is pottery that has been fired at a temperature too low to allow it to be even partly converted to a brittle, hard glass or glasslike material. This change, which requires high temperatures, is called vitrification. One method of classifying pottery, based on progressively higher firing temperatures, is the division into earthenware, stoneware, and porcelain.

Pottery may be glazed or unglazed. Glazing is the process of applying to the surface of the pottery a thin layer of a material that vitrifies under heat. This forms a hard coating that protects the ware, increases its impermeability (water resistance), and usually enhances its appearance. The production of glazed ware usually involves two separate firings. First, the ware is fired to produce a strong, pale-colored pottery called biscuit; then the glaze is applied, and a second firing causes vitrification of the thin glaze layer. In the case of porcelain, which is the highest quality pottery, the second firing is at a much higher temperature than the primary firing.

Pottery can also be categorized by the amount of water it will absorb when unglazed and immersed. Absorption of water occurs through fine pores in the surface of the fired material. As a general rule, absorption—which may cause a 2- to 15-percent increase in weight—depends on the firing temperature: the higher the temperature, the smaller the pores will be and the lower the absorption. Unglazed pottery allows water to pass through it, which can be

FIRING AND GLAZING POTTERY

Modern pottery made in the Taos Pueblo in New Mexico.

Firing is the process by which irreversible changes are caused in the clay, which is converted into a form of stone or glass. This conversion is called densification and occurs through a process called liquid-phase sintering, in which residual water in the clay is driven out. Clays contain finely ground feldspar, which melts to form a viscous liquid and promotes densification.

Modern kilns are lined with refractory materials that will withstand very high temperatures. The lowest temperatures commonly used in kilns are for the firing of common earthenware. For this, a temperature of 1650–2190°F (900–1200°C) is used. The color of the resulting article depends on the clay used and may range from dull yellowish through red, brown, or even black. Stoneware is fired at temperatures of 2190–2340°F (1200–1280°C). At these higher temperatures, the result is a white, gray, yellow, or red material, which is then usually covered by an opaque glaze. The firing of porcelain differs from that of other pottery. The initial firing to produce the biscuit is done at 1830–2190°F (1000–1200°C), which is similar to that used for earthenware. But the final firing is done at the maturing temperature of the glaze, and may be as high as 2730°F (1500°C) .

Glazes may be transparent or opaque and come in a range of different colors. With clays containing various impurities, changes in color can be effected by altering the oxygen inside the kiln by opening or closing air vents. This is because different metal oxides have different colors, and these can be selected by altering the availability of oxygen.

Glazing can be done over the whole surface of the object or only outside or inside. Often, the bottom surface—on which the article rests—is left unglazed, but in commercial practice, the item is often supported on three or more fine points for the second firing so that the bottom can be glazed. There are three elements to glazes: the materials that melt to form the glass (mainly silica or boron); the body or stiffener, such as clay, that gives thickness to the glaze; and the flux or melting agent that helps silica to liquefy at a lower temperature. Fluxes are made of lead or sodium compounds. The most common element in glass is silica (silicon dioxide), which is derived from minerals such as sand, flint, quartz, or feldspars (aluminosilicates) and is finely powdered.

Glazes can be applied by dipping, brushing, or spraying. They can be applied to the unfired clay article or, more commonly, to the article after the initial biscuit firing. Glazes must be able to melt and partially penetrate the surface of the biscuit at a temperature that does not adversely affect the biscuit. The melting temperature is critical, since the glaze must not become so liquid that it runs.

A CLOSER LOOK

an advantage in that liquids can be cooled through slow evaporation from the outer surface. The latent heat of evaporation is taken partly from the contents of the container (see HEAT EXCHANGER). Garden pottery is usually unglazed.

Terra-cotta is unglazed earthenware made from yellow, red, or brown clays. This type of pottery has long been used for large pots, statues, sculptures, and other pieces of art. Earthenware is also used for common and inexpensive white or ivory-colored tableware, which is usually glazed. This type of pottery is called creamware.

Stoneware, which is a heavy, strong pottery, usually of a cream or pale-brown color, is often left unglazed. China is always glazed. It is white and strong enough to be made so thin that it is translucent (light can pass through it). Because it must undergo heavy and sometimes careless usage, hotel china is generally made thick and strong and is not translucent. Some chinas contain powdered glass; bone china contains animal bone that has been calcined (strongly heated) and powdered.

Porcelain is a fine ceramic material that uses kaolin clays (also called China clays) to form thin, delicate shapes. The first firing of a porcelain piece is done at a comparatively low temperature, but the second firing, after the application of the glaze, is done at an extremely high temperature, resulting in vitrification. At such high temperatures porcelain becomes very soft and sometimes has to be supported if it is to retain its shape.

Various terms are used to describe pottery that has been decorated in different ways. *Majolica* is the name of a pale red or gray pottery that is covered with an opaque (nontransparent) glaze made from bright metallic oxides. *Faience* is a soft, porous red or yellow pottery covered with an opaque glaze made from tin compounds.

Shaping clay

Clay that is suitable for pottery has a plasticity that allows objects to be modeled from it in various ways. Plasticity can be adjusted for each particular object either by adding water or by allowing water to evaporate. If necessary, clay can be made almost liquid and strained to remove large particles before being poured into a mold. This strained liquid form of clay is known as slip.

There are various traditional methods of shaping clay for domestic utensils. For some objects, a lump of clay can simply be pinched and shaped into the desired form with the fingers. Alternatively, the clay can be rolled out flat on a board and pressed into some kind of mold, or the flat clay can be draped and formed over the outside of the mold. It can also be rolled between the palms of the hands into long thin ropes, known as coils, which can then be formed into circles or spirals from which the walls of a vessel can be built. Sometimes the coils are left visible to create a particular effect, but more commonly they are smoothed out using the palms of the hands and slip to produce an even surface.

Today, the most familiar and popular method of shaping bowls and similar utensils is on a potter's wheel. A potter's wheel is a simple turning lathe that takes the form of a small circular table, which is rotated in a horizontal plane by a treadle mechanism or by a variable-speed electric motor. In order to maintain momentum and smooth rotation, the vertical rotating shaft, which bears the weight of the table, sometimes carries a heavy flywheel situated below the tabletop.

Before putting any clay onto the wheel, the potter will ensure that its consistency is suitable for the object to be made. The clay is thrown onto the center of the table and pressed down to ensure that it adheres (sticks). The wheel is then rotated at high speed, by foot treadle or electric motor, and the potter's wetted hands center the clay. This process requires a lot of practice and great precision, since the potter must prevent the clay from flying outward as a result of centrifugal force (see CENTRIFUGE). Once the clay is perfectly centered, the speed of rotation can be reduced. The potter works with the force of the wheel, ensuring that accurate centering is maintained at all times. To make a bowl or pot, a cavity must be formed in the clay lump, which is a process known as opening. This requires great care in order to avoid dynamic imbalance in the clay from unequal thickness of the walls.

Generally the potter will work with both hands simultaneously, one inside and one outside the walls of the emerging object. This has the result that, as the object becomes taller, the walls gradually become thinner. When the basic shaping is complete, variously shaped metal tools can be applied to the surface of the clay as it continues to rotate, in order to form simple decoration.

Objects made of wet clay cannot be fired immediately but must first be thoroughly air dried. If there is any excess water in the clay when it is fired, it will be turned to steam, which may cause breakage or other damage. Although the drying process may take several days, it is essential that it is accomplished slowly and evenly, because clay shrinks as it dries, and any uneven drying may cause the clay to crack. Cracking happens because clay has a platelike molecular structure, and as the water evaporates, the plates are no longer able to slide as freely over each other. As a result, the clay becomes hard, rigid, and brittle and is easily broken.

Clay that is partially dried and stiff, which is often referred to as leather hard, can have a pattern embossed upon it by pressure. Alternatively, it can be decoratively incised, with holes cut through or colored pieces pressed into it.

Industrialized pottery

The application of large-scale industrial methods to pottery production, while greatly altering the quantities manufactured, has not changed the underlying principles. Conventional drying in the open atmosphere is, however, unacceptably slow, and in modern pottery factories, greenware (unfired articles) is

Pottery plants use large machines to mix clay ready for shaping.

dried on conveyor belts in hot drying tunnels. This stage removes easily evaporable water. It is not part of the firing process itself.

Although some mass-produced articles are still shaped by turning at the leather hardness stage, this limits production and is seldom feasible when large output is required. Instead, purified and processed clays are pressure molded to produce items. Firing is done by gradual heating in tunnel kilns, through

JOSIAH WEDGWOOD

Josiah Wedgwood (1730–1795) was born into a family of potters in Burslem in Staffordshire, England. At the time of his birth, local pottery was primitive and most quality goods were imported from China. As a young man, Wedgwood was barely able to read or write. At the age of 14, an attack of smallpox affected his right leg, which was later amputated, and hindered his work at the potter's wheel. Despite these setbacks, he opened his first pottery factory at Burslem in 1759.

Wedgwood's initial success came from a cream-colored ware, which became known as Queen's ware after Queen Charlotte ordered a complete table service from him. This form of pottery was patented in 1763. As he became better known, Wedgwood was able to obtain—on loan—specimens of ancient vases, cameos, sculptures, medallions, and seals, which he used as models. The result was a unique and widely imitated design of pottery, with an unglazed blue jasper background and raised designs in white and black basalt. To this day, this design is known as Wedgwood.

By 1785, Wedgwood had built a village of potteries, and in the now greatly enlarged pottery district of Staffordshire, 20,000 people were employed and 60,000 tons of clay and flints were being imported annually. Wedgwood became a fellow of the Royal Society and died rich, respected, and widely honored.

PEOPLE

THE MAIN STAGES IN MAKING PORCELAIN AND GLAZE

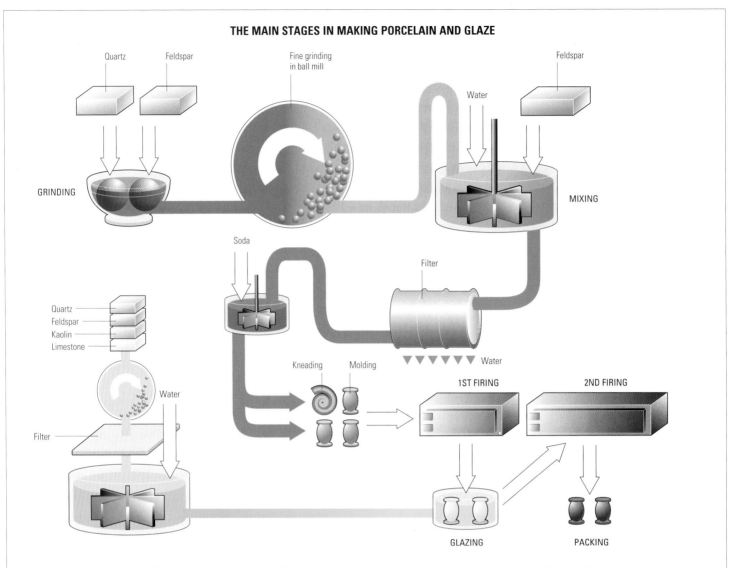

Quartz Feldspar Fine grinding in ball mill Feldspar

Water

GRINDING

MIXING

Soda

Filter

Quartz
Feldspar
Kaolin
Limestone

Water

Filter

Kneading Molding

Water

1ST FIRING 2ND FIRING

GLAZING PACKING

The raw materials are ground, mixed with water, filtered, then shaped into pots. The pots are fired, glazed, then fired again before being packed.

which items are carried on conveyor belts or on vehicles running on rails. The items are carried through zones of rising temperature until optimum baking or vitrifying temperature is reached. The fired items are then taken through zones of decreasing temperature to avoid cracking through thermal shock.

R. YOUNGSON

See also: CERAMICS; GLASS AND GLASSMAKING; MATERIALS SCIENCE; PLASTICS; PREHISTORIC TECHNOLOGY; TECHNOLOGY IN ANCIENT CIVILIZATIONS; WOOD AND WOODWORKING.

Further reading:
Cohen, L. *Art of Clay: Timeless Pottery of the Southwest.* Santa Fe: Clear Light Publishers, 1993.
Cosentino, P. *The Encyclopedia of Pottery Techniques.* Philadelphia: Running Press, 1990.
The Emergence of Pottery: Technology and Innovation in Ancient Societies. Edited by W. Barnett and J. Hoopes. Washington, D.C.: Smithsonian Institution Press, 1995.*Encyclopedia of British Art Pottery, 1870–1920.* Edited by V. Bergesen. London, England: Barrie & Jenkins, 1991.
Fournier, R. *Illustrated Dictionary of Practical Pottery.* Radnor, Pennsylvania: Chilton Book Co., 1992.
Gibson, A. *Prehistoric Pottery for the Archaeologist.* Washington, D.C.: Leicester University Press, 1997.
Godden, G. *Encyclopedia of British Pottery and Porcelain Marks.* London, England: Barrie & Jenkins, 1991.

BERNARD LEACH AND SHOJI HAMADA

British potter Bernard Howell Leach (1887–1979) studied at the Slade School of Art in London before traveling to Japan to be a teacher at the age of 21. There he also studied pottery. In 1920, Leach returned to England and, in partnership with a great Japanese potter named Shoji Hamada (1894–1978), set up the Leach potteries at St. Ives in Cornwall. Hamada had been a professor at the Institute of Pottery in Kyoto, Japan. Leach and Hamada established styles of stoneware and Japanese *raku* ware that combined artistic quality with cheapness, using local materials. Leach's aim was to make fine ware readily affordable. One of his pupils, Michael Cardew (1901–1982), became a leading figure in the 20th-century revival of interest in craft pottery making.

PEOPLE

POWERBOAT

Powerboats are high-performance, motor-powered boats used for sport and leisure

The first true powerboats made their appearance with the invention of the steam engine and the screw propeller during the 19th century. A wide range of steam pinnaces (small vessels) and launches were built that had graceful lines and room for picnic parties or small groups of paying passengers. But the modern powerboat evolved from the invention of the internal combustion engine. By the early 20th century, motorboats that used modified automobile engines had become highly popular in both Europe and North America.

Three major innovations brought about this popularity. The first was the invention of the outboard motor by Ole Evinrude (1877–1934) in 1909. This was a self-contained power unit that had an adjustable clamp with which it could be fitted to any suitable boat or even moved from one boat to another. The second innovation was more efficient hull design, which allowed boats to plane on top of the water surface instead of plowing through it, greatly cutting drag (water resistance) and allowing speeds to rise. The third innovation was the gradual replacement of traditional wooden hulls by metal or fiberglass hulls for greater strength and durability (see BOATBUILDING AND SHIPBUILDING).

Basic powerboats

Today's powerboats are built for a wide variety of uses, all of which influence hull design and power requirements. For sheltered inland waters, the most basic powerboats have simple, flat-bottomed hulls, which curve upward at the bow (front) and stern (back). These allow the boat to plane on smooth water and make it easy to beach, but they can make for a wet and unstable ride in rougher water.

The skiff or sharpie has a similar flat-bottomed hull, with the bow shaped to a point so that it produces less spray in choppy water. Some skiffs have the bow faired (smoothed) into a more deliberate V-shape at the bow, so that the boat cuts through the waves to produce a smoother ride. But when the hull starts to plane, its flat bottom produces a very bumpy ride in choppy water.

A three-person Fountain powerboat planes at high speed across the waters of Lake Washington in Seattle, Washington.

The answer to this problem, the deep-V hull, which has a long, wedge-shaped bottom and a V-shaped cross section, was developed in the United States in the late 1950s. Because this hull lacked the flat surface to help planing at speed, the designers added strakes on either side of the point of the V. Strakes are steps in the contour of the bottom of the hull that provide lift and hoist the boat into the planing position. This design proved so efficient that it became the basis of all specialized high-speed racing powerboats (known as hydroplanes), in which most of the the hull leaves the water altogether, leaving only the screws (propellers) and the rudder below the surface to propel the vehicle forward.

As a result, powerboat speeds have increased enormously since the beginning of the 20th century. In 1904, the average speed of the winner of the

CORE FACTS

- The first successful outboard motor was invented by Ole Evinrude in 1909 and made powerboating more popular.
- Powerboats can plane over the water surface to produce high speed or ride behind their own bow wave for more economical running.
- Flat-bottomed hulls give stability but are uncomfortable in rough and choppy seas.
- The Boston whaler was made of a sandwich of fiberglass and polyurethane foam; it could float even after being sawed in half.

CONNECTIONS

● While powerboats skim across water to minimize drag, **HYDROFOILS** rise up on vanes to minimize cutting through the water.

American Power Boat Association's first Gold Cup race was only 23.6 mph (38.0 km/h). In 1950 the hydroplane Slo-Mo-Shun IV set a new record speed of 160.3 mph (258 km/h) at Seattle; 10 years later the Hustler raised it to 285.2 mph (459 km/h). The Spirit of Australia recorded an even higher speed of 319.6 mph (514.3 km/h) in 1978.

The fastest boats have inboard engines, which can occupy a large part of the hull; outboard engines are smaller and less powerful. The 100-mph barrier was not broken by an outboard-powered boat until 1954, when Massimo Leto di Priolo of Italy reached 100.4 mph (161.5 km/h). In 1989, U.S. boat *MACH Propeller Specialties* reached 176.6 mph (284.1 km/h)—a record that still stood in 1999.

SPECIAL HULLS

This racing powerboat has a pickle-fork tunnel hull.

Because flat-bottomed boats are more stable than V-shaped hulls but give a very rough ride in choppy conditions, designers have tried to find an efficient compromise. The popular Boston whaler used the flexibility of fiberglass as a building material to produce a hull bottom with a corrugated profile, like a series of shallow V-shaped hulls side by side.

The whaler was made from a sandwich of fiberglass outer hulls and polyurethane foam filling inside. Not only was it unsinkable, even when sawed in half during a demonstration or with the drain plug removed, but it gave a more stable and comfortable ride than either deep-V or flat-bottomed hulls.

Another successful design used a hull with a V-shaped cross section in the center, flanked by sections on either side that were angled downward. The cross-section was similar to an inverted W and gave better stability and rough weather performance. Later variations included trihulls, with three V-shaped profiles side by side in a single hull.

For greater speed, catamaran (twin) hulls have given way to pontoon boats, with a single platform over two small hulls set side by side. For high-performance powerboats, another development of the catamaran is the tunnel hull, where the gap, or tunnel, between the twin hulls and below the main hull platform creates lift and helps the boat to plane. When the twin hulls project in front of the platform, the design is called a pickle-fork tunnel boat. It can be extremely fast even when powered by an outboard motor.

A CLOSER LOOK

Displacement hulls

While most fast powerboats have planing hulls, heavier freight powerboats have displacement hulls. These hulls remain immersed in the water and displace a volume of water equivalent to the weight of the boat—including its cargo. The maximum speed is lower than that of a planing hull and is governed by the laws of hydrodynamics (liquid and gas motion) rather than the power of the engines: maximum speed increases with the waterline length of the hull (see HYDRODYNAMICS AND HYDROSTATICS).

The theoretical maximum speed of a displacement hull in knots (nautical miles per hour, where one nautical mile is equal to 1.15 miles or 1.85 km on land) is approximately equal to 1.5 times the square root of the waterline length in feet. This means a powerboat with a waterline length of 36 ft (10.9 m) has a maximum speed under ideal conditions of 9 knots. Any attempt to move the hull at a faster speed requires an enormous increase in power to move the bow wave out of the way.

However, the great advantage of displacement hulls is that at any speed below the maximum they need less effort to move them through the water. Under these conditions, a powerboat with a displacement hull may cover a given distance using only a fifth of the fuel that a planing boat would burn to operate at its most efficient speed.

Motor cruisers

Powerboats for short trips or for lake or river fishing are usually completely open. Some have a deck covering the bow section for stowing food or equipment. Others, particularly when fitted with inboard engines, may have a sheltered steering position. But powerboats designed for cruising usually have bunks and cooking facilities inside a closed cabin so that users can live aboard. While smaller cruisers are often powered by outboard motors, larger cruising powerboats usually have inboard engines. The largest of all are seaworthy enough to navigate offshore routes; they have twin engines for extra performance and in case of breakdowns.

Some cruisers use both sail and power. Sailboats often have an auxiliary engine for use while maneuvering in harbor, to maintain progress in calm weather, or to steer clear of hazards, while some larger power cruisers have auxiliary sails. These are called motor sailers. They have powerful engines and a powerboat hull form, but they are able to operate under sail with a fair wind.

D. OWEN

See also: BOATBUILDING AND SHIPBUILDING; HYDRODYNAMICS AND HYDROSTATICS; MARINE ENGINEERING; PROPELLER; RUDDER; SAILING; SHIP AND BOAT; SHIP AND BOAT, HISTORY OF; SUBMARINE; WARSHIP.

Further reading:

Pike, D. *An Introduction to Powerboat Cruising.* New York: Hearst Marine Books, 1989.

POWER STATION

A power station produces electric power in bulk for industrial, commercial, and household uses

At the heart of any power station are the alternators, also called generators, which are machines that produce electricity when a shaft inside them is made to rotate. This rotation is powered by a turbine, which may be driven by falling water in a hydroelectric plant, by expanding hot gases in a gas-turbine plant, or by high-pressure steam in a thermal plant (see TURBINE).

A thermal power station uses a heat source to produce steam from water. The heat may be provided by a nuclear reaction (see NUCLEAR POWER) or by burning fossil fuels, such as coal, oil, or natural gas. The steam drives a turbine, which turns generators to produce electricity. The voltage from the generator is then changed to a convenient value to feed a network of cables, which carries the electricity from the power station to the customer (see ELECTRICITY TRANSMISSION AND SUPPLY).

The first power plant, built by Thomas Edison (1847–1931), was operated in New York in 1882. A power station built in London in 1889 provided energy for half the city's population.

Electricity generation

The amount of electricity a power station generates is measured in megawatts (MW), which are millions of watts. A power station may contain more than one generating unit, and the outputs of the different units may vary considerably. Large coal-fired or nuclear generating units produce between 800 and 1200 MW. Typical oil- or gas-fueled units generate between 300 and 600 MW. Small, gas-turbine units generate 100 MW or less. A 1000-MW power station will supply the electricity demand for about one million people in a developed country.

The breakdown of total electricity generated using each fuel type varies considerably between countries and is determined mainly by the fuel reserves and the economic and ecological policies of the different countries. France has invested heavily in nuclear power: it generates about 80 percent of its power in nuclear power stations. The United States generates 70–80 percent of its total power by burning fossil fuels, the remainder being produced by nuclear or hydroelectric power stations.

Worldwide, at the start of 1999, the total electric-generating capacity was about 2 million MW. Of this, fossil-fuel power stations account for about

CORE FACTS

- The first power station was built by Thomas Edison and began operation in New York in 1882.
- A 1000-MW power station can supply the electricity needs for a city with a population of about one million people in a developed country.
- A modern fossil-fuel power station can convert up to about 40 percent of the heat energy from the fuel into electric power; the other 60 percent is wasted.

CONNECTIONS

- **DAMS** are part of **WATER RESOURCES TECHNOLOGY** projects to harness **WATER POWER**.

- A modern power station would use the latest **PUMP AND COMPRESSOR** technology and **PRESSURE MEASUREMENT** systems.

The smokestacks of the New York Edison Power Company in 1940, a steam-producing plant located at 40th Street and 1st Avenue.

Electricity distribution

Electricity is often generated away from the areas where electricity consumers are concentrated. Hydroelectric power stations have to be situated close to reservoirs that provide the pressure of water required to drive their turbines, while thermal power stations require a plentiful supply of cooling water, such as a river, to condense steam after it has passed through their turbines. Furthermore, nuclear power stations are usually situated in remote locations to reduce the potential for damage to human health in the case of an accident.

Several power stations are linked to each other and to the consumers by a network of high-tension (high-voltage) cables known as a grid. Some electrical power is lost as heat when current flows through the grid, and the amount lost is proportional to the square of the current. For this reason, very high voltages are used to reduce the size of the current needed to deliver the same power (see ELECTRICITY AND MAGNETISM). The output from the generators—typically 22,000 V alternating current (AC)—is stepped up (increased by transformers) to 400,000 volts or more before it is fed into the grid. Such high voltages require pylons with cables hung from long insulators to avoid losses of current to the ground, and underground cables require thick insulation for the same reason (see TRANSFORMER).

Near the consumer, the power is spread through local networks at progressively lower voltages provided by substations (transformers that are fed by the grid and that reduce the voltage of the supply). Industrial users may require 33,000 V; distribution to neighborhood substations may be 11,000 V; and household supplies are typically 110–240 V. Local grids, therefore, have a number of substations that provide the required voltages.

The quantity of electricity demanded from the grid at any time is known as the load. The load varies widely throughout a 24-hour period, and peaks can be caused by a variety of events, such as large numbers of people arriving home at roughly the same time and switching on electrical appliances. There may be several peaks in one day, and the number of generators in use and their combined output have to respond accordingly.

The base load—the lowest level of demand in the daily cycle—is provided by large, efficient power stations that produce the cheapest electricity but take longest to start up and shut down. These are typically coal-fired or nuclear power stations. Medium-sized generating units are started up to fulfill periods of increased average demand at higher cost (they are less efficient). The smallest stations (and normally the most expensive to run) can be put into operation rapidly to cope with short-term peaks in the load. These small stations are typically gas turbines.

62 percent, of which coal is 40 percent, oil about 7 percent, and gas about 15 percent. Hydroelectric and nuclear power divide the remaining 38 percent about equally. Wind, solar, and geothermal energy made a tiny contribution to global capacity.

FOSSIL FUELS AND GLOBAL WARMING

The concentration of carbon dioxide in the atmosphere has increased from about 280 parts per trillion parts of air by volume in preindustrial days to about 360 parts per trillion parts of air by volume today. This increase is mainly due to human activities, particularly the burning of fossil fuels. Carbon dioxide remains in the atmosphere for many decades, and if emissions were to continue at the 1999 levels, the concentration of carbon dioxide in the atmosphere would reach roughly 500 parts per trillion by volume—about twice the preindustrial concentration—in 200 years. Experts believe that this concentration of carbon dioxide is already causing significant changes in the global climate.

The efficient removal of carbon dioxide from gaseous discharges is technically difficult and prohibitively expensive. To lessen global climate change, it is argued that future energy supplies should rely more on renewable energy resources, such as solar and wind power, and much less on fossil fuels.

WIDER IMPACT

Fossil-fueled thermal power stations

A fossil-fueled power station comprises a fuel-processing facility that delivers the coal, natural gas, or oil to be burned; a furnace and boiler to produce steam; and turbines that use steam to turn electric generators. Condensers turn the steam back to water and thereby create a vacuum that helps draw the steam through the turbines. There are pumps to provide high-pressure water to the boiler and low-pressure water to the condenser, and many stations also have facilities to remove pollutants from gases before they are discharged into the air.

Handling the fuel. The way that the fuel is handled in the power station depends on the type of fuel used. By far the simplest fuel to handle is natural gas, which is received by pipeline and fed directly into the furnace, where it burns. No special handling or storage arrangements are needed. Oil may also be delivered to the power station by pipeline, but it is usually transported in tankers by ship, road, or rail. It is stored at the power station in large storage tanks from which it is piped to the furnace to be vaporized and burned. Usually, a few months' oil supply is kept in the tanks at the power station.

In a coal-fired power station, coal is delivered to the power station by road, rail, or ship. It is stored, often in large stockpiles that contain enough coal to supply the power station for perhaps six or more months in case there are interruptions in supply. Coal is taken from the stockpile and crushed into a powder in a mill (pulverized coal burns more efficiently than solid lumps).

Producing steam. The type of furnace used in fossil-fueled power stations depends on the fuel used. Gas-fired furnaces are the smallest and simplest; oil-fired furnaces are intermediate in size; coal-fired furnaces are the largest and most complicated. The size and complexity of coal-fired boilers also varies with the energy content of the coal used. Brown coal and lignite have the lowest energy content per unit weight and require the largest furnaces to produce the same quantity of heat.

Water is pumped at high pressure into pipes that run through the furnace. The heat energy released by the burning fuel turns the water into high-pressure steam that is then fed through steam turbines. The expanding steam causes the turbine to rotate and turn an electric generator connected to the shaft of a steam turbine. At the turbine outlet, the steam is cooled with water, which makes it condense.

Water contracts on condensation from steam to liquid water, and the process of condensation produces a partial vacuum, which draws the steam through the turbine and increases the mechanical energy delivered to the turbine. The hot water from the condenser outlet then returns to be reheated.

Condensers often use water from a large body of water—the sea, river, or lake. Usually, most of the condenser water's heat is removed in cooling towers before the water is returned to its source. This minimizes the impact of the hot water on aquatic lifeforms near the power station. Sometimes, waste heat may be used in the central heating systems of buildings, a practicable use when the power station is in a built-up area. In other cases, the heat can warm a body of water for fish farming.

GAS TURBINES AND COMBINED-CYCLE PLANTS

The generator hall of a power station. The generators are linked to turbines.

Some power stations use gas rather than steam turbines to drive the electric generators. They are normally fueled with natural gas or light oils, have a low power output of a few tens of MW, and a low thermal efficiency. However, they can be brought onstream (be in a condition to generate electricity for the grid) in minutes, rather than the hours needed for larger units. Typically, therefore, they are used to supply peak loads.

A compressed-air and fuel mixture is burned in a combustion chamber. The gases produced by the combustion are allowed to expand in the turbine before being discharged to the atmosphere.

Both gas and steam turbines are used in combined-cycle power plants to improve thermal efficiency and save costs. Heat from the gas turbine exhaust is used to produce steam for the steam turbine.

A CLOSER LOOK

Improving efficiency

The thermal efficiency of a power station is the percentage of the heat generated in the furnace that is converted into electricity. In the 1940s, the thermal efficiency of a typical thermal power station was less than 30 percent. By the end of the 20th century, thermal efficiencies had increased to nearly 40 percent. Much of this improvement was due to the introduction of new alloys, such as a chromium-manganese-molybdenum-nickel alloy, for making the steam piping. These pipes can withstand steam pressures of up to 600,000 pounds per square feet (2.9 million kg/sq m) and temperatures of about 1200°F (650°C). These figures represent an increase in steam pressure by about four times, and a steam temperature about 30 percent higher than would be possible using older pipe materials such as cast iron. The higher pressure and temperature of the steam allow it to drive the turbine more efficiently.

Further improvements have been achieved by passing the steam through a series of turbines so that more mechanical energy can be extracted from the

The twin domes of a nuclear power plant on the North Anna River, Virginia.

steam. Some units reheat the outlet steam from the turbines to about 1060°F (570°C) before passing it through a second set of turbines.

As the world's resources of fossil fuels are used up, interest in improving thermal efficiencies will continue to increase. At the rate of fossil fuel consumption at the start of 1999, oil reserves will be used up in about 40 years, gas reserves in 60 years, and coal in 250 years.

Controlling emissions

Gaseous and liquid wastes from fossil-fuel power stations are treated before they are discharged to the atmosphere to reduce the amount of pollutants in them and therefore minimize damage to the environment. National regulations often limit the amounts of pollutants—solid, liquid, and gaseous—that can be discharged (see POLLUTION AND ITS CONTROL).

The main pollutants are solid particles and gases. Power stations that burn natural gas do not produce particles to a significant extent, but those burning coal and oil do: coal produces large quantities of pulverized-fuel ash (PFA), and oil produces soot (amorphous carbon).

Particles in flue gases can be removed using electrostatic precipitators, in which the particles are given an electrical charge by passing the flue gases through a metal comb that is at high voltage. The charged particles are then passed over plates that carry the opposite electrical charge. The particles become stuck and are removed from the gas stream.

The main gaseous pollutants are carbon dioxide, nitrogen oxides, and sulfur dioxide. Carbon dioxide and nitrous oxide contribute to global warming; sulfur dioxide produces acid rain.

The pollutant from fossil-fuel power stations of greatest environmental concern is carbon dioxide gas. The burning of one ton of carbon produces almost four tons of carbon dioxide. The carbon dioxide is released into the air, where it contributes to global warming (see the box on page 1040).

Sulfur dioxide can be removed from flue gases by desulfurization equipment, which uses alkaline substances, such as lime, limestone, sodium, magnesium, or other compounds to remove the sulfur dioxide. Limestone slurries are commonly used. The slurries are either thrown away or used to produce gypsum as a by-product (see HAZARDOUS WASTE).

Nitrogen oxides are sometimes removed by injecting ammonia into the flue gas and passing the mixture through a catalyst (see CATALYST, INDUSTRIAL). This process is used less commonly than flue-gas desulfurization.

After these processes, which are collectively known as scrubbing processes, the flue gases are generally reheated, which helps carry them upward in the atmosphere. They are discharged through a tall chimney so that the gases are dispersed effectively.

F. BARNABY

See also: ELECTRIC MOTOR AND GENERATOR; GAS TURBINE; GEOTHERMAL ENERGY; HYDROELECTRICITY; STEAM TURBINE; WAVE POWER; WIND POWER.

Further reading:

El-Hawary, M. *Electrical Power Systems: Design and Analysis*. New York: Institute of Electrical and Electronics Engineers, 1993.
Grainger, J. *Power Systems Analysis*. New York: McGraw Hill, 1994.

PRECISION FARMING

Precision farming is the use of technological systems that precisely deliver inputs on a field-by-field basis

Farmers have traditionally separated their land into enclosures or fields in which different activities can be pursued. Precision farming involves farming practices that vary according to differing conditions in a field. This site-specific approach makes more efficient use of inputs such as labor, machine running time, and chemicals.

Using satellites on the farm

The core of precision farming is modern satellite tracking technology. The Global Positioning System (GPS) is a satellite network that can be used, with appropriate receiving equipment, to identify precisely the latitude and longitude of any site, typically to within a few feet (see NAVIGATION).

A GPS receiver can be installed in any farm machine so that its location can be tracked constantly. Other information can then be recorded in combination with this positional data. For example, a GPS-equipped combine harvester can be fitted with a meter to measure the volume of grain being harvested. Data is held on an electronic recorder in the cab and can be transferred later to a personal computer for analysis (see HARVESTING MACHINERY).

Data analysis in precision farming is often in the form of a yield map (see the diagram at right), which is a plan of a field showing grain yield. This map can be used to identify areas that perform above or below average and to make management decisions based on this knowledge. For example, the farmer may decide to take a low-yielding area out of cultivation to cut losses, or to take soil samples to identify any local nutrient deficiencies that may be depressing the yield. More comprehensive maps of field conditions may also include other yield-determining factors, such as weed infestations. Improvements in the capabilities of field recording equipment and sensors should further expand the scope of precision farming (see TRANSDUCER AND SENSOR).

Increasing farm efficiency

An important aspect of precision farming is the use of yield maps and similar data to control fertilizer dosage. The best rate of application can be calculated from yield data, and this can be programmed into an electronically controlled fertilizer dispenser, drawn by a GPS-equipped tractor. This releases the desired amount of fertilizer for the current location as the tractor moves across the field. The application of herbicides or pesticides can be controlled in the same way. The total dose of chemicals is reduced, cutting costs and giving environmental benefits.

Precision farming places the computer at the center of the farm. Information from diverse sources can be added to that derived from GPS to build an extensive body of management data. For example, digital images from remote-sensing satellites, giving

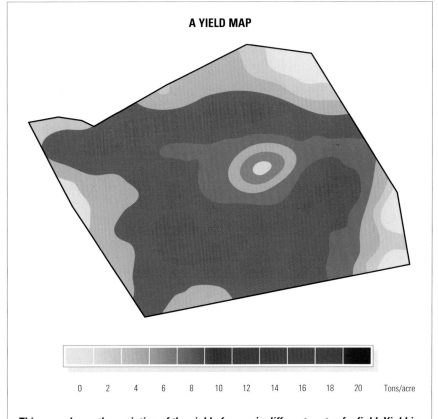

A YIELD MAP

| 0 | 2 | 4 | 6 | 8 | 10 | 12 | 14 | 16 | 18 | 20 | Tons/acre |

This map shows the variation of the yield of crops in different parts of a field. Yield is determined by factors such as soil type, topology, streams, high trees, and fertilizer.

pictures of large areas of cropland or rangeland, can be studied. Computer data can also be archived to give an accurate record of past management.

Precision farming offers previously unprecedented control over many aspects of agriculture and is certain to be an area of development in the future. It will increase farm efficiency by making optimum use of inputs such as chemicals; this is cost-effective and minimizes wasteful overuse and environmental pollution. Full automation of farm machinery is likely to be the next development in countries with advanced agriculture. Research is proceeding into the use of GPS systems to steer tractors and other farm machinery electronically, without operators. The prospect of an arable farm controlled by a single worker from the farm office is a distinct possibility for the future.

T. ALLMAN

See also: AGRICULTURAL SCIENCE; AGRICULTURAL TRANSPORT AND MAINTENANCE MACHINERY; AGRICULTURE, HISTORY OF; ARABLE FARMING; ORGANIC FARMING AND SUSTAINABLE AGRICULTURE.

Further reading:
Emmert, B. *Precision Farming*. Beltsville, Maryland: National Agricultural Library, 1994.

CONNECTIONS

● Precision farming equipment can be used to deliver exact amounts of **FERTILIZER** and **PESTICIDE AND HERBICIDE** to farmland.

● Precision farming depends heavily on **SATELLITE** technology and **COMPUTERS**.

PREHISTORIC TECHNOLOGY

Prehistoric humans made and used tools to obtain food, work the land, and increase their chances of survival

The Stonehenge monument on Salisbury Plain, England, was used by ancient peoples, probably for religious ceremonies linked to the rising and setting of the sun and moon. Researchers estimate that it was built in three stages between c.3000 and 1500 B.C.E.

CONNECTIONS

● Prehistoric farming communities used their knowledge of **ANIMAL BREEDING** to increase the productivity of their herds.

● **MINING AND QUARRYING** were vital prehistoric technologies because they provided materials to make metal and stone implements.

With the knowledge that history is widely considered as the record of the past as derived from written texts, it may seem evident that prehistory should be defined as the period before writing was invented. However, literacy did not appear all over the world at once, nor did it spread evenly throughout societies. Thus the line dividing prehistory from history cannot be simply drawn. To further complicate definition, some groups lived after history began but did not themselves have writing. Examples of such communities, known as protohistorical communities, would be the peoples of northern Europe who were contemporary with the early literate civilizations in the Mediterranean, or indigenous communities of Africa and the Americas when they were first settled by European explorers four or five hundred years ago.

For the purposes of this article, prehistoric peoples are considered to be those without any writing skills or extensive contact with literate neighbors. Prehistoric societies were generally small in scale, without major divisions of labor. This definition not only implies that prehistory ended at different times in different regions of the world, but also that, in a very few, extremely isolated areas, prehistory may be said to continue to this day.

The Stone Age

The story of the human race begins in East Africa, with the appearance of the earliest human ancestor, called the hominid, some 4 or 5 million years ago. By around 2.5 million years ago, hominids were beginning to make stone tools (see the box on page 1046). The earliest part of the Stone Age, from around 1.6 million to 200,000 years ago, was called the Lower Paleolithic age and was dominated by a humanlike species called *Homo erectus*. Before becoming extinct, *Homo erectus* spread throughout Africa as well as much of Europe and Asia. The path taken by *Homo erectus* can be traced not only by its fossil remains but also by its characteristic teardrop-shaped ax heads, fashioned by knocking off flakes from both sides of a suitably sized stone (see HAND TOOL).

In addition to toolmaking, another major evolutionary contribution of *Homo erectus* was the ability to make fire. Burned animal bones have been found in a South African cave in a stratigraphic layer about 1.5

CORE FACTS

■ Fire was first used for cooking and hardening materials, and flint working techniques were developed in the Paleolithic or Old Stone Age.

■ The end of the Ice Age saw the dawn of the Neolithic or New Stone Age, when agriculture began and the wheel was invented.

■ Settled communities drove the need for technologies such as pottery and metalworking and provided the opportunity for their development.

■ The transition from prehistory to the historical period began with the development of writing 5000 years ago.

million years old. Fire provided for human comfort and allowed food to be cooked and preserved. Since heated flint was easier to work with than the unheated stone, fire permitted the further development of toolmaking techniques. Wooden implements could also be hardened by fire. Observation of the hardening of clay near the fire soon led to the fashioning of small terra-cotta figures of humans and animals. But the Paleolithic period saw no pottery vessels, since there was little use for it: people were nomadic, and pottery vessels were too heavy to carry (see POTTERY).

Homo sapiens emerged during the Middle Paleolithic age, which is designated as the period between 200,000 and 40,000 years ago. The modern human subspecies, *Homo sapiens sapiens*, is believed to have arisen in Africa around 100,000 years ago. By 10,000 years ago, most areas of the world were populated by humans, except for Oceania, where the Polynesian islands were colonized progressively between c.1000 B.C.E and c.1000 C.E.

The Upper Paleolithic age, from around 40,000 to 15,000 years ago, was characterized in some regions of the world by the development of blade technology. A cylindrical core of rock was split using a punch and hammer stone into a number of thin parallel blanks that were then trimmed into blades for knives, scrapers, and borers. Microliths, which were tiny, geometric stone tools that could be used as barbs in composite weapons, were a feature of the Mesolithic or Middle Stone Age. This period started about 15,000 years ago with the end of the last Ice Age, known in geologic terms as the Pleistocene epoch, and heralded the beginning of the Holocene, which is the current geologic epoch.

In the Neolithic, or New Stone Age, around 10,000 years ago, agriculture began in communities in the Middle East and Latin America. In other areas, such as Japan, settled communities developed around the availability of resources from the sea. Established communities opened the way to the development of many technologies, because infrastructure could be built and information readily passed on. A more complicated society also created more needs, such as more permanent housing and better food production and storage. Large ovens were first built in the Middle East c.8000 B.C.E. to parch grains for easier threshing and to bake bread. Such ovens also provided the opportunity to better control the firing of pottery, and the higher temperatures enabled the development of metalworking. In the naming system of Old World archaeology, the subsequent period, the Bronze Age, began c.4000–3000 B.C.E. and was followed by the Iron Age (see IRON AND STEEL PRODUCTION). As Middle Eastern civilizations developed writing during the Bronze Age, it is then that history can be said to have begun.

Skins and bones
Stone was not the only material used for prehistoric tools—it is just the best preserved and so most readily available for study. Objects made of animal

products, such as animal bones, hides, antlers, and shells, are more fragile, and minor modifications made to them can be harder to distinguish from natural deterioration.

Bone was an especially useful material, being strong but easier to shape than stone, and readily available as a by-product when animals were hunted for food. In Africa, bone splinters were sharpened into weapon points similar to those used in modern times by the San of the Kalahari Desert in Botswana and Namibia. Animal skins were the primary material used for clothing and shelter; leather was also used by the inhabitants of Ireland during the Bronze Age to make sturdy shields for battle (see ARMOR).

Prehistoric woodworking
In most regions of the world, wood is one of the most important materials available. But most wooden structures and tools of prehistoric times have long been lost, having rotted away. Wood may be preserved in certain special environments, which range from the dry heat of the desert areas of Egypt to the bogs of England. Timbers preserved in wet

This idealized painting shows a prehistoric man chipping a stone tool in his firelit cave. His neckwear has been crafted from bones.

FLINT WORKING

These prehistoric Native American flint arrowheads were found in New Mexico.

Many prehistoric tools such as weapon points, blades, scrapers, and shredders were made from stone in a process known as flint working, knapping, or flaking. This involved fracturing the stone to leave an edge, or other shape, and create a useful implement. The first step was to choose the right stone as the raw material. Toolmakers sought hard, homogeneous stone such as flint, chert, or quartzite in pieces fairly close to the size and shape of the end product. Archaeologists often find evidence of test flakes, which were apparently done to check whether a stone would be suitable.

In order to fracture the stone, a force must be applied. Pressure flaking is a technique in which a gradual pressure is applied. In percussion flaking, another stone is used to hammer on the one being worked. The result of a fracture is the separation of a flake of stone from the main part, or core. Usually it was the core that was being worked into the tool by the removal of flakes. But sometimes the flake itself was used, perhaps after being retouched by having further flakes removed from it.

Since techniques tend to be passed down within communities, it is important for archaeologists to be able to classify stone tools by their features. When a flake is separated from the core, fracture features are left on each piece, where they were formerly in contact. On the flake, this is called the ventral surface. The reverse images of the features on the flake appear on the core as negative or flake scars. The types of features that appear on these surfaces are given standard names so that they can be compared from one tool, community, region, or time to another. Classifying the features left by intentional stone fracturing also helps archaeologists to distinguish between tools and stones fractured by heat, ice, or other natural phenomena.

A CLOSER LOOK

environments are especially useful because they often still show the marks of woodworking. This enables archaeologists to learn not only about the wooden object itself but also about the tools and techniques used to create it. Great care must be taken to distinguish tool marks in wood from natural marks, such as those left by the teeth of rodents. Large wooden objects such as coffins, trunks, bridges, waterfront structures, and buildings survive in recognizable form more often than small wooden implements.

A very important product of woodworking in prehistoric times was the wheel (see WHEEL). In the Old World, wheeled vehicles first appeared in the 4th millenium B.C.E. They were sometimes placed in graves along with other goods that the deceased was expected to need in the afterlife.

Early wheels were solid disks cut from planks of wood; spoked wheels were not developed for another few thousand years. In the Americas, wheeled vehicles were not seen until the arrival of the Spaniards in the 15th century C.E.

The use of fibers

Because plant and animal fibers deteriorate readily, like wooden objects, they have mostly been preserved in either extremely dry or cold conditions, or where they have been completely waterlogged and not exposed to air at all. Thus archaeologists have been able to study the prehistoric textiles and basketry of several regions in the Americas, Siberia, Egypt, Britain, and Northern Europe.

In attempting to learn how the prehistoric textiles of a particular region were made, one clue is to study traditional practices of indigenous peoples in the area. The collection of these observations is called ethnographic data.

Early colonial and explorers' records can be useful, because they sometimes captured the practices of the indigenous society before it was changed by contact with the outside world. But the best data comes from studying the textiles themselves. When they are well preserved, the exact weaving methods can be deduced by expert observation. Chromatography and other analytical techniques can help to determine the different sources of the dyes (see LABORATORY EQUIPMENT; SPECTROSCOPY).

The Andean cultures of South America were among the most advanced prehistoric makers of textiles, and many of their products were preserved because of their dry climate. By 3000 B.C.E., cotton had replaced the stiff reed and rush fibers used earlier, and many different weaving techniques were devised. The Nazcas of Peru had over 190 vegetable-dye colors in their palette.

Pottery

Early pottery was hardened in open hearths, but the use of kilns allowed a number of vessels to be fired together at higher temperatures. The pottery was generally built up with coils or slabs of clay; the earliest evidence of a potter's wheel is 5000-year-old Egyptian tomb paintings. The materials used to make clay depended on the resources available in the area. These might include crushed shell or pottery, sand, grass, straw, or even sea sponge.

Pottery is a durable substance, and potsherds (fragments of pottery) are as common at Neolithic and more recent archaeological sites as stone tools are at Paleolithic ones.

Understanding the types and variations of pottery made by particular cultures has been extremely important in enabling archaeologists to understand

ANALYSIS OF POTTERY

Archaeologists specializing in the analysis of prehistoric pottery and other ceramics may use a variety of methods, including examining modern objects and attempting to duplicate prehistoric techniques, clays, firing, and glazing. But the most important method is to examine the potsherds (fragments of pottery) themselves, attempting to discern their form, function, style, and technology.

Often the shape of a vessel must be determined by looking at small pieces. Potsherds that preserve the shape of the rim or shoulder of the original are particularly important. Potsherds found in the same place may be fitted together like a jigsaw puzzle. Unfortunately, the removal of pieces by collectors or tourists often interferes with this process.

From the form of a vessel, it is often possible to deduce its function. Changes in the predominant form of a culture's pottery may indicate changes in its way of life. For example, pots designed to hold liquid appearing at the same time as an increase in findings of cattle bones may indicate an upward trend in the consumption of cow's milk.

Stylistic changes in decoration, color, and surface finish have little to do with function except in distinguishing ceremonial vessels from ones that were in everyday use. In general, changes in style reflect cultural choices, and in the American Southwest the style changes have been used to study cultural variations over thousands of years. Migration or trade patterns can result in patterns being seen in different geographical areas over time. Conclusions may also be drawn from the variation or homogeneity (sameness) of styles in a given region. For example, Mayan pottery was much more standardized around 300 B.C.E than it was five hundred years earlier. It has been argued that this reflects a much less flexible social system during the later period.

Advanced techniques of material analysis can provide a great deal of information about the clays from which the pottery was made and about how it was fired and glazed. If trace-mineral analysis indicates that a vessel could not have been made from clay indigenous to where it was found, then this provides evidence of trade between communities.

Archaeologists examine potsherds at a cliff dwelling in Arizona.

A CLOSER LOOK

the development and migration of civilizations and glean information about their contact and trade with other groups (see the box above).

From burrows to pyramids

When humans first learned to build their own shelters, they greatly extended the range of environments in which they could live. No longer were they dependent on trees or caves for protection from the elements. Rock piles that may have been built as shelters some 1.75 million years ago were found in the Olduvai Gorge, an important early site in East Africa. Some 300,000-year-old remains of temporary shelters built of wooden poles and animal skins were found on the French Riviera. In areas where wood was scarce, the bones of mammoths were sometimes used as poles to hold up the shel-

ters' makeshift roofs. In cold climates, humans imitated animal behavior by digging pits in the ground that were covered with wood, branches, or skins. The insulation and windbreak provided by these houses enabled their inhabitants to survive the long cold winters. Earth shelters were the direct ancestors of the sod houses built by 19th-century American pioneers.

In hot, dry climates, the most common types of dwellings built were mud houses. The mud could be fashioned into slabs or bricks, which were then left to bake in the sun. Alternatively, a framework of sticks could be erected to hold a paste of mud, not unlike the lath and plaster method used in later construction techniques. The roof of a mud house generally consisted of wooden beams that were covered with sticks or brush. In some parts of the world,

ROCK PAINTING AND ENGRAVING

Shepherd and cattle rock engravings on the Djado Massif in Niger.

Just as people today use photography, art, or writing to record significant events, Stone Age humans also created images that depicted important moments in their lives. In areas where people depended on hunting rather than farming, images of wild animals can provide scientists with important information on the distribution of mammals that are either no longer found in a specific area or are extinct, like mammoths. Pigments used in cave paintings were made from minerals found in the area that were generally bound with water. Charcoal or manganese dioxide were used for black, and iron oxide commonly provided a striking red. Depending on the custom of the particular community, the paint may have been applied by finger, brush, or pad or by blowing it through a reed. Archaeologists often find changes in pigments and superimposed lines, indicating that the pictures were altered over time.

As well as painting, many communities engraved images directly into the rock. To do this effectively, the rock surface had to be of a softer stone, such as sandstone, than the engraving implement.

WIDER IMPACT

especially in developing nations, many houses are still constructed using the same basic techniques and materials (see BUILDING TECHNIQUES, TRADITIONAL).

In general, stone was a relative latecomer to building construction because of the difficulty of moving large stone blocks. However, piles of stones were used for burial sites, probably to discourage animals from digging to reach the corpses. Stone tombs gradually increased in size as societies grew more complex and as powerful leaders arose who were able to marshal the resources in order to commemorate themselves. The megalithic tombs in Europe and the pyramids of Egypt and Latin America were constructed using ingenious lever and roller techniques to maneuver heavy stones. Other megalithic sites such as Stonehenge in England were probably used for astronomical sightings, which were crucial to agricultural communities needing to track the seasons, or for other spiritual purposes. In many cases, controversy still remains over exactly how and why these monuments were built.

The beginnings of agriculture

The idea of food production by means of domesticated plants and animals seems to have taken hold independently in several regions of the world after the end of the Ice Age, approximately 15,000 years ago. Of course, the specific type of farming depended on the resources of each area.

By c.8000 B.C.E., beans, squash, and peppers were being grown in Latin America, followed by manioc (cassava), potatoes, and some grasses. The cultivation of corn, which was to become an important staple crop, began c.5000 B.C.E. Farming was well established in the Middle East by 8000 B.C.E, mainly for wheat, barley, sheep, and goats.

Agriculture spread to Europe by c.6500 B.C.E. Independently of European agricultural development, communities in China arose following the cultivation of millet around 5000 B.C.E.; at the same time, rice farming began in southeast Asia. In sub-Saharan Africa, millet and sorghum wheat were being grown by the 3rd millenium B.C.E.

Early farmers used simple digging sticks, and later spades and hoes with blades made from stone, bone, or horn. While individual farming efforts often failed, the overall enterprise grew and prospered, in some measure thanks to a few serendipitous accidents of nature. While the first farmers knew nothing about fertilizer, their fields still benefited from the nutrients in the manure deposited by domesticated animals, as well as in human waste and garbage. Furthermore, the wheat used to make bread, which became such an important staple crop worldwide, was the product of accidental hybridization, when the fields of native wheat cultivated in the Middle East spread into the range of a wild grass indigenous to Iran, allowing cross-fertilization to take place.

With the incorporation of grains as the centerpiece of the human diet came the need for more elaborate food processing. Prehistoric communities shared kitchens that were equipped with husking trays, grindstones, and pottery vessels used for cooking and storage. In some cases, there may have been an outdoor oven for baking bread that supplemented an indoor hearth used for other cooking.

Metallurgy

The use of metal began with the simple shaping of copper nuggets found in nature. The copper could be cold-hammered into simple artifacts seen in Middle Eastern villages by 7000 B.C.E. and in the cultures of the northern United States and Canada between the 4th and 2nd millenia B.C.E. Later, kilns provided sufficient heat to soften the copper for shaping into ingots. The copper could also be hammered while hot in a process called annealing. Annealing results in a product that is much less brittle than if it were made by cold hammering.

Copper ores are relatively rare and are generally concentrated in specific regions. One copper-rich area is the Andes Mountains on the west coast of South America, where sophisticated mining and smelting operations existed among the Incas during the period before the arrival of Spanish explorers in the 16th century. Rich mines were surrounded by hundreds of furnaces, in rows that were carefully lined up so that the prevailing winds would carry their heat and noxious fumes away from settlements. Copper ore was transformed into metallic copper and slag by heating it to 2280°F (1250°C) in the presence of air. Workers kept air circulating through the furnaces by blowing into them through very long tubes. When the furnace cooled, the copper was picked out of the slag residue, and then it would be either remelted to form ingots or annealed into sheets or other forms.

Pure copper is too fragile to be very useful for tools, weapons, or other implements. Alloying, which means combining the copper with arsenic or tin, results in a much stronger and far more workable product. Some copper ores are rich in arsenic to begin with, which makes them immediately easier to manipulate. In other areas, arsenic minerals were probably first added in order to provide a silvery coating, and then they became recognized for their strength benefits. Smiths in the Middle East and in Southeast Asia around 3000 B.C.E. discovered that copper combined with tin created an alloy called bronze that was easier to work with than either metal on its own. They continued to experiment with proportions, eventually finding that a combination using 10 percent tin seemed to be the ideal solution for maximum workability and durability. The Bronze Age, and history, had begun.

S. CALVO

This bronze incense burner, dating from the eighth or seventh century B.C.E., is now housed in the Museo Nazionale Tarquiniese, Italy.

See also: AGRICULTURE, HISTORY OF; ARCHAEOLOGICAL TECHNIQUES; COLORANTS AND PIGMENTS; DYES AND DYEING; FASTENING AND JOINING; FISHING INDUSTRY; HAND WEAPONS; LEATHER; METALWORKING; POTTERY; TECHNOLOGY IN ANCIENT CIVILIZATIONS; TEXTILES AND THEIR MANUFACTURE; WOOD AND WOODWORKING.

Further reading:

Early Human Occupation in British Columbia. Edited by R. Carlson and L. Bona. Vancouver: University of British Columbia Press, 1996.
Earwood, C. *Domestic Wooden Artefacts in Britain and Ireland from Neolithic to Viking Times.* Exeter: University of Exeter Press, 1993.
Renfrew, C., and Bahn, P. *Archaeology: Theories, Methods and Practice.* New York: Thames and Hudson, 1991.

PRESSURE MEASUREMENT

Pressure measurement determines the pressure exerted by a gas or a liquid

An aneroid barometer designed to indicate likely changes in the weather.

CONNECTIONS

● Pressure measurement devices are an important part of **TORPEDO AND DEPTH CHARGE** weapons, allowing the depth of the water to be calculated.

● **PUMP AND COMPRESSOR** systems must be able to measure the pressure of the fluid being pumped.

Pressure measurement began with the need to measure the pressure of air in the atmosphere. At sea level, this is approximately 14.7 pounds per square inch (100,000 N/cm²). Since pressure varies with height above sea level or with changes in weather patterns, accurate pressure measurements can reveal the height of a place above sea level or warn of approaching weather changes.

The first pressure measuring instrument was the barometer, which was invented in 1643 by Italian physicist and mathematician Evangelista Torricelli (1608–1647), a pupil of the astronomer Galileo Galilei (1564–1642). Torricelli used a U-shaped glass tube sealed at one end and containing liquid. The space between the liquid and the sealed end was a near-perfect vacuum, and the other end was open to the air. The pressure of the outside air forced the open end of the liquid column down to a lower level than the sealed end, and this difference in level was a measure of the air pressure.

A question of density

Most conventional barometers of the Torricelli type used mercury because of its high density. Since the height of the sealed liquid column is inversely proportional to the density of the liquid (the height decreases as the density increases), a dense liquid such as mercury makes for a much more compact barometer than water, for example. Normal atmospheric pressure can support a column of mercury of approximately 30 inches (760 mm) in a tube, so the barometer needs to be a little larger than this. If water were to be used instead, the barometer would need to be more than 33 ft (10 m) high.

Pressure is measured in many different units, such as pounds per square inch and newtons per square meter. Some units are directly related to atmospheric pressure. Standard atmospheric pressure is enough to maintain a 29.92 in (760 mm) mercury column, and this is equivalent to 1 atmosphere or 1 bar. Air pressure for weather forecasts is measured in millibars (thousandths of a bar). Pressures above 1000 millibars (or standard atmospheric pressure) are classified as high pressure, and those below 1000 millibars as low pressure.

Other types of barometers

Torricelli's original barometer was really a modified manometer—a U-shaped tube capable of comparing pressures from two different sources. Instead of a closed end with a vacuum to provide a reference for measuring atmospheric pressures, manometers usually have both ends open so that pressures from two sources can be compared. For example, if the pressure of a gas supply is connected to one end of a manometer with the other end open, the difference in liquid levels shows the difference between the gas pressure and atmospheric pressure.

A simple barometer consists of a single tube with one sealed end that is filled with mercury and then dipped in a trough of mercury. A vacuum forms when the tube is placed upright, and the height of the top of the column of mercury above the surface of the mercury in the trough indicates the pressure (see the illustration on page 1051). If the diameter of the tube is far less than that of the trough, the level of the mercury in the trough will change little as the column rises and falls, and a scale on the tube can be used to give reasonably accurate pressure readings.

A Fortin barometer has a trough with a flexible bottom and an adjusting screw. Before each reading, the screw is adjusted so that the surface of the mercury in the trough aligns exactly with the zero point of the pressure scale. This removes inaccuracies caused by changing mercury levels in the trough.

CORE FACTS

■ The first pressure-measuring instrument was the mercury barometer, invented by Italian physicist Evangelista Torricelli in 1643.

■ If water were used in place of mercury to measure air pressure, a barometer would need to be approximately 33 ft (10 m) high.

■ Pressure measurement instruments can tell a pilot the height and airspeed of an airplane.

Instead of a mercury column, an aneroid barometer uses a metal box assembled from two thin corrugated diaphragms with a sealed, airtight joint. The air is pumped out from inside the box, with one diaphragm anchored to a base plate and the other to a strong spring to prevent the box from collapsing. The box expands and contracts with changes in atmospheric pressure, and this small movement is amplified by an elaborate system of gears and levers, which are connected to a rotating pointer in front of a marked scale.

Why measure pressure?

The aneroid barometer is much more stable and easier to transport than a mercury barometer, so aneroid instruments can be used for a wide range of applications; weather forecasting is perhaps the best known. Changes in weather produce changes in atmospheric pressure over a period of time. Pressure tends to be higher in stable, dry weather systems and lower in changeable, wet conditions.

Weather forecasting depends on plotting changes in pressure over a period of time. The barograph is an adaptation of the aneroid barometer with the pointer replaced by an arm that inks a trace on paper wrapped around a slowly rotating drum. The trace shows whether air pressure is rising (indicating the onset of more settled conditions) or falling (showing a period of damp weather is on the way). It also indicates the rate at which conditions are changing, and this information can be used to estimate the severity of an approaching storm.

Aneroid barometers are also used in pressure switches in automatic control systems to trigger different actions if pressure rises too high or falls too low (see TRANSDUCER AND SENSOR). With very high pressures, as in steam boilers, safety valves use strong springs deflected by increasing pressure. When the pressure reaches the safety limit, the spring deflects enough to allow steam to escape and the pressure to fall (see VALVE, MECHANICAL).

Aircraft and submarines

Air pressure falls with increasing height, so a barometer can measure altitude. This is the principle of the altimeter used in airplanes to show their height above sea level. At sea level, pressure can change from place to place, or from time to time, so the instrument needs to be adjusted to match local variations. Pressure in liquids increases regularly with depth below the surface, and pressure instruments can calculate a submarine's depth.

Pressure instruments include the rate of climb and descent indicator, which uses the rate at which pressure changes to tell a pilot how quickly the aircraft is climbing or descending. An air-speed indicator shows an airplane's speed through the air by measuring the pressure of the airstream using a device called a pitot-static tube—a forward-facing open-ended tube—and comparing it with the static air pressure at that height.

D. OWEN

A SIMPLE MERCURY BAROMETER

A mercury barometer using the same principles as Torricelli's. The air pressure forces mercury up the tube. The height of the mercury is a measure of the pressure.

See also: MEASUREMENT; MEDICAL MONITORING EQUIPMENT; METEOROLOGICAL INSTRUMENTS.

Further reading:
Pavese, F. *Modern Gas-based Temperature and Pressure Measurements.* New York: Plenum Press, 1992.

MEASURING BLOOD PRESSURE

Doctors measure a patient's blood pressure using an instrument called a sphygmomanometer. Like barometers, these instruments use a column of mercury or an aneroid chamber and pointer to reveal the pressure reading. The construction is similar in both cases, although aneroid instruments need to be recalibrated (have their scales adjusted) at intervals against more accurate mercury sphygmomanometers.

Pressure is measured using an inflatable cloth sleeve, connected by rubber tubing to the sphygmomanometer. The sleeve is wound around the patient's arm between shoulder and elbow. It is fitted with an adjustable one-way valve and is pumped up until it fits tightly enough to press against the patient's brachial artery (the main artery in the upper arm).

More air is pumped into the sleeve until the pulse in the brachial artery can no longer be detected. This means the pressure in the sleeve is high enough to prevent the heart from pumping blood through the restricted artery. Air is released very slowly from the sleeve until the pulse reappears, and the instrument reading is then equal to the patient's systolic pressure (the heart pumping blood out). The other important pressure reading, the diastolic pressure (the heart taking blood in), is taken by listening through a stethoscope for the brachial artery pulse to return to its normal rate.

A CLOSER LOOK

PRINTING

A newspaper being printed on a printing press.

CONNECTIONS

● Because of the large machines and great number of **MACHINE TOOLS** used in the printing industry, adequate **SAFETY SYSTEMS** must be put in place to insure the safety of printing workers.

The development of printing methods from the time of German printer Johannes Gutenberg (1400–1468) and others was at first very slow (see the box on page 1055). But from about 1850, there was a rapid increase in the complexity of printing technology. In the last few decades of the 20th century, the rate of evolution and change accelerated further. Elaborate and expensive printing methods were invented, enjoyed a brief vogue, and then had to be scrapped because cheaper and quicker methods were pioneered. A powerful recent influence on the evolution of printing technology has been the development of personal computers (see COMPUTER).

The printing industry enjoyed unprecedented expansion throughout the 20th century. In 1997, at the International Print '97 Exhibition in Chicago, equipment sales totaled more than $300 million.

Printing is the process of reproducing text or images by applying ink to paper

This was the largest such exhibition ever held in North America and was attended by more than 100,000 visitors. But the expansion of the industry has not been without a price. The changes in technology have often led to the obsolescence (becoming out-of-date) of laboriously acquired skills; the rapid evolution of printing methods has called for much flexibility and retraining of people working in the printing industry itself and in related industries.

HIGH-VOLUME PRINTING

Typesetting
Typesetting is the setting of text in type by any method. For several centuries, from c.1450 until c.1890, print was cast as individual letters. Typesetters—also known as typographers or compositors—worked entirely by hand, setting lines of print backward in composing sticks. Each letter had to be picked out individually from the type case and set into the line, with blank spaces of different widths between words to justify the lines (make sure they were of equal length). An attempt was sometimes made to speed up this process by casting together pairs of letters that often occurred next to each other—*er*, *th*, and *qu* are examples of pairs of letters *th*at frequently occur in English text.

Print shops were equipped with many fonts (typefaces). Each font contained numerous copies of complete sets of type in particular sizes and designs, which included everything necessary to print each design. Once the sticks were assembled, with thin metal strips called leads between the lines, they were locked into a rectangular steel or cast-iron frame called a chase to make a complete page for printing. This structure was known as a form. Forms were very flat and were set up on a table known as a stone.

Hot-metal machine typesetting was the first significant advance over manual methods. One of the most successful machines was the Linotype, which was patented in 1884 by German-born U.S. engineer Ottmar Mergenthaler (1854–1899). As the keys on its keyboard were pressed, blocks with a character

A tray of type, consisting of different-sized blocks with raised letters and symbols on them.

engraved on one face would be brought down from a magazine and placed in order in a block called a line mold. After each line had been completed, a lever would be pulled to cause molten metal alloy of relatively low melting point to flow into the line mold. The metal would then cool and solidify to form a slug—a bar with a line of raised type on one face (see CASTING). A Linotype machine could produce type at a rate of about five characters per second. In the similar Monotype system, each letter was cast individually from hot metal. Lines of type could then be set up into pages. Type that was no longer required was melted down again.

Straightforward letterpress printing is known as a monotone process, because in a single impression it prints solid areas of ink on a background of no ink at all—that is, either completely black (or any other ink color) or completely white, with no intermediate shades. This is acceptable for printing text but produces a very crude effect for pictures, which normally have a wide gradation of tone (a range of gray shades). To overcome this difficulty, letterpress printing makes use of a system known as halftone, which produces gray shades using an optical illusion. Illustrations are photographed through a screen of very fine mesh, ranging from 60 to over 300 mesh lines per inch. This converts the image into a large number of small dots. Although the centers of these dots are equally spaced, the dots vary in area according to the intensity of tone. The dots are too small to be seen with the naked eye, but differences in their sizes expose different proportions of white background, giving the illusion of a range of tones.

Hot metal systems were succeeded by phototypesetting methods. The earliest of these used photographic samples of all the required letters, symbols, and so on. These were reproduced photo-graphically, enlarged by lenses to the required sizes, and then projected onto light-sensitive paper or transparent film. Once a page had been produced by such methods on paper or film, it had to be converted into a form that enabled printing to be done. This stage is still required for most high-volume printing and is called platemaking (see the box on page 1056).

PRINTING INKS

Printing inks are similar to paints (see PAINT AND SURFACE COATING). They consist of fine-powder pigments (coloring substances; see COLORANTS AND PIGMENTS) dispersed in the ink medium, which is typically a vegetable oil such as linseed oil, a synthetic oil derived from petroleum, or a mixture of the two types.

A common pigment for black ink is carbon black (carbon in the form of a fine soot produced by burning hydrocarbons in a limited supply of oxygen). Pigments for inks of other colors include compounds of metals such as iron, chromium, cadmium, and molybdenum. Most are insoluble in the ink medium. Metallic inks contain actual elemental metal in finely-powdered form. Metals such as copper, gold, or aluminum, or alloys such as bronze may be used. Magnetic inks, such as those used on computer-readable bank checks, contain powdered magnetic iron.

The function of the ink medium is to carry the pigment onto the surface to be printed. After printing, the oil "dries" (hardens) as it is oxidized by air; the pigment is then held in place by the hardened medium. Often, a type of catalyst called a drier is added to accelerate the oxidation process (see CATALYST, INDUSTRIAL).

Different printing processes require inks of different viscosities. Offset and sheet-fed printing presses use viscous (thick, sticky) inks to minimize blurring of the printed image. Gravure processes require much more fluid inks that flow easily into the cells (pores) in the gravure plate and then transfer quickly onto the surface to be printed (see page 1057). Low-viscosity printing inks can be formulated by using low-viscosity oils and adding some solvent, which evaporates after printing. Alternatively, less or no solvent is added and the ink is applied hot, which temporarily reduces its viscosity.

A CLOSER LOOK

PRINTING SURFACES

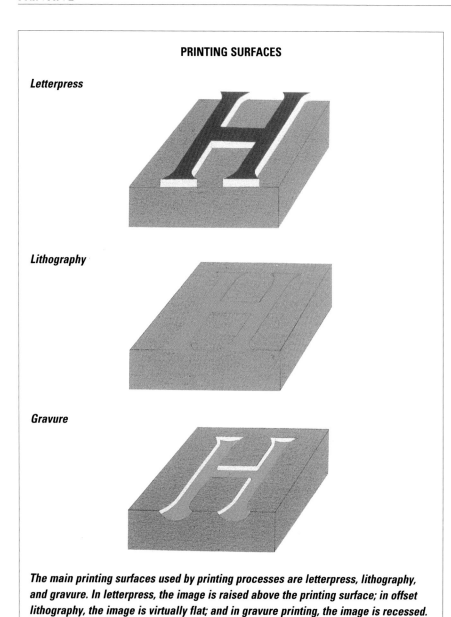

Letterpress

Lithography

Gravure

The main printing surfaces used by printing processes are letterpress, lithography, and gravure. In letterpress, the image is raised above the printing surface; in offset lithography, the image is virtually flat; and in gravure printing, the image is recessed.

The traditional typesetting methods already described have been superseded by wholly electronic systems. This is largely a result of the power and storage capacity of personal computers. Thousands of different fonts have been prepared and stored as computer files, and these are widely available for computer typesetting. The quality of printed typefaces produced in this way is assessed in dots per inch. Professional standards require a minimum resolution of about 1200 dots per inch, but twice this resolution is common.

Phototypesetting has been incorporated into the more general activity of page makeup, which is most conveniently done on a computer using one of the many available desktop publishing (DTP) programs. Work in progress is saved to the computer hard disk at regular intervals and backup copies are made as a precaution against system failure. The final version can then be printed on a laser printer or sent to a typesetter or platemaker.

High-volume printing machines have now eliminated all manual stages between the production of the saved DTP files and the printing of the finished book, magazine, or newspaper. Purely electronic and laser systems of printing are rapidly surpassing mechanical systems. High-capacity electronic printing systems that can compete with lithographic printing systems (described on page 1056) are now being sold in their thousands annually. These systems are particularly suitable for printing color brochures and other marketing material.

Letterpress

Letterpress is the general term for the kind of simple block printing that has been commonplace since the time of Gutenberg (see the box on page 1055). Letterpress is printing from type or blocks in which the areas to be printed are in relief (raised). The raised surfaces are covered with ink by rollers, and paper is then pressed onto them so that the ink is transferred to the paper. Letterpress requires a fairly stiff or sticky ink that will adhere to the raised area without running. In the process of printing, the thin ink film cleaves in two so that one layer is transferred to the paper and the other layer remains on the raised surface of the type or plate.

As in other fields of printing, letterpress has evolved considerably since the time of the flatbed, hand-operated press. The earliest presses used a flat platen (block) that forced the paper down onto the inked print using a screw press.

An important development in presses was the flatbed cylinder press. This uses a bed of type that moves back and forth. The cylinder carries the sheet of paper and rotates over the bed while the impression is being made. While the bed is returning to its original position and being inked, the cylinder is separated from it to receive a new sheet of paper. There are various forms of flatbed cylinder presses, some with the print bed horizontal, some with the print bed vertical. The main disadvantage of the flatbed cylinder press is its slowness.

A much faster and more widely used type of printing machine is the rotary letterpress. This is almost a standard for high-volume printing and is extensively used for printing from a web (continuous roll) of paper for producing newspapers and magazines. Printers that use continuous rolls of paper that need to be cut as part of the printing process are called web-fed printers.

The great majority of rotary high-volume printers are now web-fed. Rotary presses, whether they are used for letterpress or for some other form of printing, are characterized by a large number of rollers and other cylindrical structures, which all rotate continuously at high speed. In rotary printers, both the type surface and the surface carrying the paper are cylindrical and rotate continuously, which results in very rapid printing. The plate cylinders are inked by a series of hard rollers and soft rollers, which apply and evenly spread the ink. Printing happens first on one side of the paper. This is followed by very rapid drying with heat, then by cooling with cold rollers, then by immediate printing, heating, and cooling on the other side of the

EARLY HISTORY OF PRINTING

German printer Johannes Gutenberg in his workshop, showing his first proof sheet.

The first known printer was a Chinese craftsman named Pi Sheng. Sometime between c.1041 and 1048 C.E., he made movable type from earthenware (see POTTERY). Unfortunately this idea was doomed to failure because the Chinese written language has a different pictogram (picture symbol) for each of the 80,000 words in the language—far too many to catalog and use practically. By contrast, European languages such as German or English use about 100 characters, including the letters of their alphabets (some with accents), numerals, and symbols. For these alphabet languages, the invention of movable type—usually attributed to the goldsmith Johannes Gutenberg (1400–1468) of Mainz, Germany—proved to be an advance of major importance. Gutenberg, however, really became famous as the first person to print a Bible. He developed a sticky ink that could be daubed onto the type and then transferred to paper by pressure exerted by a screw press (the kind used to press grapes for wine). Later, rollers were used to apply the ink evenly.

The first book printed in England by the Gutenberg method was *The Dictes and Sayenges of the Phylosophers*, written by Earl Rivers and produced in 1477 by Englishman William Caxton (c.1422–1491). Movable type had the great advantage that the individual characters could be separated after printing, cleaned, and used again.

There was no real change in this system until 1796 when Aloys Senefelder (1771–1834) invented lithography. Soon afterward, in 1813, the cumbersome and slow screw system for pressing the paper to the type was replaced by a system of levers that applied the required pressure and so speeded up the process.

Almost simultaneously, in 1811, the first press to use a revolving cylinder (instead of a flat block or platen) to press the paper against the type was invented by Friedrich Koenig (1774–1833). In Koenig's machine, the bed with the print moved under inking rollers after each impression. This machine was to revolutionize large-scale printing. On November 14, 1814, a steam-powered Koenig machine printed *The Times* newspaper in London. This was the first newspaper to be printed by steam power, and a rate of more than 1000 sheets per hour—four times faster than had been possible until then—was achieved.

From then on, improvements came fast. The next major advance was the development of the full rotary press by U.S. inventor and industrialist Richard M. Hoe (1812–1886). This was patented in 1847 and was used by the *Philadelphia Public Ledger* and the *New York Tribune* newspapers. Hoe's press abandoned the flatbed of print and replaced it with a cylinder or drum of print. The press printed on rolls, or webs, of paper.

The final triumph of the high-speed, web-fed rotary cylinder press came in the 1870s with the solution to the problem of casting curved plates. First, a flatbed would be prepared with the page to be printed. Then, a papier-mâché or soft pasteboard sheet (called a mat) would be pressed firmly onto the flatbed to take an impression. The mat would then be dried, curved into a semicylindrical form, and used as a mold to cast a metal half-cylinder. Pairs of semicylindrical plates would be joined to make rollers, and electrically driven presses, using pairs of rollers of this type to print both sides of the paper at the same time, were virtually the sole option for printing large newspapers until well into the 20th century.

HISTORY OF TECHNOLOGY

OFFSET LITHOGRAPHY

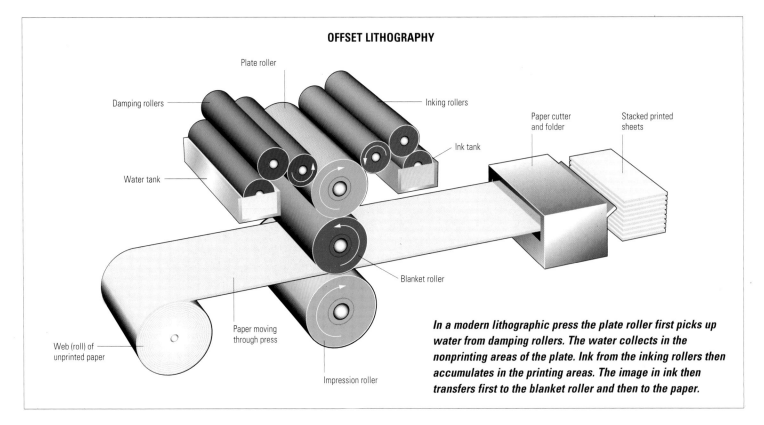

Plate roller

Damping rollers

Inking rollers

Paper cutter and folder

Stacked printed sheets

Ink tank

Water tank

Blanket roller

Web (roll) of unprinted paper

Paper moving through press

Impression roller

In a modern lithographic press the plate roller first picks up water from damping rollers. The water collects in the nonprinting areas of the plate. Ink from the inking rollers then accumulates in the printing areas. The image in ink then transfers first to the blanket roller and then to the paper.

same web of paper. The paper then passes to a section of the machine where it is cut into sheets of a specified size and folded.

Letterset is a rotary printing process in which ink is transferred indirectly from the inked type to the paper by way of a rubber roller. Flexography is a form of rotary letterpress printing suitable for printing on metal foil or plastic. Low-viscosity inks are used, and the printing plate is made of a flexible plastic that is not softened by the solvents used to reduce the viscosity of the inks.

MAKING PLATES FROM PHOTOGRAPHS

Photopolymeric plates are produced using a solution that forms a solid plastic by polymerization when exposed to UV light (see PLASTICS). The solution is spread on the metal or plastic sheet that is to be the backing for the plate. UV light is then shone onto the coated sheet through a film of the negative image. The lighter areas of the negative (which correspond to the darker areas of the positive image) allow more UV light to pass through them, which causes more polymerization in these areas. After exposure, the solution that has not been exposed is still liquid and can be washed away to leave a pattern of solidified polymer that corresponds to the positive image.

Photogravure uses a positive image that has been photographed through a fine screen. Light is shone through the image onto paper coated with a light-sensitive gel. The gel hardens least where the image is darker and, since the image was photographed through a screen, the result is a pattern of dots of underexposed gel of varying size in a sheet of light-hardened gel. This sheet is then stuck to a copper plate and the unhardened gel and paper backing removed by soaking in water. When the plate is treated with acid, pores are formed to depths that correspond to the varying darknesses of the dots in the positive image. The plate is then used in gravure printing (see page 1057).

A CLOSER LOOK

Offset lithography

Lithography differs from letterpress in that the areas to be printed are not raised but are made ink-receptive in a different way. The term *lithography* derives from the Greek words *lithos,* meaning "stone," and *graphos,* meaning "writing." Invented in 1798 by the Prague-born Bavarian playwright Aloys Senefelder (1771–1834), lithography is a system of printing that uses a flat stone surface on which the image to be printed is formed with a greasy, water-repellent ink. Senefelder discovered this when drawing on limestone with a grease pencil in an attempt to engrave plates for the publication of his plays. Once the design was completed in grease, Senefelder would dampen the whole stone with water, which would be absorbed into those parts of the surface of the stone where there was no grease. He would then apply ink to the surface of the stone. Being oil-based, the ink would be repelled by those parts of the surface that were penetrated by water and would collect in the greased areas. A sheet of paper pressed against the stone would then pick up a very accurate reverse (mirror-image) reproduction of the original design.

A limitation of the original process was that it was of no use for printing hard surfaces, since any imperfection in the inked surface or the surface of the object to be printed would interfere with the contact that is necessary for a good image. This limitation was overcome by U.S. printer Ira W. Rubel around 1905. Rubel's technique—offset lithography—used a blanket roller (a rubber-coated roller) to pick up the ink from the lithographic plate and then offset, or transfer, the ink to the surface to be printed. The flexible surface of the blanket roller ensures an even contact with hard surfaces and results in a high quality reproduced image, even on metal and plastic.

Modern offset lithography machines use a metal plate roller, usually made of aluminum, instead of a stone slab. A polymeric coating is applied to the parts of the roller that are to accept ink, usually by photopolymerization (see the box on page 1056). First water and then ink are applied to the plate roller by damping rollers (see the illustration on page 1056). The ink and water separate on the plate roller to form an image that is picked up by the blanket roller. The blanket roller then offsets the image to the surface to be printed. If more than one color is to be printed, the layers of ink can be applied one by one to the blanket before offsetting. Flexible surfaces such as paper are held against the blanket by an impression roller.

Web-fed offset rotary printers operate at 250 or more revolutions per minute, which is ideal for fast production runs such as overnight newspaper printing. Offset lithography is by far the most commonly used form of high-volume color printing. Until the recent development of high-volume commercial laser color printers, it was virtually unrivaled.

Gravure

Also known as intaglio, gravure is a form of printing in which the image to be printed is engraved, etched, or otherwise cut into the surface of the printing late. The whole plate is then inked and the surface wiped using a blade, leaving the ink in the recessed parts. Paper that is then pressed to the surface will have the desired image transferred to it.

Gravure has an advantage over letterpress in that, because the recessed wells into which the ink runs can be of variable width and depth, it is capable of reproducing a reasonable effect of tone gradation without having to resort to a halftone method. In addition, the system allows heavy inking, which produces rich colors. For these reasons, gravure is often selected in preference to offset lithography for printing high-quality artwork.

Some gravure platemaking processes include photoengraving (see the box on page 1056), machine engraving, and, rarely, hand engraving. Thin copper plates were once the conventional media, but plastic plates are now commonly used. As in other forms of high-volume printing, high speeds in gravure printing can be obtained only by rotary presses. This explains why much of gravure printing is called rotogravure—it involves cylindrical plates similar to those used for other printing purposes.

Color printing

From the time of the invention of lithography in 1796 until around 1900, almost all color printing was done by lithography from hand-drawn images on a stone surface. Then, following the publication of the trichromatic (three-color) theory of vision by German physiologist Hermann Helmholtz (1821–1894), it became apparent that an almost infinite range of colors could be produced using only three inks. It is now known that the human retina is, in fact, sensitive only to blue, green, and red—the

A printer applies ink to a stone cut in the Cape Dorset print cooperative in Cape Dorset, Northwest Territories, Canada.

primary colors. The thousands of different hues that can be distinguished are formed from combinations of varying proportions of these primary colors.

In practice, printing uses cyan, magenta, and yellow inks, which are complementary to red, green, and blue. Yellow, magenta, and cyan therefore absorb red, green, and blue light respectively, producing any color by a subtractive process (see COLOR). Added together, these three complementary colors produce black. However, it is common to use a separate black ink, which results in more consistent quality.

Color lithography is most commonly a halftone process that deposits a pattern of closely spaced tiny dots of the three colors and black. A separate plate is used for each color, and each has its own separate ink supply. One major difficulty is to achieve accurate registration (alignment) so that the three or four printed dots in each color lie close together in the correct relationship. This requires adjustment at the

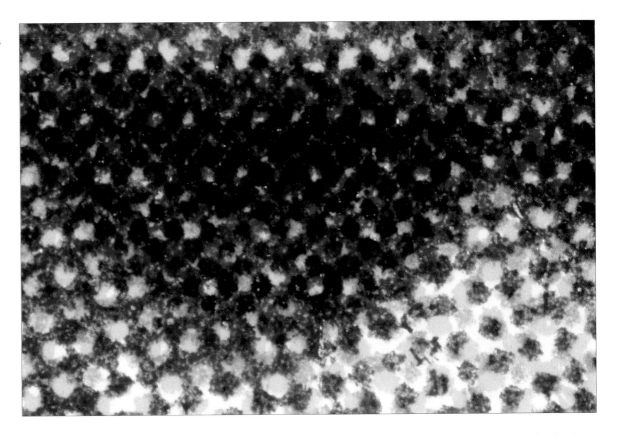

A macro (close-up) image of tricolor layers on a print of an eye.

start of each print run but once the press is set up, further adjustment is rarely necessary. Loss of registration gives a blurred, apparently smudged effect.

LOW-VOLUME PRINTING

Low-volume printing includes hand or manual printing on small, flatbed machines; artistic methods such as screen or silkscreen printing; printing from hand-engraved wooden or linoleum blocks; and batik printing of fabrics, in which areas not to be dyed are protected by wax. The most common low-volume printing systems, however, are the printers used with personal computers.

Computer-controlled printing

The ready availability of inexpensive personal computers (PCs) and desktop publishing (DTP) software has revolutionized low-volume printing, both for

---

PRINTING A NEWSPAPER

Until the personal computer revolution, most newspapers were typeset by letterpress using linecasting machines such as Linotype or Monotype machines (see page 1054). However, linecasting is labor-intensive and inflexible. Newspapers are now rapidly composed on personal computers using desktop publishing (DTP) software. This allows quick, effective composition and rapid last-minute changes as new stories are reported.

Once the page makeup is completed, a process called phototypesetting is used to produce relief print and halftone images on lithographic cylinders for the presses. Web-fed offset printing is used universally. On a great number of newspapers, color printing of illustrations is also common. Present-day high-speed rotary printer drums are able to turn at nearly 600 revolutions per minute, consuming paper at the rate of 1600 ft (500 m) per minute, and producing as many as 100,000 copies of a newspaper in one hour.

Newspapers come off the press on a conveyor belt.

A CLOSER LOOK

business and personal applications. Most popular DTP and word processing programs are capable of doing the things once done by typographers, typesetters, and printers and are now available for a few hundred dollars. Mass production has also reduced the cost of high-quality printers to a level at which the smallest businesses—or home users—can afford to buy and use them.

Monochrome (black-and-white) laser printers that have a print resolution of 600 or 1200 dots per inch are now commonplace and readily affordable. On good quality paper, these machines produce print quality that compares favorably with professional printing. Higher resolutions are available at a modest increase in cost. Monotone desktop inkjet machines are even more inexpensive than laser printers and are very well suited to small-scale work. There have been extraordinary developments, too, in the quality of color printing available from color laser and inkjet printers and in the reduction in price of these machines.

The current trend in laser printers is to supply the consumables, such as the toner powders that form the printed image, in a cartridge that also contains the special rotating drum on which the image drawn by the moving laser is formed. There is a limit to the number of good copies a drum surface can produce. Therefore, when the toner is exhausted, the cartridge is discarded and a new one is inserted. In this way, all the wearing parts of the printer are replaced at regular intervals, with the result that high-quality work can continue to be produced. Most laser printer cartridges are able to print as many as 4000 sheets.

Inkjet printers use a matrix of very fine jets that squirt ink a short distance onto the paper under the control of computer software. In some cases, the ink supply and the jets are integrated into a single unit, which insures that the jets are unblocked when a new ink cartridge is inserted. Color inkjet printers can be made at just a little more expense than the monochrome type, but the cost of the ink cartridges is significantly higher. Color inks are often used in the form of solid, waxy rods that are instantly liquefied by heat. The fine jet of the resulting ink is then projected by heat expansion.

For each new design of PC laser or any other kind of printer, a special print-driver software program must be supplied. This tells the computer exactly how to translate its print instructions into a form that the printer is able to understand. Installing a PC printer (setting up a computer to use it) used to be a laborious and complex process, but modern software requires computer users to do no more than select a printer from a list of those suggested; in many cases, the computer is loaded with software that figures out what device is connected, and the user simply has to confirm this.

Systems of this kind provide an extraordinary degree of control over the whole process of printing. A wide range of fonts is available in software and these may be accurately reproduced on the monitor

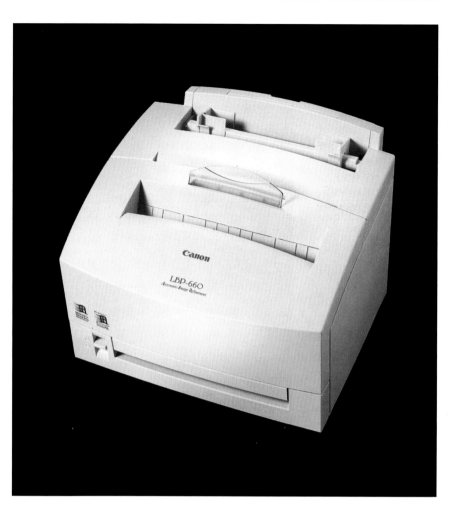

in precisely the form that will appear on the printout. It is even possible for the artistically inclined printer to design an entirely new typeface.

Desktop publishing programs—and even many of the more advanced word-processing software packages—provide a wide choice of print sizes in bold and italic type. They also facilitate the spacing of lines and the alignment of both the lines and the columns of text, as well as the positioning of diagrams and photographic images.

R. YOUNGSON

Desktop printers, such as this Canon LBP 660, are used in offices of all sizes and in the home.

See also: BOOKBINDING; COMPUTER; PAPER AND PAPERMAKING; PHOTOGRAPHY.

Further reading:
Barnard, M. *Introduction to Printing Processes.* London, England: Blueprint, 1991.
Bednar, B. *Resists in Microlithography and Printing.* New York: Elsevier, 1993.
Books and Printing: A Treasury for Typophiles. Edited by P. Bennett. Savannah, Georgia.: F.C. Beil, 1991.
Bowman, J. *Greek Printing Types in Britain in the Nineteenth Century: A Catalogue.* Oxford, England: Oxford Bibliographical Society, 1992.
Cost, F. *Pocket Guide to Digital Printing.* Albany: Delmar Publishers, 1997.
Craig, J. *Production for the Graphic Designer.* New York: Watson-Guptill, 1990.
Sassoon, R. *Computers and Typography.* Oxford, England: Intellect, 1993.

PRODUCTION ENGINEERING AND PROCESS CONTROL

Production engineering is the technology of mass production; process control improves quality

Robots weld an automobile body together in a German auto plant. The robots can repeat this exact task many times, and their speed can be matched to that of the production line.

CONNECTIONS

● Accurate prototypes are central to **AIRCRAFT DESIGN AND CONSTRUCTION** and to the manufacture of **SPACE PROBES**, where 100 percent reliability of all parts is required.

● Computerization of manufacturing processes has improved the precision of mass-produced implements used in **SURGERY** and **DENTISTRY**.

Modern manufacturing industry is based on the economy, efficiency, and consistency of mass production. Since its introduction in the late 18th century by industrial pioneers such as U.S. inventor Eli Whitney (1765–1825; see the box on page 1062), technological development has enabled the principles of mass production to be widely applied in the manufacture of progressively lower-cost and higher-quality products.

For mass production to work, the whole production operation has to be split into a series of specialized tasks, each one involving an essentially simple operation on a highly repetitive basis, with as little handling or movement of the workpiece as possible. Where workers are involved, hand and eye movements can then be carried out rapidly and consistently after a short period of practicing and without the need for a great deal of special training. Where operations are performed automatically by machines, movement paths must be along the shortest route, but they are also designed not to conflict with other manufacturing machines so that all movements can be achieved as quickly and efficiently as possible (see MECHANICAL HANDLING; ROBOTICS).

The same process simplifications must be applied to the components of the finished product. The more these can be standardized in terms of size and shape and material and fastenings, the greater the efficiency of the whole production process. Each machine on the production line is designed to carry out a particular operation, with minimum human input and maximum accuracy, consistency, and speed.

In recent years, machine tool developments have produced machines that are more versatile and can perform far more operations on a workpiece, turning and relocating it as required. Not only does this reduce the time and cost of transferring the workpiece from one machine to another, but it also maintains higher levels of accuracy throughout the operations performed on it. By allowing the machines to cope with larger and more complex parts, the assembly of the finished product is made simpler and more efficient.

CORE FACTS

■ The world's first production line was set up in 1798 by U.S. inventor Eli Whitney, who used semiskilled workers to produce 10,000 army muskets in two years.
■ Computer-controlled robots have replaced human operators on many production lines.
■ In chemical plants, control computers can measure and manage thousands of different stages of a process through hundreds of control loops (feedback systems).
■ Computer-controlled machine tools can change settings and cutting tools to match the specifications of a particular workpiece.

Design for manufacturing

In modern manufacturing, the processes required to make a product are considered from the very beginning of its design. The production engineer has to take into account the assemblies, subassemblies, and individual components that make up the whole, the materials from which they will be made, and how they will be cut, shaped, drilled, machined, and fastened together in order to meet the desired functional and tolerance specifications. All the necessary components must be available in the correct numbers at the same time for the finished product to be assembled as efficiently as possible.

Computers are now heavily involved in design and manufacturing, so that the whole production process can be carried out on a virtual production line before actual production begins, thereby highlighting weak points and potential trouble spots in the manufacturing process.

The software used in modern aerospace production can simulate each pass of a specific machine tool across a piece of material that is being manipulated, registering the precise amount of material it will remove and the actual path of the high-speed cutting tool so that possible collisions with other machine tools on the same line can be avoided.

Because different tools and operations in a plant are controlled by the same central computer system, the accuracy of the size and position of the holes drilled in different components by different tools can be guaranteed all along the production line so that all parts will fit perfectly at the assembly stage.

Rapid prototyping

An essential step in turning out any product by mass production is the making of one or more prototypes of each individual part. Originally, prototypes had to be made by hand and were expensive and time-consuming to produce, but methods have now been developed to turn out highly accurate prototypes at a fraction of the time and cost.

The modern prototyping process begins with the engineer, who designs a part by computer-aided design (CAD). This software model is then sliced by the computer into a series of thin layers approximately 1/25 inch (1 mm) deep, which are used to create a physical prototype built one layer at a time using one of three main techniques: stereolithography, lamination, or laser sintering.

Stereolithography uses an ultraviolet laser, controlled by the computer, to trace a two-dimensional pattern of each layer, one after the other, onto the surface of a special fluid resin that solidifies when exposed to the laser beam. As each layer is formed, the component is lowered by one thickness and covered by another layer of the resin. Then the next layer is formed in the surface of the liquid resin.

Laminated-object manufacture works in a similar way but uses layers of a special paper material to achieve the same effect. The resulting prototypes are accurate physical replicas of the designed part that can be used to check fit and to assess reactions to

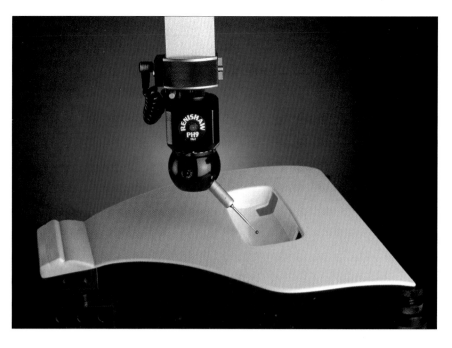

A computer-aided probe tracks a component of a gear in three dimensions and stores the information for use in future mass production of the gear.

its design. However, the use of these specialized materials means they do not perform to the same specifications as the designed component in terms of strength and other mechanical properties.

To produce fully functional prototypes, engineers use selective laser sintering. Sintering is a process that uses a laser in combination with a heat-fusible powder (one that melts easily and forms into a solid when cool) to build the component layer by layer. A carbon-dioxide laser draws the first layer of the component onto the powder in the same way as the other similar processes, raising the temperature of the powder to the point where the powder melts. It then solidifies in the shape of that layer. A roller then

THE EARLY YEARS OF MASS PRODUCTION

Eli Whitney is credited as the inventor of mass production.

The principles of mass production were first developed in the United States by American inventor Eli Whitney (1765–1825), who in 1793 invented the cotton gin—a machine for separating the seeds of the cotton plant from the surrounding fibers so that the fibers could be spun and woven into cotton fabric.

In spite of its economic importance, Whitney made little money from this and his many other inventions, until, in 1798, he was given a U.S. government contract to manufacture 10,000 muskets for the U.S. Army over a period of two years.

Making such a large quantity by hand was impossible in the time available. Instead, Whitney set up a series of precision lathes equipped with guides so that semiskilled workers could turn and shape large numbers of identical parts very quickly. Because of the accuracy of the process, individual musket parts were completely interchangeable, and the finished weapons could be assembled by unskilled labor. Furthermore, replacement parts could easily be fitted to extend the muskets' service life.

Early mass production had dramatic economic advantages. In 1802, when the British Royal Navy needed thousands of wooden pulley blocks for the rigging of sailing warships, British engineers Marc Brunel and Henry Maudslay built an integrated series of 43 machine tools that carried out the whole manufacturing process— from sawing the rough elm logs to cutting grooves for the ropes in the finished blocks. The machines, staffed by 10 men, produced 100,000 blocks a year in three different sizes.

The concept of mass production was extended by U.S. automobile manufacturer Henry Ford, who turned out his mass-market Model T automobile. His concept of a production line that moved the components through the factory was initially used in making just the automobile's ignition system in 1913, but it was later extended to cover the manufacture of the whole vehicle.

HISTORY OF TECHNOLOGY

deposits another layer of powder on top of the first layer, and the process is repeated to build the finished replica of the designed part.

This method can produce prototypes made from certain types of plastics that can be used as patterns for short production runs (see PLASTICS). Components made in this way can also be used to make molds for metal castings. By incorporating metal granules in the powder, prototypes can even be made tough enough to be used as molds for producing plastic products.

Types of production lines

Most production lines fall into one of two types: batch or continuous. A batch production line turns out different products at different times to meet the exact demands of different customers. This involves a line that uses general-purpose machines that can be set to work to specific sizes and sequences to produce a relatively small output batch of a specific product. When one batch is complete, the machine tools must then be reconfigured to match the requirements of the next batch so that they can be used to make a completely different product using the same production line.

Computer-aided manufacturing (CAM) has revolutionized batch production line: a single production line can be used to produce a variety of workpieces by changing the computer instructions that control the tools on the line. The ability to change quickly from one batch of components to another makes the production of small batches of components more economical; CAM lines also have the advantage of being better able to respond to changes in demand.

Continuous production systems use assembly lines that are dedicated to one particular product. The production process is divided into a series of simple operations that are performed by machines designed specifically for each operation. Productivity is improved by eliminating the time taken to change tools or programs on batch-production lines.

Sometimes both types of production lines are combined in a single overall operation. In the making of a product like a computer or an automobile (see the box on page 1605), the end products may be largely identical but may include different features according to different customer options. In this case, components will be made on continuous-production lines and then a series of subsidiary production lines will assemble these components to produce batches of finished products with slightly different specification options. The two stages may be done within one plant or at a number of subcontracted factories.

Control of flexible manufacturing

Flexible manufacturing is a form of batch manufacturing that uses computer control to enable a production line to produce more than one model of a product at a time. This kind of system is particularly useful when demand for each individual model is relatively low or liable to change sharply. Each system has a series of computer-controlled machine tools linked to a central computer, which performs successive machining operations, and automated inspection stations, which maintain quality control.

Parts arrive at the manufacturing line by conveyors and are loaded onto the first machine in the sequence by workers or, increasingly, by automatic handling (see CONVEYOR). Originally, staff had to feed information into the computer on the product to be made and the computer would then control the machines. When the next product came in, workers would then have to change the machines' operating tools to match the requirements of the next run. The latest, most sophisticated production lines are able to carry out all these procedures automatically. Computers instruct machines which workpieces and tools to select for a particular assembly and these instructions change when a different assembly is to be made. Computer-controlled machines can even monitor their own performance and carry out their own inspection functions, and they can decide when it is time to replace a worn-out tool.

Computer control of manufacturing processes has been taken further in the production of materials such as chemicals, food, metals, oil, and gasoline. This is because of the large volumes involved and their ease of handling compared with engineering products. Sensors measure quantities such as pressure, temperature, and production rate and feed this information to the computer. If there is any departure from the most efficient values, the computer can then operate valves, switches and controls to restore the correct balance. The basic principle of this type of control is the negative feedback loop. When a particular property changes in a specific way, the computer program is designed to carry out actions that have the opposite effect, thus making that particular property return to normal.

In a chemical production plant such as an oil refinery (see OIL REFINING) an increase in pressure will trigger the computer to open a valve that will reduce that pressure. If the pressure continues to fall past the optimum value, then the computer will reverse the action and close the valve so that the pressure will start to rise again toward the correct level.

In some cases, depending on the nature of the process, many thousands of different properties are measured at regular intervals. The control system involves hundreds of feedback loops. If a particular reading exceeds safety limits, the computer will sound alarms or carry out emergency procedures to

prevent a hazardous situation from developing. In other cases, changes in process conditions may result in the computer changing the critical boundaries of some of the feedback loops to make the process control function respond more efficiently.

Quality control

Where a production operation produces a relatively small number of complex and expensive products, such as automobiles, quality control is usually maintained by giving every product a detailed inspection. Where simple products are produced at a much higher rate, carrying out inspections on each one would create an unacceptable production bottleneck.

Sometimes computerized inspection systems can carry out checks without slowing down the output of the production line. One of these artificial-intelligence inspection systems checks automotive

Quality control workers in an Italian pharmaceuticals factory examine drug containers for flaws.

An architect designs the pipework of a petroleum refinery using a computer-aided-design (CAD) program.

components, rejected components, or those to be sent back to the production line for reprocessing (see PATTERN RECOGNITION; VIDEOGRAPHY).

Because many production line faults tend to be progressive, statistical quality control is often used to monitor output. This involves inspecting regular samples of the product leaving the production line and displaying the results on a control chart that shows if a particular measurement is continuing to rise or fall within the acceptable upper and lower limits. Any trends that show errors approaching either limit can then be detected early enough for the process control system to correct matters. As far as random faults are concerned, the sampling technique will reveal how often they occur and help to determine what type of further action is needed to determine the factors causing the problem.

Another quality control technique is known as acceptance sampling, where a customer takes regular samples from a large order of components from a particular producer and records the number of items that fail to reach the agreed quality standards. This sample information can then be used to decide whether to accept or reject the entire order. Statistics are used to calculate how many samples must be taken to be representative of the whole batch and at what interval the samples should be taken. Otherwise there is the risk of rejecting high-quality work because a small sample happened to contain a number of defective parts. Alternatively, a sample from a poor-quality order may contain no defective parts at all and give the impression that the batch is of better quality than it is in reality.

valve stem seals by using a bank of video cameras to feed images of the finished components to a computer running an image-processing program. This checks the finished components for shape and surface flaws before sorting them into bins of accepted

Human factors

In spite of the automation of production lines, people are still involved, both in the process itself and as users of the finished products. At one time, human factors were largely ignored in the design of industrial machinery, giving rise to cases such as a lathe that, when analyzed by ergonomics engineers, was found to require an ideal operator 3 ft (0.9 m) tall with the reach proportions of a gorilla.

Today, ergonomics (human-factors engineering) is involved in every kind of product and production machinery. After extensive trials when designing the push-button telephone, for example, it was decided to adopt a different arrangement of numbers from the already widely used pad of numerical keys on calculators and computer keyboards. On a telephone keypad, the numbers increase from left to right and from top to bottom, whereas on the other two products they increase from left to right and from bottom to top (see ERGONOMICS).

When the typewriter keyboard was first designed, an attempt was made to place keys of frequently used letters so that their related arms would not become entangled during fast typing. It has since been found that other combinations are easier and quicker to learn and use, but unfortunately standardization prevented their adoption, and the old layout was extended to the vast computer market.

TIME AND MOTION STUDY

Time and motion studies are used in mass production design to analyze different parts of the process. In 1881, U.S. inventor and engineer Frederick W. Taylor (1856–1915), of the Midvale Steel Company in Philadelphia, began studying and timing operations such as the shovelling of raw materials, which laid the foundations for modern production planning. He suggested that production could be enhanced by eliminating the waste of time and motion caused by the way workers did their jobs. Taylor was the first person to attempt to quantify the efficiency of different aspects of production processes. Despite his work being unpopular with many factory workers, Taylor became a very successful industrial engineering consultant and went on to develop the first high-speed steel production process. The results of his lifetime of research into productivity maximization was published in *The Principles of Scientific Management* in 1911.

Taylor's ideas were further developed by U.S. engineer Frank Gilbreth (1868–1924) and his wife, engineer Lillian (1878–1972), who used movie cameras to film production workers and analyze every step of an operation. The resulting data was used to redesign production sequences to make them easier, quicker, and more economical. Their book *Motion Study*, published in 1911, was the first to use the phrase *time and motion study*.

HISTORY OF TECHNOLOGY

PRODUCING AUTOMOBILES

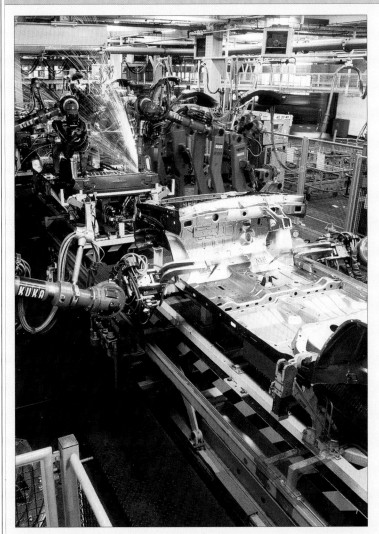

Robots at the Ford car plant in Dagenham, England, perform a task on a car chassis before it moves to the next stage on the production line.

The modern production line originated in the automobile industry, and auto factories still offer one of the best examples of production-line efficiency in action. The production line on which the finished automobile is assembled is often the final link in a highly complex chain: suppliers, subcontractors, and even sub-subcontractors all contribute in layers of mutual dependence.

At one time, auto plants had two main production lines: one for the body of the car and the other for the chassis (supporting frame), onto which all the major mechanical parts would be fitted. Today, the construction of body and chassis is a single, complex, integrated process. The sequence usually starts with the welding together of the panels that make up the reinforced body-chassis. This is often done by assembly robots with parts that have been produced within the plant on a separate line of presses or that have been trucked in from an outside supplier.

The heavy lifting tasks are performed at intervals down the line, often by machines operated by highly trained people. A hoist swings the engine into position, and assembly line workers fit it to its mounting points and connect the transmission system and other services. Some tasks, such as the fitting of seats and interior trim panels, still tend to defy automation and call for skills best provided by more dextrous human workers. Otherwise, workers are specialists in the use of their own particular tools and repeat individual tasks over and over again as the moving line brings forward each new vehicle in turn.

Where components arrive from outside contractors or from elsewhere in the plant, they have to be matched very accurately to the specifications of the line. A concept known as just-in-time deliveries, pioneered by the Japanese auto industry, involves parts being supplied as required, which minimizes the need for space to store large quantities of spares on the production floor. This system can cause costly delays, however, when shortages halt the line and interrupt production. The supply situation is made even more complicated by the pressure on auto makers to offer customized cars with a choice of colors, accessories, and options. In these cases, production engineers have to insure that the sequence of cars on the line matches the orders from dealers or customers, and that all alternative parts have standard fittings.

A CLOSER LOOK

Ergonomics is particularly important in automobiles and aircraft. At one time, car designers favored rows of identical switches on the dash panel, which meant drivers had to take their eyes off the wheel to find the right one. Instruments were placed in inconvenient locations, where readings might be obscured by the driver's hands on the wheel. On aircraft instrument panels, one confusing design for an altimeter caused pilots to mistake their altitude by 1000 ft (305 m), sometimes crashing as a result. Ergonomics is used on the production line itself in the design of computer displays, in keypads for the input of data or instructions to machine tools, and in instruments or displays for inspection systems.

D. OWEN

See also: AUTOMOBILE; AUTOMOBILE, HISTORY OF; CHEMICAL ENGINEERING; CHEMICAL INDUSTRY, ORGANIC; COMPUTER; CONTROL SYSTEMS AND CONTROL THEORY; DESIGN, INDUSTRIAL; DIGITAL SIGNALS AND SYSTEMS; ELECTRONICS; INFORMATION THEORY; MACHINE TOOL; MECHATRONICS; SAFETY SYSTEMS.

Further reading:
Foulard, C. *Product Development and Production Engineering in Manufacturing Industries.* New York: Hemisphere Publishing Company, 1990.
Hitomi, K. *Manufacturing Systems Engineering: A Unified Approach to Manufacturing Technology, Production Management, and Industrial Economics.* Bristol, England: Taylor Francis, 1996.
Shores, A. *Reengineering the Factory: A Primer for World-Class Manufacturing.* Milwaukee: ASQC Quality Press, 1994.
Winch, G. *Managing Production: Engineering Change and Stability.* New York: Oxford University Press, 1994.

PROPELLER

Propellers transfer energy between the rotational motion of a shaft and the linear motion of a fluid medium

Workers repair the giant propeller of a container ship in dry dock.

CONNECTIONS

● **PRODUCTION ENGINEERING AND PROCESS CONTROL** and innovations in industrial **DESIGN**, such as the use of computer-aided design (CAD), have greatly improved the manufacture and efficiency of propellers.

Although many large aircraft are jet propelled, the propeller is still the most efficient means of driving slower airplanes. Some marine craft, such as small jet skis, use water rushing out of the rear to push them forward, but most are driven by propellers. Propeller-shaped turbines convert wind thrust into rotational power in windmills and wind turbines and move fluids (gases and liquids) in fans, pumps, and compressors (see AIR-CONDITIONING AND VENTILATION; PUMP AND COMPRESSOR).

A propeller consists of a rotating hub to which are attached two or more blades set at an angle to the axis about which the hub rotates. The blade design varies depending on the medium in which the propeller works and the intended rotating speed.

Theory of propellers

A propeller acts like a screw, moving forward through air or water in a helical (spiral) path in much the same way as a screw moves through wood when it is rotated. For this reason, the term *screw* is commonly used to describe both aircraft and marine propellers. *Pitch* is the term for the angle each blade makes to the axis of the hub; it also refers to the distance traveled by a craft in one propeller revolution.

The cross section of a propeller blade is the same shape as an airfoil. This is the cross section of an aircraft wing, curved on top and flat or slightly concave on the underside, which produces upward lift. In the case of a propeller, the airfoil blades produce a force parallel to the axis through the hub; by accelerating a column of air or water backward, a propeller provides forward thrust. As well as thrust, a propeller experiences drag, which is the force of air or water resistance acting in the opposite direction to (and thus reducing) the thrust. For this reason, propellers are designed to be of a shape and size to maximize thrust and minimize drag.

Because air is much less dense than water, propellers for the two media differ considerably in shape, size, and speed of rotation.

Aircraft propellers

An aircraft propeller may have as few as two or as many as eight blades. The higher the speed and power of the aircraft, the more efficient it is to use multibladed propellers. Any action produces an equal and opposite reaction (see MECHANICS), so a single propeller produces a torque (rotational force) that tends to rotate the entire aircraft in the opposite direction. Dual propellers rotating in opposite senses cancel this effect.

Propellers are most efficient at airspeeds under 500 mph (800 km/h): at their cruising speed, aircraft propellers have an efficiency of 85–90 percent. Efficiency is much affected by changes in speed. A propeller fixed at the ideal pitch for cruising speed would be very inefficient at lower speeds. For this reason, most propeller-driven aircraft have adjustable-pitch screws. This means that the pitch of the blades can be altered during flight so that the optimum blade angle is maintained at different airspeeds. Usually the propeller is designed to rotate at an almost constant speed, while the pitch is

---

CORE FACTS

■ Air and water propellers function in the same way, converting the torque (rotational power) of an engine into thrust to propel an aircraft or marine vessel.

■ On aircraft, propellers are more efficient than jet engines for speeds below 500 mph (800 km/h); they can achieve efficiencies of up to 90 percent.

■ Most aircraft propellers are of adjustable pitch (the blade angle can be altered); most marine propellers are of fixed pitch.

mechanically, hydraulically, or electrically adjusted for different airspeeds. The pitch is set at a shallow blade angle for takeoff and a steeper angle for maximum speed. The shallow angle also allows the engine to reach maximum power (thrust) at takeoff speeds.

A further advantage of variable-pitch propellers is that, if one engine fails, its propeller blades can be feathered (set parallel to flight direction) to minimize drag while the remaining functioning engines keep the aircraft flying. Blades can also be set to a negative pitch so that the engines produce reverse thrust, which slows the aircraft during and after landing.

Aircraft propeller tips travel at a speed approaching that of sound. Very strong centrifugal forces are involved, so blades must be of high tensile strength (resistant to pulling forces), securely attached to the hub, and well balanced to avoid damaging vibrations.

Marine propellers

Marine propellers function in a similar way to aircraft propellers, but because water is more dense and more resistant than air, they are designed differently. There are commonly two, three, or four blades, but up to seven may be used. The blades are shorter, much wider, and thinner than airplane propellers. They are often elliptical in shape but may be skewed to look like the blade of a scimitar (curved saber). The total propeller diameter (twice the blade length plus the diameter of the hub) is seldom more than three-quarters of the draft of the vessel (distance from the water line to the deepest part of the keel). Marine propellers become much less efficient if the blades approach the water surface. Their depth must take into account pitching movements of the ship.

Propellers for different marine applications are often selected using propeller pitch. A pitch of 17 means that, in ideal conditions, the craft will travel 17 in (43 cm) forward in one revolution. The higher the pitch, the higher the top speed of the craft. The lower the pitch, the more load it can carry. A craft with a propeller pitch of 17 will be better able to pull several skiers at one time than one with a pitch of 21.

Marine propellers have two great disadvantages: they corrode and they suffer from the effects of cavitation in water. Normal steel, which rusts easily, is thus an unsuitable material, and in most cases an alloy of copper, such as manganese brass, is used. Stainless steel is also suitable. Cavitation occurs above a certain rotational speed and involves the formation and collapse of bubbles of low-pressure vapor at various points on the blades. This reduces efficiency by increasing drag and causes pitting of the blades. Cavitation is one of the main challenges of designing marine propellers for ships traveling at normal speeds. For high-speed craft in which cavitation cannot be avoided, superventilated propellers are used. These channel a supply of gas through the propeller shaft to reduce the formation of low-pressure bubbles. Alternatively, the blades may be only partially submerged and designed to draw in air from the atmosphere to relieve cavitation.

R. YOUNGSON

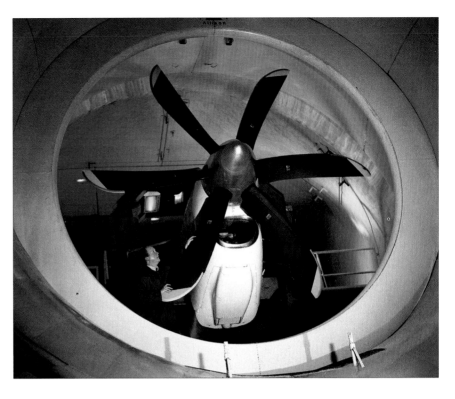

See also: AERODYNAMICS; AIRCRAFT ENGINE; FLIGHT, PRINCIPLES OF; SHIP AND BOAT; WIND POWER.

Further reading:

Carlton, J. *Marine Propellers and Propulsion.* Boston: Butterworth-Heinemann, 1994.
Gerr, D. *Propeller Handbook: The Complete Reference for Choosing, Installing and Understanding Boat Propellers.* Camden, Maine: International Marine Publishing Company, 1989.

This Allison Engine Company (Rolls-Royce) AE2100 propeller engine is used to power military transport aircraft and regional airliners.

THE INVENTION OF THE PROPELLER

Francis Pettit Smith was born in England in 1808. From boyhood, he was intensely interested in model boats, of which he made many. In 1834 he made a boat propelled by a wooden screw driven by a spring, which achieved a remarkable performance.

Until then only paddle wheels similar to waterwheels had been used to propel ships and boats, but Smith was convinced that his screw system was better. He made a succession of improvements and in 1836 took out a patent on the idea of an underwater screw propeller.

One of Smith's best innovations happened by accident. His wooden screws were originally like drill bits with a groove that encircled the shaft twice. His first full-sized, steam-driven craft was performing well when the screw struck a rock and its rear half was broken off. The craft immediately shot ahead. From then on a single-turn screw was used.

The British naval authorities were unconvinced by the screw propeller and raised many objections to its use. A few years later, in 1839, a ship of 237 tons (215 tonnes) called the *Archimedes* and driven by a single-turn screw was tried out. It was an outstanding success.

By 1856, when his patent expired, Smith had been financially ruined. However, by public demand, his great contribution to the future of the shipping industry was eventually recognized: in 1871 he was given a knighthood and a pension by the state. By the time of his death, in 1874, thousands of ships of many nations were being driven by propellers.

HISTORY OF TECHNOLOGY

PROSPECTING

Prospecting involves exploring or surveying a region for deposits of valuable minerals

A placer is a sediment of small particles of gold or other precious metals found near the Earth's surface, and the people who went searching for placers were known as placer miners. Placer miners searched the beds of streams for gold dust and nuggets eroded from soil by natural water flow. Panning was the conventional method of separating the gold particles from gravel or soil. This involved partly filling wide, shallow plates with water to agitate and wash out lighter debris (of lower density) than the gold, which would be left in the pans. Sometimes crude washing machinery was used.

When the yield from panning was exhausted, prospectors began to dig in the areas through which the streams flowed, and from which it was believed the gold particles were eroded. Tons of rock were dug up for crushing and panning, and the results were, more often than not, negative. If the yield was encouraging, the diggings were extended into deep mines, but this meant the costs rose considerably. Many prospectors became discouraged and moved on or gave up the search.

The greatest of all the U.S. gold rushes was in northern California and started in January 1848 when gold was found at Sutter's Mill on the American River. The principal inrush of people seeking their fortunes was in 1849, and thereafter the prospectors were known as forty-niners. The effect of this was an enormous increase in the population of California, which, in ten years, rose from about 14,000 to some 380,000 people.

The process of prospecting

In most areas, minerals are distributed widely in low concentrations that are not economically advantageous to extract. Prospecting is concerned with finding areas in which there are localized high concentrations of the desired minerals. The essence of modern prospecting is to detect land areas that show significant differences from what would normally be expected and then to investigate these further. Areas of unusual mineral distribution may appear different in various ways. They may show differences in soil

Miners use prospecting equipment to check for the presence of silver.

CONNECTIONS

● In some cases, a **DETONATOR AND FUSE** is used to detect areas where minerals may lie.

● The **ORE EXTRACTION AND PROCESSING** industry relies on effective prospecting methods.

Prospecting was originally based on chance findings of minerals and precious metal ores, especially gold and silver, but is now a high-tech activity involving sophisticated equipment. Modern geological, geophysical, and geochemical techniques have helped to direct attention to those areas of Earth's outer crust most likely to produce economically exploitable deposits and have eliminated the need for often hopeless random searching.

History of prospecting

Until the beginning of the 20th century, prospecting was conducted by people who wandered around looking for rock and land formations known to be associated with particular valuable mineral deposits. The more experienced prospectors were familiar with the physical appearance of the ores (mineral-containing rocks) of various metals and with the appearance of precious metals, such as gold, that occur in pure form.

CORE FACTS

■ Crude methods of prospecting, such as panning for gold, have been replaced by complex technology that ranges from satellite surveillance to the deliberate production and tracing of seismic waves.

■ Prospectors take particular interest in igneous (volcanic) rocks, since they frequently contain large quantities of metal ores.

■ Large deposits of otherwise valuable minerals may be ignored if the costs of mining and processing are likely to be greater than the profits obtained.

A CROSS SECTION OF EARTH'S CRUST

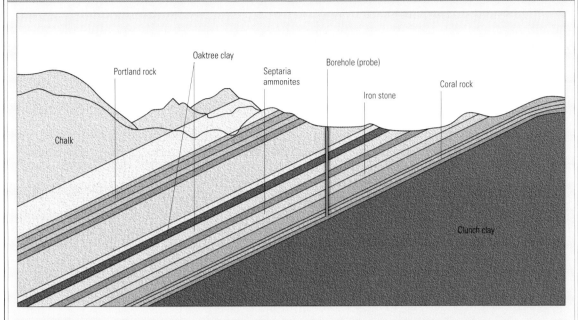

Oaktree clay

Portland rock

Septaria ammonites

Borehole (probe)

Iron stone

Coral rock

Chalk

Clunch clay

Core samples from a borehole can be analyzed to determine the compositions and depths of rock strata.

One of the most valuable techniques in prospecting is the drilling of boreholes for core sampling. A core is a long cylinder of material about 2 in (5 cm) in diameter and often hundreds or even thousands of yards (meters) long. The core is sampled with a special diamond-tipped drill that cuts out a section and brings it to the surface in a continuous length. The lengths of core are stored in boxes, and the operators carefully note the order of their extraction so that it is known at what depth they were found.

Although a single borehole can only give precise information about the depths of strata in the location where it is drilled, the results from several boreholes can be compiled to give a three-dimensional map of the rock strata in the area of study. Details of the morphologies (shapes and forms) and changing compositions of the rock strata can be deduced, as can the location of geologic faults (planes where there is a discontinuity in the depths of rock strata caused by past Earth movements).

A CLOSER LOOK

color and texture, differences in rock formations and type, and even differences in vegetation that are caused by the minerals.

Today, mineral deposits are most quickly detected by aerial surveys or by television surveillance and photography from satellites (see SATELLITE). On the ground, several different techniques are used to detect unusual concentrations of minerals. These include chemical analysis of soil and rock samples and physical analysis of density, electrical conductivity, magnetic properties, and radioactivity of the soil.

In prospecting for metals, the presence of igneous rock is of special interest. Igneous rock is derived from molten material (magma) from Earth's mantle —the layer between Earth's crust and core—that has been thrust up to or near Earth's crust and cooled. Such rock may contain large quantities of metals such as copper, lead, and zinc. Outcroppings (veins of minerals exposed at the surface) can be mapped to suggest the extent of deposits. Drilling can then be used to confirm or deny the initial analysis.

Core sampling over an area (see the box above) is a valuable method of reducing the risk of wasted expense and effort. It is used mainly when there is

evidence of fairly well localized medium to small deposits at various levels below ground that are sharply delineated from the surrounding crust. Core samples are useful for assessing whether exploitation is likely to be economical.

Prospecting equipment

The equipment used in prospecting varies with the mineral being sought. Metals such as iron are magnetic, and their presence can be established using sensitive magnetism-detecting instruments known as magnetometers. Many minerals are physically more dense than other materials. If they are present in adequate concentrations, their increased density can cause a tiny change in the gravitational field of Earth. This can be detected by instruments called gravimeters. Some minerals conduct electricity well; others are insulators. This property has been exploited in the design of instruments to detect areas of relatively low electrical resistance (good conductance). Some minerals in the process of oxidation (combining with oxygen) create electrical currents that flow in the ground that can be detected by sensitive instruments. Sulfide mineral deposits can be found in this way.

THE GREAT KLONDIKE GOLD RUSH

Klondike prospectors display gold nuggets.

The Klondike, which is named for the Klondike River, is an isolated and sparsely populated part of the Yukon Territory in Canada near the border with Alaska. In 1896, some gold nuggets were discovered in a tributary of the Klondike at Rabbit Creek, renamed Bonanza Creek after the gold strike. Within a year, rumor of the strike spread and prospectors, mostly amateurs and adventurers, began to arrive, mainly from the United States. This was the start of the great gold rush, and during the ensuing 13 years more than 30,000 people moved into the area. Dawson, the major town of the Klondike, provided the prospectors with the opportunity to relax from work and spend a lot of money. By 1910, more than $100 million worth of gold was said to have been removed from the Klondike and the gold rush was over.

Mining for gold, silver, lead, and zinc continues on a small scale in the Klondike. Elsewhere in Canada, substantial deposits of copper, lead, zinc, and silver, especially in the Kootenay region of southeastern British Columbia, have proved to be far more important. They have promoted railroad construction and urban development and have brought in many permanent residents.

HISTORY OF TECHNOLOGY

Seismography is used increasingly for prospecting. This involves detecting planes (boundaries) between different strata (layers) of rocks and providing information from which the nature of the rocks may be deduced. Shallow holes are drilled in the surface of the ground and explosive charges are placed in them. A wide array of detectors is laid on the ground in the form of a grid. When the charges are detonated, shock waves similar to those caused by a miniature earthquake are sent down into the ground. These shock waves are reflected off the boundary planes between the rock layers back to Earth's surface. On the surface, the reflected vibrations are recorded by the detectors. The results are detailed charts from which a great deal of valuable information can be deduced about the geologic structures under the surface (see SEISMOGRAPHY).

In prospecting for radioactive ores such as those of uranium, thorium, and radium, much use is made of radiation-detecting equipment such as Geiger counters. These operate by detecting the changes in the electrical conductivity of a noble (inert) gas that occur when one or more atoms of the gas are turned into ions (atoms with too many or too few electrons) by the action of high-energy gamma rays and fast-moving particles given off by the radioactive ore. Because ionization turns neutral atoms into charged ions, any high voltage across the ionized gas will attract or repel the charged ions, resulting in scintillations (tiny pulses of current) that can be amplified and counted (see RADIATION DETECTION).

Assaying
Although any random rock sample contains traces of a range of minerals, this does not necessarily mean that it is worth mining. Material that is believed to be of high enough grade (having a high enough proportion of desired mineral present) to be exploited profitably is called ore. Any material of lower grade than this is classed as waste (see ORE EXTRACTION AND PROCESSING).

Grade varies widely from deposit to deposit and also within a particular deposit. If a deposit contains only low-grade ore it will seldom justify the expense of mining. The grade of an ore below which it is thought likely to be profitable to mine is called the mine cutoff grade. And, because deposits vary in grade, a proportion of mined material contains so little mineral that it will be unprofitable to process. This level is called the mill cutoff grade. Break-even grade is the level at which the total costs of mining and processing are equal to the expected profits from the sale of the mineral.

The process of determining the grade of a sample of mineral is called assaying and is performed in a laboratory by chemical analysis. Assaying is extremely important: it is the major factor that determines whether or not a particular deposit is of high enough grade to be worth mining. It is not, however, the only factor. The depth of the deposit and the difficulty and cost of extracting it also carry great weight, as does the current price being paid for the mineral in question.

R. YOUNGSON

See also: IRON AND STEEL PRODUCTION; METALS; MINING AND QUARRYING; NONFERROUS METAL.

Further reading:
Clark, A. *Seeing Beneath the Soil: Prospecting Methods in Archaeology.* London, England: B.T. Batsford, 1990.
Ettinger, L. *The Rockhound and Prospector's Bible: A Reference and Study Guide to Rocks, Minerals, Gemstones and Prospecting.* Reno, Nevada: L. J. Ettinger, 1992.
Evans, A. *Ore Geology and Industrial Minerals.* Boston: Blackwell Scientific Publications, 1993.
Kozlov, E. *Migration in Seismic Prospecting.* Rotterdam, Holland: A. A. Balkema, 1990.

PUMP AND COMPRESSOR

Pumps and compressors are mechanical devices that move liquids and gases or increase their pressure

The world's most important pump, the human heart, beats two billion times in an average lifetime. Few mechanical devices are as critical or as dependable, but reliable pumps and compressors have nevertheless become the artificial hearts of the modern world. Airplane and automobile engines, oil refineries, refrigerators, chemical plants, and fire engines all depend on them.

The term *pump* is usually taken to mean a mechanical device that pumps liquids; the term *compressor* usually refers to a gas pump. However, most pump and compressor designs work equally well with liquids or gases. This is because both liquids and gases are examples of fluids and behave according to similar physical laws (see HYDRAULICS AND PNEUMATICS; HYDRODYNAMICS AND HYDROSTATICS).

TYPES OF PUMPS AND COMPRESSORS

Some types of pumps and compressors work better than others for a particular application. The choice of which pump or compressor to use depends on a number of factors, including capacity (the amount of fluid the pump can move in a particular time), simplicity (intricate pumps tend to be less reliable), cost, ease of control, and quietness in operation.

Displacement pumps

All displacement pumps operate by repeating a cycle of steps. The pump extracts a fixed amount of fluid from a source during one part of the cycle and expels it during another part. Displacement pumps fall into two categories: reciprocating and rotary.

Reciprocating (up-and-down) pumps use pistons and one-way valves to take in a fixed amount of fluid during one stroke and expel it during another stroke (see VALVE, MECHANICAL). Bicycle pumps, hand-operated well-water pumps, and diaphragm pumps used in automobile fuel systems are all reciprocating pumps. A well-water pump uses a three-stage cycle. First, the handle is pressed down, causing a piston to rise. This creates a partial vacuum inside the pump that draws in water through a one-way inlet valve at the base. Second, the handle is pushed up, which closes the inlet valve and opens an outlet valve in the piston. As the handle is raised, the open valve in the piston allows it to move down through the trapped

This large pump is housed at a waste management facility in Thief River Falls, Minnesota.

water. Third, the handle is pressed down again, which forces the piston upward and pushes water out of the spout. At the same time, more water is drawn in below the piston in the first stage of the next cycle.

As their name suggests, rotary pumps use a rotating device to draw fluid from an inlet pipe to an outlet. In a gear pump, this is done by two intermeshing gear wheels (see GEAR). A sliding-vane pump has several spring-loaded vanes fastened to an eccentric (off-center) axle within a circular chamber. As the axle rotates, the vanes push against the outer casing, moving fluid through the chamber from the inlet to the outlet pipe, like a revolving door.

Similar to the sliding-vane pump is the widely used vacuum pump, which uses an eccentrically mounted wheel (known as a rotor) to draw gas into the pump and push it out again in a continuous process. The entire casing of a vacuum pump is immersed in oil to prevent gases from leaking. Vacuum pumps are used to reduce gases to

---

CORE FACTS

- A displacement pump moves a fixed amount of fluid during each cycle; a rotary pump operates continuously, drawing fluid from an inlet to an outlet pipe.
- Vacuum pumps are used to remove gases from inside electron microscopes and television tubes.
- Axial-flow pumps are used as the compressors in aircraft engines.

CONNECTIONS

- **STEAM ENGINES** were initially developed to pump water from underground mines.

- **VACUUM CLEANERS** rely on pumps to suck dust from carpets.

EARLY WATER PUMPS

This water-lifting device in Sudan feeds a system of irrigation canals.

Pumps did not always look like they do today. Water-lifting devices were the earliest pumps and also among the earliest machines. The *shaduf*, which dates from c.4000 B.C.E. but is still used today, is a seesaw with a bucket at one end and a stone or lead counterweight at the other. A human operator lowers the bucket into the water source, raises it up with the help of the counterweight, swings it to where it is required, and then empties it (see IRRIGATION AND LAND DRAINAGE).

The *shaduf* is a primitive reciprocating pump; later devices moved greater quantities of water using rotational motion. In the third century B.C.E., Greek mathematician Archimedes (c.287–212 B.C.E.) developed a device that lifted water along the turning thread of a screw. Around the same time, Greek engineer Ctesibius (c.250 B.C.E.) was the first person to use pistons in a reciprocating water pump. Roman architect Vitruvius (c.first century B.C.E.) wrote of the tympanum, a waterwheel with hollow compartments that lifted water as it turned, which was operated by a human- or animal-powered treadmill. The *noria* was an undershot waterwheel with jars attached to its rim that raised water as it turned in the flow of a stream (see TECHNOLOGY IN ANCIENT CIVILIZATIONS; WATER POWER).

In the 17th century, the development of better pumps was spurred on by research into the properties of gases. French physicist Denis Papin (c.1647–1712) developed first the centrifugal pump, then a forerunner of the steam engine. Early steam engines were developed as large-scale reciprocating pumps to remove water from underground mines; in 1698 English engineer Thomas Savery (c.1650–1715) produced the miner's friend—a steam-powered water pump.

HISTORY OF TECHNOLOGY

extremely low pressures, which is useful inside television tubes, electron microscopes, and lightbulbs, which all require low pressures of gas.

A displacement called peristaltic pumping is used in heart-lung machines. Rollers pinch and release sections of a flexible pipe, pushing fluids through it.

Dynamic pumps

Dynamic pumps, or kinetic pumps, are always rotary. They operate continuously and at high speed, moving a greater volume of fluid in a given time than displacement pumps of similar dimensions. The two principal types are centrifugal and axial-flow pumps:

Centrifugal pumps. Centrifugal pumps comprise a rotating paddle wheel—the impeller—in a disk-shaped chamber. Fluid is drawn in near the center of the impeller and thrown toward the outlet in the rim of the chamber by the impeller's fast-spinning vanes.

Axial-flow pumps. Axial-flow pumps use a propeller mounted inside a cylinder with its axis inline with that of the cylinder. The propeller blades accelerate fluid through the pump as they rotate. They are widely used as compressors in jet engines.

At high speeds, dynamic pumps for liquids may suffer from cavitation. This occurs when local suction pressures become so low that vapor bubbles form in the liquid and the pump efficiency is much reduced. When the bubbles collapse, the resulting shock waves cause noise and vibration, as well as wearing away the internal surfaces of the pump and reducing its working life.

Other types of pumps

Although most pumps operate by displacement or dynamic action, other designs have been developed for specialized applications. Electromagnetic pumps work by magnetizing metallic fluids and moving them through pipes using electromagnets. They are used to pump liquid sodium metal, which is used as the cooling fluid in fast nuclear reactors (see NUCLEAR POWER). An ion pump uses a cathode (negative electrode) to generate free electrons, which collide with gas molecules and turn them into positive ions. These are attracted to the cathode, in effect producing a gas flow. Ion pumps are used to create a vacuum in particle accelerators (see PARTICLE ACCELERATOR).

USES OF PUMPS

Most devices that move liquid or gas use a pump to do it. The cylinders in automobile engines are reciprocating piston pumps (see INTERNAL COMBUSTION ENGINE). Refrigerators pump a gas called a coolant around their compartments to extract heat (see REFRIGERATION). Oil and natural gas are pumped from underground reserves to tanks on the surface, then pumped onward through pipelines. Some hydroelectric power plants generate electricity by draining reservoirs through turbines during the day (when electricity is expensive), then using some of the power produced to pump water back to the reservoir at night (when electricity is cheap). This is known as pumped storage (see HYDROELECTRICITY).

C. WOODFORD

See also: HEART-LUNG MACHINE; TURBINE.

Further reading:
Cheremisinoff, N. *Pumps and Pumping Operations.* Englewood Cliffs, New Jersey: Prentice Hall, 1992.

RACE CAR

Specially built race cars, and ordinary vehicles modified for racing, compete in speed contests all over the world

Members of the pit crew work on the Mistral race car at an Indianapolis 500 race.

The human need for speed has existed for as long as people have been going places, with most modes of transportation subjected to speed and racing contests over the years. Motor racing began almost as soon as the automobile was invented. Today, races for specially built race cars, or modified mass-production vehicles, are held worldwide.

The raceway has prompted the development of technologies for making cars faster, lighter, and safer. Many of these innovations have become modified and used as standard equipment on ordinary automobiles. Manufacturers sponsor motor racing because of the publicity it brings.

Types of race cars

The best-known international car races are the Grand Prix (large prize) events, which include dozens of laps of a circuit. In some cases, such as the U.S. Grand Prix in Detroit, the route includes local roads, which are cleared for the occasion. Grand Prix races are for Formula One race cars, which can reach 200 mph (322 km/h) on straightaways (straight stretches of track).

A formula is an international standard that governs everything about the race car, including its size, weight, design, fuel, and safety equipment. Formula One cars have no fenders, resulting in an open wheel design. The car must be low to the ground, with the driver sitting in an open cockpit in front of the rear-mounted engine. Formula Two and Formula Three cars are defined by similar rules, but they are smaller and not as high-powered, so they are less expensive. Many Formula One drivers started their careers in Formula Two or Three cars.

In the United States, Indy racing, named for a race called the Indianapolis 500, is very popular. Indy cars look a lot like Formula One racers, but they are heavier and sturdier, with a suspension designed to give the best grip on the track. This allows them to reach speeds of over 230 mph (370 km/h) on the banked Indy tracks, taking hundreds of laps over the course of a race. Indy cars must withstand 500 miles (805 km) of racing, in contrast to Formula One races, which never exceed 200 miles (322 km).

Karting is racing in miniature and often serves as a training ground for Indy and Formula drivers, although the events are popular in their own right. Karts are low, open vehicles of various sizes that are driven on short dirt or asphalt tracks. Midget and

CORE FACTS

- Automobile racing began in 1895 with the earliest automobiles.
- Many racing classes exist, each with its own rules and specifications on which types of cars can compete.
- Race cars are a valuable proving ground for new automotive technologies.
- In addition to speed, power, and maneuverability, safety and ergonomics are important considerations in race car development.

CONNECTIONS

- Manufacturers rely heavily on the **ELECTRONICS** industry for assembling race cars.

- **COMPUTER GRAPHICS** are used to produce 3-D models of race cars before they are made.

A stretch dragster stands ready for a race at a meet in Los Angeles, California.

completely rebuilt and its body strengthened with a cage made of steel tubing, to which the suspension and steering systems are anchored. The resulting car weighs twice as much as a Formula One car, but with its powerful engine it can go just as fast. The National Association for Stock Car Auto Racing (NASCAR) has been instrumental in promoting this racing class.

Drag racing involves two cars competing at the same time in quarter- or eighth-mile (0.4-km or 0.2-km) heats on a straight, paved drag strip. The loser of each heat is eliminated until only one car is left. The most popular dragster (drag car) is the Top Fuel car, which has a long, thin frame, and the driver sits in front of the engine. Its rear wheels are much larger than those in the front, because the weight of the car shifts backward as it accelerates—to speeds of 260 mph (418 km/h)—from a standing start. The race is six seconds long or less, and the cars use parachutes to help them stop. The funny car is a dragster with a front engine and fiberglass or plastic body that makes it look like a passenger automobile. But the fake body has no doors, so the driver swings the entire body up on its hinges in order to get in or out.

sprint cars are the largest, heaviest classes and can reach over 100 mph (160 km/h). Five-year-old children can drive quarter-midget versions, reaching speeds of 45 mph (72 km/h) on straightaways.

In GT (Grand Touring) racing, regular sports cars, like Porsches, are disassembled and rebuilt lighter and faster, to produce sports prototypes (cars specially built for racing). They generally have a rear engine and a large rear wing (spoiler), like Indy and Formula cars, but differ in their enclosed cockpits and fenders. These cars take part in the Le Mans endurance race in France, in which they compete to finish as many laps as possible in 24 hours.

Stock car racing is based on regular late-model production sedans. To prepare an ordinary car to race on a banked oval track, its engine needs to be

Designed for speed

The history of race cars has been one of constant technical innovation. Engineers have developed ways to squeeze more speed out of the cars while staying within the complicated regulations for a given class.

Aerodynamic considerations are important in racing design (see AERODYNAMICS). Engineers minimize air resistance to forward motion by designing narrow, smooth cars. Drivers save fuel by drafting, which is following closely behind another car to get a "free ride" as the leading car breaks the air resistance.

DEVELOPMENT OF RACING TECHNOLOGY

1895: First motor race, Paris-Bordeaux-Paris. Among the competing vehicles was the first race car on pneumatic tires, driven by Frenchman André Michelin.
1898: First land speed record set near Paris, by Comte Gaston de Chasseloup, driving an electric car at 39 mph (63 km/h).
1902: First sponsored race, organized by the French Ministry of Agriculture, to promote alcohol as a fuel.
1903: First eight-cylinder racing engines developed in France and the United States.
1905: First front-wheel-drive race cars introduced in the United States by American manufacturer Walter Christie.
1906: The fastest steam car ever built, a Stanley Rocket, driven by American driver Fred Marriott in Daytona, Florida, boosted the land speed record to 122 mph (196 km/h).
1914: Grand Prix cars built with four-wheel brakes.
1921: American driver Jimmy Murphy won the Le Mans race in a Duesenberg, the first Grand Prix car with hydraulic brakes, becoming the first American to win a major European race.
1923: A Fiat driven by Italian driver Carlo Salamano became the first supercharged car to win a Grand Prix race.

1925: Onboard mechanics eliminated from Grand Prix races.
1929: First twin-engine race car built by Italian maker Maserati.
1934: Grand Prix formula set to limit car weight to 1653 lbs (750 kg), eliminating many existing cars.
1935: Crash helmets required at Indianapolis races.
1938: First race car with disc brakes, built by American manufacturer Harry Miller, competed in the Indianapolis 500 race.
1948: First drag strip opened, in Goleta, California.
1955: Worst accident in racing history, at Le Mans in France, when a safety bank failed to contain a car that had been deflected into a public enclosure by a collision with another vehicle. French driver Pierre Levegh and 82 spectators were killed.
1963: Dragsters began appearing with aerodynamic spoilers.
1967: The Ford-Cosworth DFV 3.0-liter Grand Prix V8 engine appeared and became the dominant racing engine for almost twenty years.
1978: Radial tires introduced into Grand Prix racing by French tire company Michelin.
1981: Driver cooling system devised for races in hot climates. A refrigerated cartridge containing a cooling gel that is pumped through capillaries (fine tubes) in a hood and vest worn by the driver.

HISTORY OF TECHNOLOGY

FASTER THAN THE SPEED OF SOUND

The **Thrust SuperSonic Car** *(SSC) is powered by two jet engines from a fighter aircraft.*

The very fastest cars do not run on racetracks. In order to develop their peak speeds, and then have room to stop, they require large expanses of hard, flat ground, such as dry lake beds or salt flats.

Cars built to break land speed records have long, thin, aerodynamic bodies and jet or rocket engines (see ENGINE). In December 1979, the three-wheeled, 50,000-horsepower Budweiser Rocket was clocked by the U.S. Air Force at 739 mph (1189 km/h), just over the speed of sound. But the achievement did not count as an official land speed record, because it is required that two timed runs be made in opposite directions.

On 13 October 1997, the land speed record was set at 763 mph (1228 km/h) over a measured mile (1.6 km) by the British *Thrust SuperSonic Car*. This speed is equivalent to Mach 1.020, or 1.020 times the speed of sound in dry air.

High-speed tests are used to predict the behavior of a car as it encounters the shock waves caused by travel at near-sonic speeds. Highly compressed air tends to lift the car off the ground, with any asymmetry (imbalance) in the car causing instability that may toss it onto its side. These effects must be compensated for in the design of the car.

A CLOSER LOOK

The second car, which has avoided driving at full throttle, then accelerates at the last minute to pull ahead. This is known as slingshotting.

Aerodynamic techniques help keep race cars on the road. Spoilers, built like upside-down airplane wings, exert a downward pressure that gives the tires better traction and help the car hold the road on turns. Attempts to improve grip by using fans and funnels beneath the car ended in 1985 when flat-bottom rules were extended to most racing classes.

Engine capacity (size) must be kept within the limit for a given class, but other features are more flexible. Whether having 8, 10, or 12 cylinders is best for a racing engine is the subject of long-standing debate. Engineers constantly strive to make engines lighter, stronger, and more fuel-efficient.

Racing tires are wide, tubeless, and designed for maximum grip for a specific road condition. In dry weather, treadless tires called slicks insure that the maximum amount of rubber is on the road for the best grip. For wet surfaces, treaded tires that can shed a lot of water at high speeds are used.

Race car bodies are designed to absorb the force of impacts, and they undergo crash tests before use. Drivers wear helmets and flame-resistant suits guaranteed to protect them from temperatures up to 1300°F (704°C) for 12 seconds. They are strapped into six-point harnesses in custom-molded seats that hold them in the cockpit.

The instrumentation in a race car cockpit resembles that of a fighter jet. Controls are positioned near the steering wheel so that the driver can see them without turning the head. Sensors in the engine and chassis transmit information to the maintenance bays (pits) so that when the driver pulls in, technicians are ready to service the car to continue the race.

S. CALVO

See also: AUTOMOBILE; BODY PROTECTION; ERGONOMICS; INTERNAL COMBUSTION ENGINE; TIRE.

Further reading:
Gabbard, A. *Vintage and Historic Racing Cars.* Tucson, Arizona: HP Books, 1986.

RADAR

A military radar operator studies his radar screen. Military surveillance is one of the principal uses of radar today.

Radar measures the position or velocity of airplanes and other objects even in the dark or through fog

The word *radar* is an acronym for *ra*dio *d*etection *a*nd *r*anging. It was developed in Britain before and during World War II under the leadership of Scottish physicist Sir Robert Watson-Watt (1892–1973) for the detection of bombers. Since then, it has become an essential part of air traffic control around the world. Ships, even small fishing vessels, use radar for navigation at night and through fog. It is also used by police officers to clock the speed of automobiles and in surveying to measure distances (see SURVEYING).

Radar systems are widely used by the military to detect enemy bombers or missiles. Strategic defense systems consist of large radar installations and airborne radars (AWACS) that continuously scan the sky (see STRATEGIC DEFENSE SYSTEMS). Military airplanes use radar systems to search out enemy planes, which are often equipped with antiradar devices or designed with shapes and materials that minimize their radar profile (see ELECTRONIC COUNTERMEASURES). Missiles use radar for guidance by scanning the terrain with radio pulses and comparing the echoes to electronic maps.

Basic operation

Many radar systems operate in a similar way to sonar, but instead of sending out pulses of sound and detecting their echoes as the pulses are reflected by distant objects, they send out high-energy pulses of radio waves. The pulses are triggered by a signal from a timing circuit, generated by a device called a magnetron (see ELECTROMAGNETIC RADIATION), and directed to the antenna by a switching device called a duplexer (see the diagram on page 1077). Once the pulse has been transmitted, the duplexer connects the antenna to the detection circuit so that any returning echo can be detected and analyzed.

The detection circuitry is sensitive enough to detect echoes that may be billionths of the power of the transmitted pulses. An important function of the duplexer is to electrically isolate the detection equipment from the outgoing pulses, which could otherwise cause damage to the detector.

The time interval between the transmission of a pulse and the return of its echo is the length of the path traveled by the pulse—twice the distance of the reflecting object—divided by the speed of light. Hence, an object's distance can be calculated by comparing the signal from the timing circuit with the signal from the detection circuit.

The position of a moving airborne object is often established using two antennas. The first rotates around a vertical axis and detects an object's position in the horizontal plane from the point at which the echo signal is strongest. A second antenna then rotates to that horizontal position and starts to scan up and down to establish the angle from horizontal at which the echo is strongest. A computer then combines the results from these two systems with the distance calculation to give the exact position of the object in space.

Design considerations

For effective working, the signal (radar echo) must be distinguished from noise (extraneous electrical signals produced by external sources or from inside the receiver). Radars are thus designed to maximize the ratio of signal to noise. Echo signal strength can be increased by transmitting pulses of higher power or by focusing the pulses into a narrow beam, which also makes the location more precise. Rain or fog absorb and weaken the signal. Signal strength can be improved by using frequencies that are less susceptible to absorption than others.

A sophisticated way of improving performance is to transmit a complex waveform of long duration. The components of a complex waveform can be distinguished separately and added coherently (so that the components reinforce one another), while the noise adds incoherently (so that its components cancel out). This increases the signal-to-noise ratio. Such a system, known as pulse compression or Chirp radar, gives the effect of a very high-power pulse from a moderate-power transmitter.

CONNECTIONS

- Radar systems are used in combination with **METEOROLOGICAL INSTRUMENTS** to track the development of weather systems.

- Radar intelligence helps military controllers to know when to deploy **ANTIAIRCRAFT WEAPONS.**

CORE FACTS

- Radar gives the location and velocity of distant objects such as airplanes.
- Radar systems are designed to maximize the radar signal and minimize electrical noise.
- Radar has many applications including air traffic control, police speed monitoring, and space exploration.

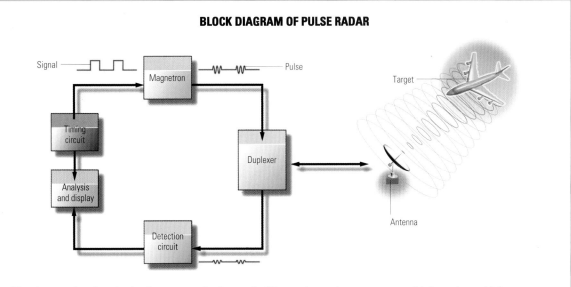

BLOCK DIAGRAM OF PULSE RADAR

The timer emits electrical pulses at regular intervals. These trigger the magnetron, which produces high-energy radio pulses that are directed to the antenna by a duplexer (a switching circuit). Between pulses the duplexer directs returning echo signals to the detection circuit.

Signal processing can also enhance the signal-to-noise ratio. One such system stores the received echoes and subtracts successive echoes from each other. Stationary targets or noise sources disappear or are significantly reduced, allowing targets in motion to stand out. This is called moving target identification (see the box below).

Doppler radar

A sinusoidal (wave-formed) signal coming from a moving source will appear to change its frequency. This is called the Doppler effect, an example of which is the perceived change in pitch of a squad car siren as it races past.

Radar systems use this frequency shift (change) to measure the velocity of a moving target. In a police speed radar, a handheld transmitter fires radar pulses at a speeding vehicle. The radar beam is reflected, changing frequency in proportion to the speed of the target. The receiver calculates and displays the vehicle's velocity using the frequency shift.

Weather radars use reflections from atmospheric particles to detect potentially dangerous weather conditions from high-velocity, downward-directed winds that are invisible optically.

Transponders

Some aircraft are fitted with devices called transponders that emit coded pulses when they detect a radar signal from the ground. The coded pulses contain information such as the flight identification number of the aircraft, which can be decoded by the radar system on the ground.

Displays

The first radars displayed return pulses on an oscilloscope (a monitor that displays graphs). Modern radars use a plan position indicator (PPI) display—in effect, a computer monitor in which the scanning electron beam is synchronized to the antenna position so that when the antenna faces north, for example, the beam scans vertically upward. A received echo appears as a brightening of the screen.

Air traffic control radar displays augment the bright spots that represent radar signals with information such as altitude and ground speed, as well as any transponder information that is received.

Extremely powerful radar systems can also be used to study the surfaces of our neighboring planets—Mars, Mercury, and Venus—by their echoes.

B. HAZELTINE

See also: AIR TRAFFIC CONTROL; ELECTRONIC COUNTERMEASURES; MISSILE; RADIO RECEIVER.

Further reading:
Cole, H. *Understanding Radar*. Boston: Blackwell Scientific Publications, 1992.

AIRPORT SURVEILLANCE RADAR

The latest version of airport surveillance radar (ASR) has been installed at over 100 airports. It has a narrow antenna beam and can locate a target 21 miles (34 km) away to within 330 ft (100 m). Moving target identification is used to separate aircraft from ground clutter, and Doppler measurements gauge aircraft velocity. Two further radar systems are used for additional purposes. One of these monitors the runways to prevent collisions between aircraft on the ground. The other, called air route surveillance radar (ARSR), monitors the airspace beyond the immediate vicinity of the the airport and guides planes en route.

Computer processing and advanced radar circuits nearly always make the job of an air traffic controller easier, but unlikely combinations of radar echoes and ground clutter can cause false readings. Fortunately these usually disappear quickly, but an operator must exercise considerable judgment even with all the electronic aids available.

A CLOSER LOOK

RADIATION DETECTION

Radiation detectors are instruments designed to measure radioactivity

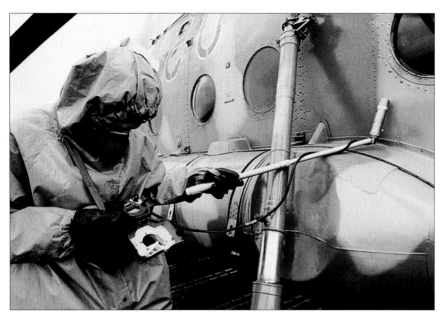

A technician uses a Geiger counter to check the radioactive contamination of a military helicopter used during the nuclear power plant disaster that occurred at Chernobyl, Ukraine, in April 1986.

Low levels of radiation are given off by radioactive elements in Earth's crust, sometimes escaping as radioactive gases. Cosmic rays continuously bombard the upper atmosphere, and some of the resulting radiation reaches Earth's surface, especially at high altitudes. In addition, nuclear power plants, atomic bomb tests, and medical equipment are sources of radiation (see NUCLEAR POWER).

Damage to biological tissue occurs because many types of radiation are capable of ionizing atoms (making them charged particles by knocking off electrons). This ionizing radiation can kill cells or damage their DNA, resulting in cancer or genetic mutations. Because it is impossible to avoid exposure to radiation, it is important to measure its presence and quantify the possible biological effects.

Alpha, beta, and gamma radiation
The principal types of ionizing radiation arising from naturally occurring sources are alpha and beta particles and gamma rays. These three radiation types occur when an unstable nucleus of a heavy element such as uranium decays into another element. The end product of decay is an isotope (one of two or more distinct forms of an element) of the metal lead (see NUCLEAR ENERGY).

Alpha particles are a tightly bound combination of two protons and two neutrons. Because these particles are highly charged and very big compared to other forms of radiation, they ionize many atoms along their path and give up their energy quickly. Thus they are quite destructive, but only over a very short range. Skin provides animals with protection from external alpha particles; however, when an alpha-particle emitter such as radioactive dust is inhaled and lodges in the lungs, alpha radiation can do extensive damage (see the box on page 1079).

Beta particles are high-energy electrons or their positively charged antiparticles, positrons, that are produce by nuclear reactions. They have a much larger range than alpha particles, but clothing is adequate protection to external exposure.

Gamma rays are high-energy photons emitted from nuclei (see ELECTROMAGNETIC RADIATION). Because they ionize fewer atoms per centimeter along their path, they are highly penetrating. For the same reason, greater numbers are required to cause extensive damage. Nonetheless, in principle, a single gamma ray could alter a cell's DNA, causing a mutation. For this reason, exposure of reproductive organs to gamma rays is particularly hazardous.

Radiation counters
Most radiation detectors work by detecting the ionization created when the radiation passes through matter. The Geiger counter, invented by German physicist Hans Geiger (1882–1945) and improved in 1928 in conjunction with his fellow German Walther Müller, is still widely used for routine radiation surveys. The sensor element is a cylindrical metal Geiger-Müller tube with a thin window on one end. The tube is filled with a gas, typically a mixture of argon and alcohol. Down the center of the tube runs a thin wire held at a positive voltage relative to the surrounding cylinder.

Radiation entering the tube through the thin window ionizes the gas, producing electrons that are accelerated toward the central wire and positive ions that drift to the edge of the cylinder. When the voltage between wire and tubes is sufficiently high, electrons rushing toward the wire gain sufficient energy to create more ions, and an avalanche of electrons results in a sizable electric pulse. In a certain range of applied voltages, this pulse is proportional to the energy of the initial radiation. (At higher voltages, the quenching effect of the alcohol limits the size of the electron avalanche and all pulses are of the same magnitude.) The pulses are then amplified to produce the familiar audible click of the detector.

Geiger counters filled with boron trifluoride can be used to detect neutrons since the boron nucleus has a high probability for interacting with neutrons

CONNECTIONS

● The safe production of **NUCLEAR ENERGY** requires the constant monitoring of radiation levels.

● Positrons and radiation emitters are used in **MEDICAL IMAGING.**

● Radiation detectors are used to measure subatomic impacts in a **PARTICLE ACCELERATOR.**

CORE FACTS

■ Naturally occurring radioactive elements emit radiation in the form of alpha particles, beta particles, and gamma rays.

■ The greatest biological dangers of radiation result from internal alpha particle decay and external gamma ray exposure.

■ Radiation is detected primarily by measuring the ions created when radiation interacts with matter.

and thereby forming an alpha particle. Geiger counters that are sensitive to gamma rays can be made by constructing the cylinder from metals with high atomic numbers, such as tungsten. A gamma ray striking an atom in the cylinder wall has a high probability of generating an electron-positron pair for subsequent detection inside the tube.

Track detectors

The simplest radiation detector is similar to photographic film. Compared to photographic emulsions, the emulsions used for particle detection are thinner—about one millimeter thick—and contain much more light-sensitive silver halide (see PHOTOGRAPHY). Microscopic examination of the developed films reveals a trail of silver grains along the path taken by charged particles. Even uncharged neutrons can be detected from the star-shaped patterns formed in the emulsion when they strike atoms and dislodge numerous charged particles. Film badges are routinely worn by persons who work around radioactive materials in order to monitor their total exposure during each week.

Cloud chambers consist of transparent containers filled with a thick mist of water vapor. The passage of charged particles is revealed by the vapor trail, caused by the ionization of water particles, in their wake. Because liquids are denser than gases, bubble chambers filled with isopentane or liquid hydrogen are better at revealing high-energy particles. In a bubble chamber, invented in 1952 by U.S. physicist Donald Glaser (1926–), the liquid is held at a temperature above its normal boiling point, but it is prevented from boiling by applied pressure. When the pressure is suddenly released, charged particles passing through the liquid leave behind a trail of small bubbles as the liquid begins to boil preferentially along the trail of ionized atoms. The tracks are photographed for later analysis.

In modern particle physics, cloud chambers and bubble chambers have been replaced by spark and streamer chambers. A spark chamber consists of a large number of parallel plates. Pairs of plates separated by a small gap have a large potential difference applied to them. When a charged particle passes, a spark is created between the plates. The trail of the original particle is revealed by photographing the gap. In a streamer chamber large electric fields are applied suddenly over larger gap distances and ionization trails called streamers are photographed.

Proportional chambers, invented in 1968 by Polish scientist Georges Charpak (1924–), are similar devices except that the voltages are applied to parallel wires that are only a few millimeters apart. Instead of sparks between wires, ions are collected on the nearest wire and recorded as an electric pulse.

In drift chambers, a later invention of Charpak, greater wire separation is used. The chamber is filled with argon gas in which electrons "drift" at a constant speed of about 1.5 inches (5 cm) per millionth of a second under the influence of an electric field. Thus, by measuring the time for the arrival of each pulse

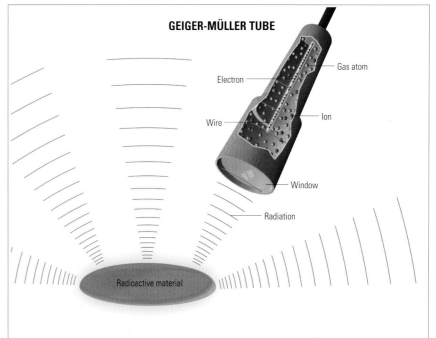

GEIGER-MÜLLER TUBE

Gas atom
Electron
Wire
Ion
Window
Radiation
Radioactive material

When radiation enters a Geiger-Müller tube, it ionizes the gas atoms inside. The electrons knocked off of these atoms move toward the positively charged wire and cause electric pulses in the wire that are amplified to form audible clicks.

of electrons, it is possible to determine how far from the wire they were created by the radiation and so locate their original position and plot the course of the ionizing radiation.

A. WESTERN

See also: MEDICAL MONITORING EQUIPMENT; METALS; NONFERROUS METAL; NUCLEAR FUSION; NUCLEAR WEAPONS; POLLUTION AND ITS CONTROL.

Further reading:
Kleinknecht, K. *Detectors for Particle Radiation.* Cambridge: Cambridge University Press, 1986.

RADON

Unfortunately, airborne alpha particle emitters occur naturally and pose a significant health hazard in some heavily mineralized areas. Each of the three natural radioactive decay series (the uranium, actinium, and thorium series) has an isotope of radon as one of its members. Radon is an inert gas. Consequently, it escapes easily from the ground and cannot be trapped by chemical means. If breathed into the lungs, it may decay into one of several non-inert elements called radon daughters. The continuing decay of radon daughters trapped in the lungs can result in extensive damage. Before the dangers were understood, it is said that every miner who worked in the Jáchymov (or Joachimsthal) uranium mines in the Czech Republic for more than 10 years died of lung cancer.

Radon gas can seep into basement and lower floors though cracks and other openings. Radon surveys are often done by using a vacuum pump to pull air through a filter paper. Radon daughters become trapped in the filter, which is later measured for radiation levels. Once radon is detected, levels can often be reduced through simple means of plugging cracks and increasing ventilation (see AIR-CONDITIONING AND VENTILATION).

WIDER IMPACT

RADIO RECEIVER

The radio receiver is a device that picks up radio frequency transmissions and converts them into audible sound

Radio has played an important role in shaping the modern world. By enabling wireless communication over great distances, it facilitated knowledge of faraway events and the sharing of ideas across geographical boundaries. Understanding how to transmit and receive radio waves led to the development of many other technologies such as television, mobile telephones (see TELEPHONY AND TELEGRAPHY), radio telescopes (see TELESCOPE), and navigation devices (see NAVIGATION).

Radio receivers that detect radio waves and transform them into audible sound are found in almost every home; because of this ubiquity, radios play a key role in standby broadcasting systems for civil-defense and weather emergencies. Since they are the part of radio communication we most commonly encounter, they are simply called radios. This article will concentrate on how radio receivers were developed and how they work.

Ideas and experiments

Natural philosophers were studying light, electricity, and magnetism for centuries before they knew that these seemingly unrelated effects were just different manifestations of the same phenomenon. In 1678, Dutch mathematician Christiaan Huygens (1629–1695) first advanced the theory that light is the result of waves traveling through a medium he called the ether. By the beginning of the 19th century, experiments with electrical current were being performed all over Europe (see ELECTRICITY AND MAGNETISM; WAVE MOTION).

The science of electromagnetism was launched by Danish physicist Hans Christian Ørsted (1777–1851). In 1820, he noticed that when he put a compass near a wire carrying electrical current, the needle jumped. In 1832, English chemist and physicist Michael Faraday (1791–1867) suggested that electricity and magnetism traveled through space as a sort of vibration. In 1864, Scottish physicist James Clerk Maxwell (1831–1879) developed the theoretical framework of electromagnetism as a series of equations describing electrical and magnetic fields. He predicted that it would be possible to produce radiation, such as radio waves, that would travel at the speed of light (see ELECTROMAGNETIC RADIATION).

Such waves were first produced by German physicist Heinrich Rudolph Hertz (1857–1894) in 1887. He set up a loop of wire with a gap in it. When an electrical current was passed through this wire the

CORE FACTS

- Radio receivers were first widely used to communicate by Morse code with ships at sea.
- Radio became popular public entertainment when receivers improved enough to allow the broadcasting of speech and music.
- When semiconductor components replaced vacuum tubes, radio receivers could be made smaller and far less expensively.
- Digital electronics helped to improve receiver performance and features.

result was a rapid series of sparks across the gap. These high-frequency oscillations produced similar—though much fainter—oscillations and sparks in another wire loop at a distance of around 200 feet (60 m). Hertz concluded that electromagnetic waves were traveling through Huygens' ether; today we know that radio waves and visible light waves differ only in their frequency.

The idea of using radio waves for wireless communication came quickly. English scientist William Crookes (1832–1919) wrote in 1892, "Here, then, is revealed the bewildering possibility of telegraphy without wires, posts, cables or any of our present costly appliances." But Hertz died in 1894 at only 37 years old, before he had learned to create radio waves that could carry information. It was left to Italian electrical engineer Guglielmo Marconi (1874–1937) to make that vision a reality.

Dots, dashes, and D-Day

Marconi, born in Italy in 1874, was an enthusiastic experimenter from an early age. He was familiar with sending Morse code telegraph signals over wires by the time he read Crookes' prediction about wireless communication. When he built his own set of wire loops to duplicate the Hertz experiments, he put a telegraph key in the circuit. The result was the first practical wireless telegraph system, which Marconi patented in 1896. Rebuffed in Italy, he took his demonstrations to England. Soon his signals crossed the Atlantic, and his invention was seized upon by navies and merchant fleets.

U.S. broadcast pioneer David Sarnoff (1891–1971) dreamed of broadcasting words and music on the radio. This required better receivers than telegraphy provided. Some of the necessary technology had already been developed, but it had been handicapped by legal and financial disputes, not to mention the lack of anything to listen to. The first broadcasting station, KDKA, began transmitting in Pittsburgh in 1920. It had an audience consisting mainly of hobbyists at first, but it created enough interest for companies to market receivers that anyone could use. While Sarnoff was its president, the Radio Corporation of America built sets with new vacuum tubes that made the signal loud and clear (see AMPLIFIER). The era of popular radio had begun.

By the end of the 1930s, most households had a radio in their living rooms, and World War II was starting in Europe. In Germany, the Nazi propaganda minister Joseph Goebbels (1897–1945) advocated a radio in every home. The Allied nations also used radio to communicate news and boost morale, with the voices of King George VI, Winston Churchill, and Franklin Roosevelt becoming familiar sounds in British and U.S. homes. Broadcast radio was at the peak of its importance during World War II, though by the 1950s it was competing with other technologies, especially television, for the attention of the public. Today, radio provides background music and news as people go about other activities in their automobiles, homes, and workplaces.

Telegraphy pioneer Guglielmo Marconi sits in the wireless room of his yacht Electra *(1920).*

Modern radio receivers

By the time radios were marketed on a large scale, the early crystal-based receivers that could only be heard through an earphone had been replaced by bulky units full of vacuum tubes. Tubes provide enough amplification to drive a loudspeaker (see MICROPHONE AND LOUDSPEAKER), but require a good deal of power and generate a large amount of heat.

After World War II, the development of semiconductor devices led to inexpensive portable transistor radios. Integrated circuits incorporating

RADIO BANDS

Radio waves have a wide range of frequencies, but many different interests compete to transmit on them. If nearby transmitters were to use frequencies too close together, the transmissions would interfere with each other, and no one would be able to hear anything. Consequently, national laws and international agreements govern the allocation of frequency bands. In the United States, the Federal Communications Commission controls the use of the airwaves.

The most familiar radio bands are the AM and FM broadcast bands for public and commercial broadcasting. AM and FM are two different technologies: AM—amplitude modulation—encodes electrical signals from a microphone or an audio source as variations in the amplitude of the carrier wave (a single-frequency radio wave) that is then transmitted. FM—frequency modulation—incoming audio signals are encoded as small variations in the frequency of the carrier wave. FM provides a high-fidelity, static-free signal. But an FM radio station takes up a bigger chunk of the frequency spectrum than an AM station.

International radio stations, such as the Voice of America and the BBC World Service, transmit on shortwave bands that can be transmitted over great distances. Other bands are reserved for use by emergency services, aviation, and marine communications. But ordinary citizens can operate radio transmitters, too. Some frequencies are set aside for radio amateurs, or ham radio operators—dedicated hobbyists who must be licensed to transmit. Citizens band, which is allocated for private communications, requires no license; walkie-talkies operate on its frequencies, and it is also popular among long-distance truck drivers.

A CLOSER LOOK

HOW A RADIO RECEIVER WORKS

This miniature receiver, manufactured in 1970, contains a variety of electrical components.

Radio waves travel though space invisibly and without making any noise. To receive them, we first must find something they will have an effect on as they pass by. An antenna made of metal and connected to ground is such a device (see ANTENNA AND TRANSMITTER). The reason that a metal conducts electricity is that some of its electrons are not as tightly bound to atoms as they are in other materials, and they can move around freely. When radio waves strike an antenna, they cause a stream of electrons (a current) to oscillate at the same frequency as the incoming waves.

Of course, the antenna is affected not only by the particular radio program we might like to hear. We have to screen out all the other radio transmissions that might be around in order to pick out the signal we want. This is the job of the tuner. Just as bells of different sizes each have their own natural frequencies of vibration that generate their tones, so the tuner is built and adjusted to select radio waves of a particular frequency. The simplest tuner is an electrical circuit consisting of a coil of wire called an inductor and another electrical device called a capacitor (see RESISTOR, CAPACITOR, AND INDUCTOR). These components have effects on the electrical current known as inductance and capacitance, respectively. The values of the inductance and capacitance determine the circuit's frequency. Either component may be constructed to be variable, so the receiver can be tuned to a range of frequencies.

The detector separates and decodes the audio signal from the carrier frequency onto which it has been superimposed. The audio signal is then boosted by an amplifier to a signal strength that is sufficient to drive earphones or loudspeakers.

A CLOSER LOOK

large numbers of miniaturized components provided the means to construct receivers small enough to build into headphones (see INTEGRATED CIRCUIT).

Miniaturized components also allow manufacturers to pack much more amplification, sensitivity, and selectivity into a package that will fit into a car dashboard or a stereo console. The advent of digital technology (see DIGITAL SIGNALS AND SYSTEMS) has brought automatic station search and memory features, as well as improved noise reduction techniques. Furthermore, digital technology allows the audio signal to be accompanied by additional signals that carry station-identity information or that can interrupt cassette playback for traffic-information broadcasts—a useful feature in automobiles.

S. CALVO

See also: COMMUNICATION NETWORK; ELECTRON TUBE; ELECTRONIC COUNTERMEASURES; ELECTRONICS; TELEVISION.

Further reading:
Orr, W. *Radio Handbook.* Carmel, Indiana: Howard W. Sams, 1991.

RAILROAD CAR

Railroad cars of many types carry passengers and freight from place to place all over the world

Passengers enjoy the view from the observation deck of the Midnight Sun Express train as it travels through Alaska.

Riding on rails is a very old idea. In ancient Greece and Rome, carts hauling farm produce and other cargo were pulled along with their wheels in parallel ruts. This helped prevent the heavy carts from getting stuck on the rough roads of the time. The wagonway, used in Europe from the 15th century, consisted of a pair of wooden tracks. Later, the wagons that traversed these tracks had special rims, or flanges, on their wheels to hold them in place.

Metal tracks were invented at the end of the 18th century. The smooth metal surfaces of these tracks caused much less friction between the tracks and the wheels, allowing heavier loads to be pulled with the same amount of power. Horses and other animals pulled the carts on these early rail systems. The invention of locomotives in the early 1800s led to the development of the many railroad cars seen today. By the 1830s, railroads in the United States and Britain were carrying both passengers and freight.

CORE FACTS

- Railroad cars evolved from wagons pulled by horses over wooden or metal tracks.
- The invention of reliable air brakes allowed trains to travel much faster than they previously had.
- The invention of the automatic coupler made it much safer to link up railroad cars.
- Containerization makes freight handling more efficient by eliminating the loading and unloading of freight cars.

Components of railroad cars

Railroad cars must be built to run on rails that are a particular distance apart, called the gauge. It is advantageous to use the same gauge in different areas whenever possible, because otherwise passengers and freight would have to be transferred from one train to another when different systems connected. The standard gauge, used over most of the world, is just under 4 ft 8½ in (1.44 m) and was based on the rails used in earlier wagonways for coal carts.

The part of the car that must be sized to accommodate the particular gauge of the rail system is the truck—the assembly of wheels, bearings, frame, and center plate on which the car body rests. A car rests on two trucks: one at each end. The earliest trucks were made of wood and employed the same design for passenger and freight trains. Later, steel was introduced, and trucks were specialized to the needs of passenger and freight cars— a smooth ride on the one hand, and sturdiness and durability on the other. In order to negotiate turns more easily, swiveling trucks were introduced.

Springs are necessary in the suspension of railroad cars so that they do not shake themselves apart. Exposed sets of four coiled springs that were 6 in (15 cm) in diameter and 7 in (18 cm) high were developed in the 1890s. Similar springs are still in use today.

One of the most important mechanisms on a railroad car is the coupler mechanism that attaches it to the cars ahead and behind. Early couplers were

CONNECTIONS

- Early rail systems were a method of **HORSE-DRAWN TRANSPORT**.

- Like railroad cars, **STREETCARS AND TROLLEYS** are vehicles that move on rails; they are used to transport passengers through main streets in some towns and cities.

A steam train tips molten slag over a bank at the Anshan Iron and Steel Works, in the Liaoning province of China.

simple linking mechanisms that had to be operated by hand. Workers rushed between the cars when the train pulled into the rail yard, connecting and disconnecting coupler pins. They were issued with long, hooked poles or paddles to help them do this without putting their hands between cars, but among many of the railroad men these safety devices were regarded as unmanly. Consequently, they recognized each other by their missing fingers, lost after being crushed between cars.

The automatic knuckle coupler helped solve this problem. Patented by U.S. inventor Eli Janney (1831–1912) in 1873, it remains in use today. Automatic couplers link on impact and release by pulling a chain or operating another mechanism. The Janney device features a revolving jaw with a locking pin that swings open and shut. Now made of heavy-duty steel, the coupler weighs around 200 lb (91 kg). Its vertical-plane design allows for a certain amount of tolerance in coupler height between cars—this is important because, despite standards, the condition of the springs and the weights of the loads vary between railroad cars.

Early railroad cars did not have their own brake systems. Of course, the locomotive had brakes, but there had to be some mechanism for preventing all the other cars from piling into it when it stopped. At the end of the train, the caboose carried an operator who controlled a set of hand brakes, which depended on the friction of a brake shoe pressing against a wheel. Even after such brakes had been installed on all the cars, they were not effective enough to stop a heavy, fast-moving train quickly in case of an emergency. So the length of trains had to be limited, and even short ones had to keep their speed down to around 30 mph (48 km/h).

Today, all cars have air brakes—invented in 1869 by U.S. inventor George Westinghouse (1846–1914)—that are operated by the engineer, with manual brakes used only for backup and for securing individual cars in rail yards (see BRAKE SYSTEMS). With more reliable brakes, even heavy freight trains can travel at 60 mph (97 km/h), and passenger trains can go much faster. Some have hydraulic mechanisms that tilt the train when sensors detect a curve, providing a more comfortable high-speed ride.

Freight cars

Most of the early freight trains were used to carry coal and other mineral ores. As the railway system developed, networks of freight lines were developed to transport raw materials to factories and carry away the finished products. Today there are many types of freight cars, and around 70 percent of the world's inland freight is transported by rail. There are over a million freight cars in the United States alone.

Coal and other materials are still generally transported in open-top cars, which can be loaded through chutes from above. Other types of freight are loaded through the side doors of boxcars. Livestock is transported in cagelike stock cars that allow air to circulate. Tankers, which may be refrigerated, carry milk, oil, and other liquids. Glass-lined milk tankers made an important contribution to public health when they came into use in the 1930s: for the first time, fresh milk could be speedily transported from rural areas straight into the cities.

Often a train will pull a mixed load of freight cars to a freight depot, where the cars are sorted according to their destinations. The cars are moved around the yard by small locomotives called switch engines. Today most yards are controlled by computers that

direct the cars onto the appropriate set of tracks. The computer also operates brake shoes built into the tracks, which press on the cars' wheels and reduce the cars' speed. Human railroad dispatchers still work at the computer consoles, but they now have many tools at their disposal to increase safety and efficiency (see RAILROAD OPERATION AND SIGNALING).

In containerized shipping, the freight remains in the same 40-ft- (12-m-) long container throughout its entire trip, from origin to destination (see MECHANICAL HANDLING). Containerized shipping is much less labor-intensive than traditional shipping practices, because there is no need to deal with individual boxes or barrels of cargo each time a transfer must be made. Cranes are used to transfer the containers between ship, truck, and train. The standard shape and size of the containers make it easy to pack them into a ship's cargo hold. Special flatbed trucks are sized to accommodate the containers. Freight trains have flatcars and gondolas to which the containers are fastened. Double-stack cars can carry two containers, one piled on top of the other, on a single flatcar. A double-stack car is lighter than two separate cars and traction costs are reduced.

Freight trains can also be made lighter by articulation. An articulated train consists of a number of permanently connected cars that share the trucks between them. Most of the heavy coupling gear is eliminated—only the end cars have unshared trucks with couplings that can be attached to locomotives. There is also less banging between the cars, which reduces the possibility of damaging the freight.

Passenger cars

Early railroad passengers rode in simple open or closed cars. By the mid 1800s, however, as the railroad became the prevalent mode of long-distance travel, wealthy travelers began demanding more comfortable accommodation. Some early trains had flatcars onto which the passengers' own horse-drawn carriages could be fastened. Horsecars were also included on some trains, or the passengers could hire fresh horses once they reached their destinations. Before long, first-class carriages were built, which were luxurious rail versions of the popular stagecoaches. Passengers sometimes rode on top of the coaches as well as inside.

By the middle of the 19th century, the standard U.S. passenger coach had taken shape, with its seating on either side of a central aisle. By contrast, European railroads have tended to favor closed compartments comprising six seats, three facing each way. Each car is made up of several compartments, with an aisle running along one side.

SUBWAY AND LIGHT-RAIL CARS

In subways and light-rail systems, each car is typically powered individually, using electrical power that is obtained either through a roof-mounted pickup in contact with overhead lines or through shoes in contact with an electrified third rail. Since trips are short, coaches are not designed to maximize comfort or the number of seats. Rather, the aisles are wide, with handgrips, to accommodate a large number of standing passengers during rush hour. There are several large automatic doors so that crowds can enter and exit easily at the frequent stops.

Safety is especially important in trains that are designed to run in underground tunnels, and each car has its own emergency brake and alarm system. Fire has always been a concern for subway travel. Modern subway cars—and sometimes even the seats—are generally constructed of metal, and no flammable materials are used. Other considerations in designing today's urban transit cars are durability, ease of cleaning, and the ability to remove graffiti. Most transit authorities fill their cars with advertising, which helps keep operating expenses down and fares affordable (see SUBWAY SYSTEM).

A CLOSER LOOK

RAIL MAIL

An American mail train worker, c.1885, uses a special device to pick up mailbags.

British shipowner Samuel Cunard (1787–1865) formed the British and North American Royal Mail Steam Packet Company (later the Cunard Line) in 1839. This company used scheduled rail services to carry mail between Liverpool, where Cunard's transatlantic steamers docked, and other British cities. The first named train in the world, the *Irish Mail*, ran from 1848 to 1985.

In the United States, the Railway Post Office service was established in 1864. Pouches of mail were suspended near the track for pickup, and as the train went by, the pouch was scooped into a net extended from its side. The interior of the mail car looked like the back room of a post office, its walls covered with pigeonholes for sorting mail. The sorted mail was bundled into dispatch bags, which were tossed out of the train into trackside nets near their destination. This system was used until the late 1960s in the United States and until 1971 in Britain. However, postal services around the world still use railroads, along with trucks and airplanes, to move ever-increasing volumes of mail.

A CLOSER LOOK

Within the basic seating configurations on railroad cars, passengers were afforded up to three classes of travel to choose from, with corresponding amenities and ticket prices. First-class travelers generally had more leg room, more luxurious seats, and exclusive dining facilities. They were sometimes placed farther from the car's wheels, which guaranteed a much smoother and quieter ride.

Railroad operators soon discovered that the more luxuries they offered, the more wealthy passengers they attracted. U.S. businessman and inventor George Pullman (1831–1897) introduced first-class sleeping cars in 1864 and dining cars in 1868. Soon, Pullman cars, with their brass fittings and inlaid woodwork, became a synonym for rail travel in style, both in the U.S. and Britain. The Wagons-Lits Company began building similar luxury railroad cars in Europe, beginning in 1876.

In 1869, when the first transcontinental rail link was completed, the railroad became a gateway to the American West for enormous numbers of immigrants on their way from the East to seek their fortunes. Many of these newcomers were stuffed into third-class compartments that were three or four times more crowded than those in first or second class. Crying babies, aromatic picnics, and occasionally even small livestock characterized third-class travel. Although most lines in the United States now have only two classes, third-class travel—with all its cramped conditions—is widely used in many developing countries. Often the main difference between first and second class is that first class is reserved, while "coach-class" passengers take their chances on getting seats. Some express trains cater only to first-class passengers.

Today many passenger trains have air-conditioned, soundproof coaches and dining cars; overnight trains offer reclining seats and sleeping compartments with berths. Trains are still very important for passenger travel in Europe, where distances are moderate and cities are fairly close together. In the United States, similar conditions make train travel practical and popular in the East Coast corridor between Washington, D.C., and Boston. In the country as a whole, however, the large distances mean that people in a hurry must fly. Still, train travel is popular among vacationers, who enjoy the journey as well as the destination. Observation cars with large side and overhead windows are often available for looking out over scenic vistas.

The AutoTrain is a special overnight service that runs between Virginia and Florida. It includes not only comfortable seating, sleeping, and dining accommodation, but also railroad cars that are designed to hold its passengers' automobiles. The AutoTrain is a popular mode of travel for snowbirds—retirees who winter in Florida and spend their summers in the Northeast.

S. CALVO

See also: RAILROAD CONSTRUCTION AND TRACK; RAILROAD LOCOMOTIVE; RAILROADS, HISTORY OF.

Further reading:
Coiley, J. *Train*. New York: Knopf, 1992.
White, J. H. Jr. *The American Railroad Freight Car*. Baltimore: Johns Hopkins University Press, 1993.

RAILROAD CONSTRUCTION AND TRACK

Railroad design, construction, and maintenance involves the track bed and the rails on which the trains run

Railroads have been a great unifying force in North America. By 1835, 50 times as many people were traveling by train as by all other types of transportation put together. For four generations, the word *road* was short for *railroad*, and what later became turnpikes were simply called trails. By 1860, the United States had 30,000 miles (48,300 km) of railroad, which was more than all the rest of the world. By 1916, this had reached 254,000 miles (409,000 km). By 1996, however, this figure had dropped to 170,000 miles (274,000 km).

The first railroads in Britain and North America developed from small tracks in mines, quarries, or construction sites called plateways, which were designed to provide a reliable path for horse-drawn wagons carrying heavy loads. Since the traditional width of wagon axles was approximately 5 ft (1.5 m), this became the generally accepted standard for the distance between the rails, called the gauge. The most widely used gauge measurement is actually 4 ft 8½ in (1.44 m), which is close enough to the 5 ft (1.5 m) standard across the outside faces of the rails.

Originally, railroads began as local enterprises serving local needs, and there was no attempt to standardize the track gauge. In some cases, such as that of the Erie Railroad, which was laid to a 6-ft (1.8-m) gauge, the decision was a deliberate measure to keep competing railroad systems off its territory. When these lines expanded and made contact with each other, progress toward a national network was hindered by people and goods having to change trains every time their journey brought them to a meeting point of systems with different gauges.

As late as 1861, railroad travelers going from Philadelphia to Charleston, South Carolina—a journey of some 660 miles (1060 km)—had to undergo a total of eight changes, and this was not unusual. At that time, more than 46 percent of the growing U.S. railroad network had tracks laid to gauges other than the standard gauge. The majority of southern railroads were actually laid to a 5-ft (1.5-m) gauge, and this network grew from 7300 miles (11,750 km) during the Civil War to over 12,000 miles (19,300 km) by 1880. To build a national rail network, most lines eventually had to be converted to the standard gauge (see the box on page 1088).

CORE FACTS

- By 1860, the United States had more miles of railroad track than the whole rest of the world.
- In 1880, more than 12,000 miles (19,300 km) of track in the southern United States ran on a different gauge from the rest of the country.
- Modern rail is often welded into sections as long as half a mile (0.8 km); then, after being fixed to the ties, the rail is welded into sections several miles long.
- Today's track maintenance machines can remove and replace rails and ties, dig out and replace ballast, check rails for alignment, grind out surface defects, and check miles of track for internal cracks and flaws.

CONNECTIONS

- **CIVIL ENGINEERING** is the branch of **ENGINEERING** that deals with the design and construction of large-scale public structures and systems, such as railroads, **BRIDGES**, and **TUNNELS**.

The last spike of the first transcontinental rail link in the United States was driven at Promontory Point, Utah, on May 10, 1869.

Grading the route

Railroads operate efficiently because of the low friction of steel wheels running on steel rails, enabling a locomotive to move a load many times its own weight with relative ease. However, this becomes much more difficult on an incline, and railroad engineers have to do their utmost to avoid gradients that are too steep. In hilly country, this means adding mileage so that the railroad follows a particular contour line with minimum changes of level. Adding extra mileage to a route means higher construction costs and higher operating costs (see the box on page 1090), which may mean that the extra cost of a more direct route is actually justified in the end.

Another problem with railroads following a contour line to create easily graded track is that sometimes sharp curves are needed. These force trains to slow down, and extra fuel has to be used to accelerate to normal running speed after the curve. In extreme cases, sharp radius curves impose design limitations on the locomotives and rolling stock (passenger and freight cars) that can use the line.

The alternative to following contours is to maintain a track level regardless of the undulations of the surrounding countryside. This means digging deep cuttings along stretches where the ground level is above the planned track bed. The spoil (excavated earth) is then moved along the route to stretches where it can be used for building embankments to carry the track over stretches where the ground level falls away. This heavy construction process produces a more direct route but adds to the cost and time needed to build the line.

In cases where the railroad route crosses a particularly deep stretch of ground, or a road or river, bridges have to be built instead of embankments. The width of the gap determines the type of bridge needed. Carrying the track across a wide valley may require a brick or stone viaduct, while bridging a narrow stream or a road can be done with a truss or plate-girder bridge (see BRIDGE). In cases where the line has to be dug through a stretch of high ground, the extra cost of boring a tunnel (see TUNNEL) may provide the only alternative to a costly and potentially inefficient diversion.

CHANGING THE GAUGE

Because of the trouble and expense of transshipping goods and passengers where gauges differed, railroads experimented with the cumbersome compromise car, which had wheels with treads 5 in (13 cm) across to enable it to run on tracks where the gauge was very close to standard gauge. Other cars had wheels that could be slid along the axle to widen or narrow the gauge. However, both these designs were implicated in a series of accidents, and as a result, safer options were devised.

On some systems, a third rail was laid so that a given route could run trains on two different gauges. In places where two networks joined, a device called an elevating hoist lifted and lowered the cars onto a new set of wheels for the next stage of their journey. This method was used in parts of Europe where long-distance trains crossed borders between two national systems operating on different gauges.

Eventually, the need for a national network in the United States led to changing the gauge of nonstandard systems. The Erie Railroad switched in 1880, and the southern section of the Illinois Central system changed 550 miles (885 km) of track on July 29, 1881 using 3000 workmen to finish the whole task by 3:00 P.M. The southern lines, totaling 13,000 miles (20,900 km), changed gauge on May 31 and June 1, 1881, switching to 4 ft 8½ in (1.44 m) to match the Pennsylvania Railroad, with which they exchanged most traffic. All remaining nonstandard track was changed to standard gauge by 1891.

A CLOSER LOOK

When a route is planned, engineers have to decide the steepest acceptable grade, which is usually called the ruling grade because it limits the loads that can be carried over the route with the available locomotive power. British engineer and locomotive builder Robert Stephenson (1803–1859) suggested a maximum grade of 1 in 100 (1 percent), but the Baltimore and Ohio Railroad built a 17-mile (27-km) stretch of line at 1 in 45 (2.2 percent) to cross the Allegheny Front. Given the extra power of the larger U.S. locomotives, this became the ruling grade for the Canadian Pacific and most U.S. lines.

The loading gauge

From the earliest days of rail transport, railroad engineers also had to decide the loading gauge—the limits of the cross section of locomotives and rolling stock—to determine the clearance of tunnels, bridges, station platforms, and lineside structures. In Britain, these dimensions were fixed in the very early years of railroad construction, when engines and rolling stock were still fairly small. Since then, the loading gauge of existing structures has limited the overall width of trains that are much more powerful and much faster and which carry much heavier loads than those for which the system was originally built.

In continental Europe and the United States, railroad engineers developed much larger locomotives quickly enough for the loading gauge to be made much bigger. With wider tunnels and bridges, and greater clearances from lineside walls and buildings, designers could build not only larger locomotives, but also more luxurious passenger cars, and freight cars with much greater load capacity.

Railroad track

The earliest railroad tracks were made from strap—rails, which consisted of iron straps fitted along the top surface of wooden rails that were fixed to large stone blocks at regular intervals. These tended to break loose and curl up under the weight of passing trains to form "snake heads," which sometimes broke through the floors of passenger cars. In Britain, engineers had already begun to use all-steel rail in a figure-eight section, known as bull-head rail, which had to be supported in cast-iron chairs (supports) fastened to wooden ties called sleepers.

U.S. engineer Robert L. Stevens (1787–1856), who was president of the Camden and Amboy Railroad and Transportation Company, developed the inverted-T rail, which had a flat bottom so that no chairs were needed. The rail was simply fixed to the ties by driving spikes into the ties at the edge of the rail, so that the broad top of the spike clamped the foot of the rail to the tie. Stevens had his idea while on a locomotive-buying trip in England; he carved a wooden model to show what he wanted and placed his first order at a Welsh ironworks. By 1831, T rails were being used on his New England railroad.

Modern rails still use Stevens' T sections, but now they are made from high-grade steel. Once the rails are rolled out, they are allowed to cool slowly in

special boxes to minimize internal stresses and avoid shatter cracks, which cause breakages in service. In some cases, rails are specially hardened to reduce the wear in areas where especially heavy loads are carried, or on sharp curves where stresses are high.

Laying the roadbed

The best foundation for steel rails and wooden (or, increasingly, steel or concrete) ties is a layer of ballast made from crushed rock, slag, or volcanic ash. This is usually a foot (30 cm) deep and is compacted around the ties to hold them in place and to absorb

Workers lay track for the Great Northern Railroad at Stevens Pass, Washington, in 1959.

TEN MILES IN A DAY

In the 1860s, the Central Pacific and the Union Pacific companies were racing to meet one another in Utah to complete the first transcontinental railroad. The Central Pacific laid a mile (1.6 km) of track per day, with construction gangs living aboard specially fitted work trains that moved forward over each stretch of newly built track. Special cars held equipment, tools, stores, kitchens, dining rooms, bunks, and workshops.

The Union Pacific had an 80-car work train, with a bath car, a bakery car, and a butcher's car, which prepared meat from a herd of beef cattle driven alongside the train. Mule trains brought in timber for ties and bridge construction, and fuel for the locomotives on the open plains. The company reached a rate of 2 miles (3.2 km) of track laid per day.

The Central Pacific responded by setting up a $10,000 wager that said they could lay 10 miles (16 km) of track in one day. Before the set date—April 28, 1869—loads of rails, ties, fishplates, bolts, and spikes were delivered along the route by horse-drawn carts. A group of workers was detailed to carry tea and drinking water on yoked pails, to refresh the gangs who were lifting and laying the rails. By 1:30 P.M. in the afternoon of Ten Mile Day, the gangs had laid 6 miles (9.7 km) of track. By 7:00 P.M. that evening, after a full 12-hour working day, they had beaten their target by 56 ft (17 m), laying 3520 rails on 25,800 ties. Each member of the gangs had lifted a total of 111 tons (100 tonnes) of iron.

HISTORY OF TECHNOLOGY

A steam shovel excavates a section of ground that runs along the route of the Everett Interurban railroad line in Washington in February 1910.

Most track now used in the United States weighs 115–140 lb per yard (48–58 kg per m). Although the standard U.S. rail section has a length of 39 ft (12 m), U.S. railroads first experimented with welding rails together to produce longer lengths of track in 1933. This technique has been widely used since the 1950s, with rails welded into sections ranging from 320 yards (293 m) to half a mile (0.8 km). When these are laid on the track bed, they are then welded into sections that may be several miles long. To minimize expansion and contraction of these very long pieces of track, they are usually held by strong fixings in heavy ballast, and before being laid they are heated or cooled to a temperature equivalent to the mean levels prevailing in the region.

Mechanizing the work

Every phase of laying and maintaining railroad track has been mechanized with modern machinery. Backhoes, graders, bulldozers, and scrapers (see CONSTRUCTION AND EARTHMOVING MACHINERY) excavate cuttings and lay embankments. In areas where the roadbed is unstable, concrete grout can be injected below the roadbed.

To speed up tracklaying or track replacement, sections are often loaded onto railroad flatcars as complete sections, with track already fastened to the ties. These are hoisted into position by a crane, and then the ballast is forced into place. Rail grinding machines are then driven over the track to remove irregularities in the rail surface. Track measurement cars are run over the new stretch of track to record track alignment and ride quality, and to carry out electronic inspections of the rails in order to locate any internal cracks or flaws.

Specialized maintenance machines are now used to carry out the routine maintenance tasks of removing and replacing ties, excavating and replacing worn ballast, cleaning the ballast and tamping it down around the ties, spiking the rails, and tightening the bolts. Some machines can carry out combinations of these tasks in a single operation, and others can replace the rails themselves. Working with short lengths, or longer pieces of welded rail, these machines can lift old rails and load them onto flatcars. They can then lift new rail from other cars and lower them into place ahead.

D. OWEN

the shocks caused by trains passing over the track. Ballast has to be properly drained, and in areas where this is difficult—such as within tunnels—the ballast and ties are replaced by slab track, which is a continuous reinforced concrete support that holds the track in place.

See also: CIVIL ENGINEERING; MOUNTAIN RAILROAD AND FUNICULAR; RAILROAD CAR; RAILROAD LOCOMOTIVE; RAILROAD OPERATION AND SIGNALING; RAILROADS, HISTORY OF.

Further reading:
Nice, D. *Amtrak: The History & Politics of a National Railroad.* Boulder: Rienner Publications, 1998.
Spens, S. and Coel, M. *Goin' Railroading: Two Generations of Colorado Stories.* University Press of Colorado, 1998.
Stover, J. *American Railroads.* Chicago: University of Chicago Press, 1997.

THE "GREAT WAY ROUND"

In Britain, the Great Western Railway (GWR) laid out its early routes for high speed using easy gradients and wide detours to avoid high ground, so much so that people often claimed its initials really stood for the "Great Way Round." In the United States, railroads often took circuitous routes for quite different reasons. Because the main lines across the United States ran through sparsely populated country that would generate little traffic, companies were financed through government grants and given free land alongside the track, which they could sell for additional income.

This meant railroad companies had little incentive to shoulder the extra costs of direct routes, with expensive bridges and tunnels and steep gradients. If they laid extra mileage to follow the natural contours of the landscape, they cut the cost of the line and were rewarded by additional grants of land. Later, many companies spent much more money shortening routes to provide faster services.

A CLOSER LOOK

RAILROAD LOCOMOTIVE

Locomotives powered by steam, diesel fuel, and electricity pull freight and passenger trains

An artist's impression of a steam-powered express train, complete with cowcatcher, on its way to New York City in 1870.

The earliest trains, freight wagons pushed or pulled along tracks, were propelled by human or animal power. They were common in European mines as early as the 16th century. Grooved tracks were used even in ancient times to guide chariots and other vehicles over rough stone roads. But it was the invention of the steam locomotive in the 1800s that opened the way for long-distance railroad transportation (see RAILROADS, HISTORY OF).

Steam locomotives

As soon as steam engines were developed, experimenters began trying to use them to power road vehicles. But these early steam cars were so difficult to control that they caused a commotion whenever they were brought out onto the streets. Rails seemed like a good way to keep steam-powered vehicles going in the right direction, but there were many technical difficulties in making the rails strong enough to hold the weight of steam locomotives and

getting the wheels to stay on the rails when any appreciable speeds were reached. It was not until the 1820s that practical steam locomotives were built, but after that it took only a few decades until the design settled into the form that is familiar today.

The steam locomotive was instrumental in the settling of the American West. In Europe, trains connected existing cities, but in America, new towns developed along rail lines. The long distances and rugged terrain required large, sturdy locomotives. By the early part of the 20th century, some steam locomotives could pull thousand-ton loads over thousand-mile distances at an average speed of about 80 mph (130 km/h).

Running right through small towns, the locomotive had a large bell or loud steam whistle to warn of its approach. A plow-shaped cowcatcher attached to the front of the locomotive was used to fend off livestock that wandered into its path, and prevent them from derailing the train. Wood was the locomotive's predominant fuel in the American West.

Worldwide, most steam engines run on coal. The fuel is burned in a firebox. Hot gases of combustion are drawn through hundreds of parallel pipes running through a tank of water called the boiler. After heating the water, the exhaust gases proceed to the smoke box, the front compartment of the locomotive, and leave through the smokestack.

The steam generated in the boiler passes through steam pipes, past a throttle valve, and then passes into two to four cylinders, forced alternately into the

---

CORE FACTS

- Steam locomotives dominated the first century of railroading and were very important in making long-distance transportation more practical.
- Diesel locomotives began replacing steam engines just before World War II (1939–1945).
- Electric trains are clean, fast, and quiet, and are used in metropolitan and other high-traffic areas.

CONNECTIONS

● Modern maglev trains use **ELECTRICITY AND MAGNETISM** to move using the same principles as a **LINEAR MOTOR**.

A diesel locomotive at a rail yard in St. Louis. Locomotives such as this were in use mainly during the 1960s.

the tracks, driving wheels, and trailing wheels. For example, a locomotive may be designated 2-8-2, meaning it has one pair of leading wheels, four pairs of driving wheels, and a pair of trailing wheels.

Many steam locomotives were built on trucks, or wheel assemblies, that have some sideways motion to allow more flexibility on turns. Articulated locomotives, composed of two sections, are also designed to make turning easier. Locomotives with, for example, one pair of leading wheels, two sets of four pairs of driving wheels, and a pair of trailing wheels are designated 2-8-8-2.

Steam locomotives pull their supply of coal and water directly behind them in a car called a tender. They generally have a crew of two people. The fireman is responsible for stoking the firebox and monitoring the boiler's water level. If more water is required, the fireman uses an injector control to pump it in from the tender. The engineer is in charge of controlling the locomotive's speed in accordance with signals and conditions. The speed is set by operating a mechanism that controls the point during the piston stroke at which the steam is shut off. Locomotives also have air brakes (see BRAKE SYSTEMS) and a reversing mechanism.

By World War II (1939–1945), many existing steam locomotives were showing their age. Some diesel locomotives had been in use in the U.S. for freight-train switching operations since 1925, and in 1934 the Burlington Railroad introduced the *Zephyr*—the first diesel-powered passenger train. However, it was only in the postwar period that diesel and electric locomotives—some of them much more powerful than the steam engines they replaced—started to be more widely used.

Although steam power has now been replaced by other forms of traction on most lines, steam locomotives from the golden era of the railroads are very popular with enthusiasts and run on many scenic and tourist lines. Many engines are still in regular use in

spaces on either side of the pistons. The alternating bursts of steam cause the pistons to move back and forth, and the pistons push the connecting rods back and forth, which in turn rotates the driving wheels that are coupled to them.

Often locomotives are classified by the number of leading wheels, which support the weight of the front of the locomotive and help to guide it along

THE BIG BOYS

Just as the heyday of the steam locomotive was coming to an end, some of the most impressive specimens of the breed were being built. In the early 1940s, as the United States recovered from the Depression amid increased defense spending for World War II, freight trains were on the move. Union Pacific Railroad chose the American Locomotive Company to build engines capable of hauling 3600-ton (3270-tonne) loads across the Wasatch Mountains on its route between Cheyenne, Wyoming, and Ogden, Utah, which included the notorious 8103-foot (2470-m) Sherman Hill.

The result was the locomotive known as the Big Boy. As legend has it, the nickname originated from a shopman's graffiti and stuck. These 4-8-8-4 locomotives became known as the most powerful engines ever built. Although they may have been exceeded in one or another attribute by other steam locomotives, their overall capabilities were paramount. At a weight of around 594 tons

(540 tonnes) when fully loaded with coal and water, they were the heaviest land-based vehicles in history. The Big Boys were over 130 ft (40 m) long, with driving wheels almost 6 ft (1.8 m) across. They consumed 22 tons (20 tonnes) of coal and 50 tons (45 tonnes) of water each hour, as they chugged along at a maximum speed of 70 mph (113 km/h). New heavier rails and sturdier turntables were needed to accommodate these huge machines. While they were surprisingly flexible around turns, many curves still needed to be realigned to prevent the width of the Big Boys from endangering other trains that might be passing by on adjacent lines. As rail lines were improved to reduce the steepest grades, Big Boys were able to drag 6000-ton (5440-tonne) loads up Sherman Hill.

A total of 25 of the big engines were produced. Six have been preserved by railroad museums and societies around the United States, but none is currently operable.

HISTORY OF TECHNOLOGY

Asia and Africa, some of which date from before World War II. New steam engines were still being constructed in China until the end of the 1980s.

Diesel locomotives

The diesel engine is a form of internal combustion engine invented by German engineer Rudolph Diesel (1858–1913) in 1896. Diesel locomotives were introduced in the 1930s on U.S. and European passenger lines, and by the 1950s they were hauling most freight trains (see INTERNAL COMBUSTION ENGINE). In diesel-electric locomotives, the engine does not drive the wheels directly. Rather, the engine drives an electric generator (see ELECTRIC MOTOR AND GENERATOR) that provides power for the electric traction motors that turn the driving wheels.

Starting in the 1940s, some turbine-electric locomotives were built that used steam turbines or oil- or gas-burning gas turbines not unlike those on jet airplanes to drive electric generators (see GAS TURBINE). However, these locomotives were found to be less fuel-efficient than conventional steam and diesel-electric locomotives and almost all had been taken out of use by the 1990s.

Diesel locomotives are faster and easier to maintain than steam engines. They are built to be powerful, both because they are heavy in themselves and because they are often used to pull heavy loads of freight over great distances. The locomotive incorporates a comfortable enclosed cab and may be followed by a number of diesel-powered booster units, which can be added as necessary to pull the required weight. Some freight trains have diesel locomotives at each end so that they can leave in the opposite direction to which they arrived—useful when loading or unloading cargo.

In the United States, competition from the automobile and the airplane has stalled the development of long-distance high-speed diesel passenger trains. But in Europe and other regions where gasoline prices are higher than in the U.S., intercity train travel is very popular. The fastest diesel locomotives can travel up to 147 mph (237 km/h).

Electric locomotives

Electric locomotives first made their appearance as curiosities, pulling Victorian ladies and gentlemen around in circles at fairs and expositions. By the beginning of the 20th century, they were used regularly on a few short routes that had poorly ventilated tunnels; the tunnels had been filling with noxious fumes from steam locomotives.

Electric locomotives do not produce the pollution associated with vehicles that run on fossil fuels. However, unlike steam and diesel locomotives, they are not self-contained power sources—they require an expensive infrastructure to supply high-voltage electricity over the length of the track. Electric traction is used extensively in metropolitan transit systems and commuter services (see SUBWAY SYSTEM), where high traffic densities make them economic and desirable for their low level of pollution.

WHERE'S THE DRIVER?

A driverless electric train on a railroad serving London's Docklands area.

Electric trains use power from an outside source to drive their motors and do not need to generate their own power. Until the 1980s, the functioning of a train had to be controlled by an engineer aboard the train. In a growing number of light-rail transit systems and commuter services around the world, however, this function is also being performed remotely.

In U.S. and European cities, increasing numbers of urban rail systems are being controlled by computer. This is especially practical at facilities such as airports, where new systems can be designed for this purpose and built over existing installations, such as parking lots, with little need for other infrastructure to be taken into consideration.

A computerized train has a control box that receives signals from the system's central control computer, which controls the train's motors, brakes, and the opening and closing of its doors. In some cases, a human driver monitors the controls and can take over in case of emergency. Some systems are driverless, and emergency backup is provided by an operator at the central control center.

Computer technology is also being employed in more traditional train operations. On-board computers now provide the engineer with data about the state of the train's various systems. A system called cab signaling receives information from trackside devices, such as signals, and relays it to display units in the cab (see RAILROAD OPERATION AND SIGNALING).

A CLOSER LOOK

An electric train may be powered either from an electrified third rail or from overhead cables, tapped by an armlike pickup atop the locomotive or powered car. The cables or rails supply high-voltage electricity—which is good for long-distance transmission (see ELECTRICITY TRANSMISSION AND SUPPLY)—and in some cases, transformers aboard the train change it into low-voltage direct-current power (see TRANSFORMER). The current passes via cables to traction motors underneath the locomotive or the powered cars that move the train. Batteries are used to power emergency lights, sliding doors, and other electrical equipment on the train.

MAGLEV TRAINS

A prototype maglev train is tested in Japan.

Magnetic levitation or maglev trains are electric trains without wheels. Their electric motors generate a magnetic force that lifts the train a fraction of an inch off its track and pushes it along. Clean and quiet, this attractive technology also offers the benefit of few moving parts to wear out.

The idea of magnetic levitation was conceived in 1960 by James Powell, a U.S. nuclear scientist with Brookhaven National Laboratory in New York. The first maglev vehicle, called a Magneplane, was built at the Massachusetts Institute of Technology in 1975 by Henry Kolm. In 1984 the first maglev train was built in Birmingham, England, where it runs on a low-speed circuit that joins the city's airport to a nearby major railroad station. Soon after, Germany and Japan began competing to build a high-speed maglev train.

Experimental vehicles have been clocked at over 300 mph (480 km/h). The German Transrapid system employs cables under the track that act like electromagnets. The speed of the train is controlled by the current through the electromagnets. The Japanese maglevs use superconducting coils to reduce power loss; development of these devices is not as advanced. Maglev trains are still an expensive novelty, and it remains to be seen whether they will ever come into widespread use.

LOOKING TO THE FUTURE

The electric trains that run through the Channel Tunnel, offering routes between London, England, and Paris, France, or Brussels, Belgium, had to be developed with three separate sets of electrical standards in mind. The powered cars on these trains are equipped to run on the three different voltages used by the rail systems of the three countries through which their route passes.

Most new railroad technologies are based on electricity. Modern electric trains include high-speed services such as Amtrak's Metroliner, the Japanese bullet trains, and the French *trains á grande vitesse* (TGVs). Some of these trains are capable of traveling over 200 mph (320 km/h). A modified TGV set the world speed record of 320 mph (512 km/h) in 1990; standard TGVs travel at about half this speed on the faster stretches of their routes.

S. CALVO

See also: COAL; ELECTRIC ROAD VEHICLE; FUELS AND PROPELLANTS; MASS TRANSIT SYSTEM; MECHANICAL TRANSMISSION; MONORAIL; MOUNTAIN RAILROAD AND FUNICULAR; RAILROAD CAR; RAILROAD CONSTRUCTION AND TRACK; STEAM ENGINE; STEAM-POWERED ROAD VEHICLES; STREETCAR AND TROLLEY.

Further reading:
Comstock, H. *The Iron Horse: An Illustrated History of Steam Locomotives.* 2nd edition. Sykesville: Greenberg Publishing, 1992.
Garratt, C. *Steam Trains of the World.* New York: Exeter Books, 1987.
Harris, K. *World Electric Locomotives.* London: Jane's Publishing Company, 1981.
Hollingsworth, B. *The Illustrated Encyclopedia of North American Locomotives.* New York: Crescent Books, 1984.

RAILROAD OPERATION AND SIGNALING

The railroad system relies on the operation of signaling and safety systems, marshaling yards, and control centers

Safety systems on railroads to prevent trains from colliding with one another originally depended on operatives with flags who indicated to engineers whether or not their trains could proceed into a block (stretch of track). Over time, the flags were replaced with semaphore signals (see RAILROADS, HISTORY OF). However, on single lines, where there was a greater risk of more than one train operating in a section of track at a time, semaphore signals were not enough: other safeguards were needed. In Britain, trains operated over a single-track section using a train staff or token. A locomotive crew had to carry the staff or token with them to enter a section of track, and since there was only one of these, no other train could possibly be in that section at the time.

In North America, where sections were longer, the timetable and train-order system was developed to avoid delays. This involved trains up and down the line keeping to a set timetable as much as possible, passing trains going in the opposite direction only at stations that contained a short section of double track. If individual trains were running late or early, line controllers, dispatchers, or stationmasters along the stretch of line involved could use the telegraph—and later the telephone—to arrange for them to cross at other points, avoiding the whole schedule being disrupted by one out-of-sequence train.

Once changes had been agreed to, verbal or written instructions were given to train crews to inform them of the changes. In cases where traffic was particularly heavy, two or more trains might have to run through a section in quick succession. Trains would carry an identifying code on their locomotives to help the lineside crew to recognize each train and set the signals and track switches accordingly.

In Warrensburg, Missouri, on October 10, 1904, a freight train was waiting in a siding for an express train to pass in the opposite direction. On this particular day, the traffic was heavy enough for the express to be run as two separate trains, but the freight train crew failed either to read the orders or to notice the special code on the first express.

The signaling system of this German railroad is clearly visible at night.

Assuming they were free to move, they pulled onto the single-track main line and subsequently collided with the second express. Although the combined speeds of the two trains was only 30 mph (48 km/h), the leading coach of the second express was wrecked, and 29 people died.

In other cases, mistakes by controllers proved fatal. On March 16, 1906, a line dispatcher on the Denver & Rio Grande Railroad asked a telegraph operator whether a westbound express had arrived at his station. The operator was tired after a long night shift and had dozed off while the express passed through his station, so he reported it had not yet arrived. The dispatcher told him to give the express crew fresh orders to wait for the next eastbound train—which was running early—at Adobe instead of continuing to Florence, the normal crossing station farther to the west. Missing the orders, the express continued through the Adobe station

CORE FACTS

- The track circuit was introduced in the United States in the 1870s and used a battery-driven electrical circuit to tell a signalman that a particular section of track was occupied by a train.
- Today, centralized traffic control (CTC) monitors trains over more than 100 miles (160 km) of track, using satellite positioning systems to check their precise location.
- Four-aspect color light signals can tell a locomotive engineer whether the next three sections of track ahead of the train are clear.

CONNECTIONS

- Throughout the history of **RAILROADS**, **INFORMATION THEORY** has been important in the development of effective **SAFETY SYSTEMS** to prevent **ACCIDENTS AND DISASTERS**.

A railroad employee changes a switch signal for an oncoming train in Gillette, Wyoming.

without stopping and ran into the eastbound train between Adobe and Florence. Two coaches were wrecked and caught fire, and 34 people were killed.

Track circuits and interlocking

The track circuit, first developed in the United States in the 1870s, provided collision protection by communicating to a signal operator if a train was occupying a track section, even if it was at a distance too far away for the operator to see it. It passed a low-voltage current from a battery through an electrically isolated section of track that had a relay at one end. If a train entered the track section, the current passed through the wheels and axles and short-circuited the relay. At first, this was used to light up an indicator lamp in the signal box; later track circuits were interlocked with signals to prevent the circuits from being set so that another train could not enter the section until the first train had left it.

As railway stations and junctions became more complex, safety engineers developed more advanced interlocking arrangements between the switches that diverted trains onto different tracks and the signals controlling those movements. Increasingly, this meant grouping together all the levers controlling a yard, junction, or station into an interlocking tower so that signals could only be freed and switches moved in a correct sequence. If a signal operator tried to accept a train into a section of track without an earlier train having passed into the next block section, the system would not allow any of the levers to be pulled. Similarly, if the signal operator tried to move any switches or signals to allow a potentially conflicting maneuver between two trains, or if the operator tried to pull the wrong lever by mistake, the system would prevent him or her from doing so.

ATC and AWS

Several railroad accidents were caused by locomotive crews failing to see danger signals in darkness or poor visibility, or because they failed to keep a proper lookout. This led to the development of what was originally called Automatic Train Control (ATC) and later the Automatic Warning System (AWS). The system was introduced on Britain's Great Western Railway (GWR) in 1906 (see SAFETY SYSTEMS).

The GWR system used a ramp laid in between the tracks ahead of each distant signal. As the locomotive passed over the ramp, the ramp made contact with a shoe underneath the locomotive. If the signal was at "clear," an electric current in the ramp would cause a bell to ring in the locomotive cab in order to inform the crew. If the signal was at "danger," or if there was a fault in the system, no current would be picked up as the shoe passed over the ramp. A siren would then sound in the cab, and the locomotive's brakes would be applied. However, this did not occur if the engineer acknowledged the warning by operating a handle in the cab, when he could continue driving at reduced speed.

Later, this electromechanical system was replaced on European and U.S. lines by electrical AWS systems, which played a vital role in eliminating accidents. Yet even the most sophisticated AWS systems provide no protection against engineers who deliberately ignore the warnings they provide. In April 1940, a New York Central express from New York City to Chicago jumped the track at Little Falls on a sharp curve with a 45 mph (72 km/h) speed restriction. An investigation of the equipment showed that the engineer, who was killed in the crash, had canceled cab AWS warnings and had continued to run at full speed.

On September 15, 1958, in Newark Bay, New Jersey, a New York-bound commuter train ignored an AWS distant signal warning, ran through a stop signal at danger, and crossed a set of derailer switches at speed before plunging through an open swing bridge into a river. In both accidents, a total of 78 people were killed, including the engineers who might have been able to explain why they canceled the AWS warnings.

Color-light signaling

Traditional semaphore signals usually showed only two aspects: "clear" and "danger." Longer-term warnings were provided by distant signals, which showed train crews the setting of the next signal down the line. As train speeds increased, a more flexible and responsive system was needed. Color-light signals were introduced on main lines from the 1930s on: these are similar to highway stop signals, they show a green light for "clear," an amber light for "caution," and a red light for "danger."

Multi-aspect color light signals have highly directional beams. Because of this, they can be seen from a long distance down the track and are less likely to be confused with other lights in the vicinity. In addition, because they are electrically operated, they can be controlled over much longer distances than cable-operated or electromechanical semaphore signals. Many colored light signals used on main lines are four-aspect, enabling them to show a red signal to indicate that the next section of track is blocked by a train or a conflicting movement, such as the setting of switches for a junction. A single amber signal shows the next section is clear, but the section beyond that is blocked; a double amber signal shows the next two sections are clear, but the third section is occupied. Finally, a green signal confirms to the locomotive crew that at least the next three sections of track are unoccupied.

The signals are controlled by track circuits, which allows them to give the maximum possible warning of conditions ahead and allows crews to control their train's speed so that delays are minimized and average speeds are maintained as high as possible. Similar systems are used for subway signaling, since the intense beams can be seen when visibility is poor and the signals can respond quickly and automatically to train movements over a dense network of tracks that are divided into many sections.

Centralized traffic control

During the 1930s, railroads began developing a new control system for long-distance single-track routes: centralized traffic control (CTC). This system involved all the signals and switches for crossing loops and sidings over more than 100 miles (160 km) of track being controlled from each central dispatching office or control center. Because of this centralization, all the loopholes inherent in a system that involved the passing of orders to staff who were not aware of the wider picture of train schedules and movements were eliminated.

The colored lights on this automated railway signaling system indicate the positions of trains on particular sections of track in Atlanta, Georgia.

The first CTC installations were applied to lines that had previously been worked by timetable and train order, and they enabled train movements to be made by signal indications alone. The dispatcher did not have to receive telephone or telegraph messages to know the whereabouts of particular trains, since the information was provided in real time by indicator lights on a central control panel.

With CTC, the train crews did not have to receive detailed orders relating to changes in the timetable—all they had to do was obey instructions given by the railroad's own signaling system, confident that the people who controlled those signals had the complete picture of what was happening along the whole length of the line.

At first, CTC used cables, which allowed the controllers to send coded signals that activated a certain switch or signal lever. As trains moved along the line, they would trip and release successive track circuits, and this information would be passed back down cables to the control center in order to activate indicator lamps on the control panel.

RADIO CONTROL

The first recorded use of two-way radio from a moving train was on the New York Central Railroad in 1928. Since 1945, the development of reliable and compact equipment has allowed greater use of radio communications in railroad operations; in 1959, the Pacific Great Eastern Railroad in western Canada became the first system to use microwave radio for all its communications, replacing conventional lineside cable systems.

Radio communications allow dispatchers to talk directly to train crews, and train crews to talk to crews on other trains and to trackside maintenance gangs. In addition, engineers can talk to guards at opposite ends of long trains, and data can be sent from equipment on the train to trackside receivers from locomotive and rolling stock diagnostic and monitoring systems. Fiber-optic transmission systems are also used to carry large amounts of data for voice, video, and digital communications, without suffering from electromagnetic interference.

A CLOSER LOOK

AGAINST THE ODDS

Rescue teams try to save people after the collision of two London trains in 1988.

Despite strict safety systems, railroad accidents still happen. In Hull, England, on April 14, 1927, two trains collided at a busy junction with full safety interlocking. One signal operator released a lever a few seconds too early, freeing the interlocking in time for another signal operator to pull, by mistake, the one lever in 179 levers that was free to move for less than a second.

Mistakes were all too easy to make with handwritten orders, too. In July 1907, a freight train collided with a passenger train near Salem, Michigan, because the crew had been given orders written in sloppy handwriting, hinting they should have passed the oncoming passenger train one station farther down the line. Two months later, in Canaan, New Hampshire, a dispatcher wrote the wrong train number on an order for a freight train crew. Consequently, their train collided with the other train bearing the number that should have been written on the order, resulting in the death of 26 people.

Even the best mechanical safety systems can be overturned by human error. In Abermule, Wales, in 1921, trains needed an official token from an interlocked machine to pass through each section of single-track line. However, by mistake, a train engineer was reissued the token he had just handed in for the previous section of line. Without checking that he had the correct token, the engineer started off down the next section of track. He died in a collision with an oncoming express that did have the correct token for that section.

A CLOSER LOOK

Advances in computers and communications systems have greatly increased the power of CTC. Satellite-based global positioning systems (see SATELLITE) are able to monitor the locations of individual trains very accurately, and computers monitor the loads and shipments on the cars that make up a particular train, so the expected arrival times at their destinations can be checked.

Modern marshaling yards

Passenger trains are usually assembled for a particular service according to a set timetable, but freight services are much more complex. Loads in individual freight cars may have to be transferred between several different trains in the course of a long journey, and these switching operations are carried out in a marshaling yard, where the whole sorting system has become highly automated.

When an incoming freight train arrives at a yard, the cars are sorted into groups according to individual destination. To do this, the train is pushed at low speed over a hump in the track, and cars are allowed to roll toward a network of switches that link to individual sidings (see MECHANICAL HANDLING). Computers monitor the destination of each particular car in turn and set the switches accordingly. The

computer also senses the speed of each car and controls retarding devices (brake pads that clamp the cars' wheels against the rails) so that the car will make contact with other cars on the same siding with minimal impact. Closed-circuit TV allows the yardmaster to check the composition of each train against lists produced by the control system.

As each train is marshaled, yard staff enter its details into the central computer system. This data can then be passed to the train's destination, to customers waiting for shipments, to the railroad's own accounting department (for billing customers), to the maintenance department (which monitors each car's mileage), and to the control center (which can provide a schedule slot that allows the freight to reach its destination with the minimum of delay).

D. OWEN

See also: ACCIDENTS AND DISASTERS; COMMUNICATION NETWORK; RAILROAD CAR; RAILROAD CONSTRUCTION AND TRACK; RAILROAD LOCOMOTIVE; RAILROADS, HISTORY OF.

Further reading:
Stover, J. F. *American Railroads.* 2nd edition. Chicago: University of Chicago Press, 1997.

RAILROADS, HISTORY OF

Railroads are a form of transportation in which cars fitted with flanged wheels travel along parallel tracks

TGV locomotives in sidings in France. The TGVs (trains á grande vitesse— translated as "high-speed trains") are the fastest trains in public service.

It would be difficult to overestimate the importance of the role played by the railroad in the development of the modern world. Before the advent of the railroad, and despite the benefits of earlier road and canal construction, commerce was generally constrained by the difficulties involved in transporting goods and people in large numbers over long distances. The effectiveness of the railroad as a means of achieving this task can be measured by its effect on competing forms of transport.

Many of the trusts that had been established in Britain to build and maintain roads (at a profit) were ruined during the original boom in railroad construction during the 1830s. One English road on the Liverpool-to-Manchester route, on land that had been leased from landowners for £1700 in 1830, went out of business completely in 1831 after a railroad was opened along the same route and no one could be found to pay the toll on what had become considered a largely useless stretch of road.

The coach companies that had previously operated on roads suffered equally. Not one commercial coach company was operating along the London-to-Bristol road after a railroad was opened along the same route in 1843. A similar fate was suffered by many of the businessmen who had invested in the construction of canals most of whom were forced to sell out at a loss to the railroad companies, which were intent on eliminating competition. However, the men that built canals and roads found employment in building new railroads.

By increasing access to markets, the railroad had a significant effect on the growth of trade. The essentials of life, such as food and fuel, could be brought into cities from ever greater distances. This removed many of the restrictions on the economic growth of cities and nations.

In short, the railroad made the greatest possible contribution to the transition from a society that made its wealth from farming to an industrial society. If one country could be said to have benefited more than any other from the development of the railroad, it is the United States. The resources of the wide open spaces of the continent would have remained largely untapped were it not for the arrival of the railroad toward the end of the 1820s, and the country would almost certainly not have developed its economic might until much later.

Origins of the railroad

The first true railroads were used to transport coal from the coal faces in mines in Europe. Of these, the first was probably in Leberthal, Alsace, France, and dates from around 1550. Its railroad cars had wheels

CORE FACTS

- The earliest railroads were built around 1550.
- The first steam locomotive was demonstrated in 1804.
- The first passenger and freight railroad opened in 1825, between Stockton and Darlington in northeast England.

CONNECTIONS

● The development of a strong **ALLOY** of iron, called steel, allowed the development of train tracks strong enough for heavy engines to run on and led to an understanding of **MATERIALS SCIENCE**.

● Wires used for **TELEPHONY AND TELEGRAPHY** were laid alongside the first railroads that crossed North America.

The Experiment *was a horse-drawn passenger coach built by George Stephenson for the Stockton to Darlington line in 1825.*

with flanges—ridges, located at the sides of wheels' rims, that run along the sidewalls of the rails and guide the cars along the track. The flanged wheel design remains the standard to this day, although there were several variations on the design during the early days of the railroad. For example, some railroad cars were fitted with wheels on which the flanges had been placed on the outside of the track, while others were constructed with flanges on both sides of the wheel. Another approach to the problem of keeping the cars on course was to design track (rather than wheels) that had vertical flanges on each side. This design, known as a plateway, had the added advantage of allowing cars to be fitted with conventional wheels, which meant that they could be used on ordinary roads as well as the track. Unfortunately, as track systems became more complex, the design proved to be fatally flawed. Switching between different tracks was extremely difficult, with the cars prone to leaving the track system altogether, and plateways had all but disappeared by the time railroad building began in earnest in the early 19th century.

The track on which the railroad cars traveled was at this time constructed from cast iron, which was prone to snap. Power for the movement of the railroad cars was provided either by men or by horses, depending on whichever was cheaper.

The development of steam power

After 1550, railroads became an increasingly common sight at coal mines across Europe, reaching what is now Britain in the early 1600s. Railroad technology stagnated for the following two hundred years or so: there were only minor improvements in the design and construction of railroads and cars. Then,

in the 18th century, the invention of the steam-powered engine heralded a new era of rapid advancements in railroad technology.

There was nothing new about the principle of steam power. During the first century C.E., Hero of Alexandria had written a book on the possibilities of harnessing the power of steam and is believed to have designed and built a metal sphere that, when filled with water and heated over a fire, was made to rotate by steam escaping through narrow pipes set at an angle to the radius of the sphere. Although his work was forgotten until the Renaissance period, between the 14th and 17th centuries, its reappearance in Europe rekindled interest in the subject, and several fine minds went to work on finding ways of harnessing the power of steam.

The most notable of these scientists was French physicist Denis Papin (c.1647–1712). Papin, who as a result of religious persecution was driven out of his native France, worked mostly in Germany and England. In addition to inventing a pressure cooker (fitted with an all-important safety valve), Papin managed to build a steam-driven boat, which was unfortunately destroyed by boatmen concerned about the possibility of losing their livelihoods.

Steam engines first appeared at collieries around the start of the 18th century. At this time their power was harnessed not to drive the primitive railroad cars but rather to pump water from the mines, which were being dug ever deeper into the earth to reach reserves of valuable resources, such as coal and iron ore, that were buried beneath.

In 1698, English engineer Thomas Savery (c.1650–1715) patented the miner's friend, which was described simply as an engine for raising water using fire. This had been designed to pump water out of the deep tin mines of Cornwall on the southwest tip of England but proved to be unequal to the task of tackling floods. Fellow Cornishman Thomas Newcomen (1663–1729) patented an improved design for the steam engine in 1705 and, although

inefficient and extremely costly to run, was effective in clearing floodwater from mines. By 1750, this engine was widely used in mines throughout Britain (see STEAM ENGINE). The true father of the steam engine, however, was James Watt (1736–1819), an engineer from Greenock, southwest Scotland.

RICHARD TREVITHICK

Trevithick's Catch-Me-Who-Can *was shown at a steam circus in London in 1808.*

Richard Trevithick was born in Illogan, in the tin mining region of Cornwall, southwest England, on April 13, 1771. He demonstrated a substantial talent for engineering, and at age 19 he was working as an engineer for several of the Cornish tin mines.

Although there were considerable quantities of tin and silver to be found beneath the ground in Cornwall, there were no local coal reserves and coal had to be transported from other parts of England at a cost. By harnessing the power of steam under high pressure, Trevithick was able to increase greatly the power and efficiency of the steam engine and so reduce the amount of coal it consumed. So successful was his design that by 1800 he had found takers for 30 of his improved engines. It was also at this time that he became interested in using steam engines to provide

power for vehicles, demonstrating the first of his road-going steam-driven carriages at Cambourne in Cornwall during the closing days of 1801.

Despite his valuable contribution to the development of the railroad, including the construction of the world's first steam-driven rail locomotive in 1803, Trevithick saw no material benefits from his pioneering work. His lack of commercial sense resulted in bankruptcy in 1811. In a desperate attempt to revive his fortunes, Trevithick sailed for South America in 1816 but returned without a penny to his name a little over ten years later, only to discover that the rest of the world had profited from his inventions. He died a broken man in Dartford, Kent, on April 22, 1833, and was buried in an unmarked pauper's grave.

PEOPLE

GEORGE STEPHENSON

Stephenson's **Locomotion**, *which pulled the first train from Darlington to Stockton.*

Although Richard Trevithick is rightly credited with having invented the steam-driven locomotive, it is George Stephenson who made the necessary improvements to the design and turned the invention into a practical form of transport. Born in Northumberland, England, on June 9, 1781, Stephenson was the son of a mechanic and by the age of 19 was operating a steam engine in the coal mines around Newcastle, eventually going on to become chief mechanic at Killingworth colliery.

Having already seen a primitive steam locomotive in action, Stephenson approached the owner of the Killingworth colliery and convinced him to fund the building of a much improved design. In 1814, he built the *Blucher*, a locomotive that was able to haul up to 30 tons (27 tonnes) of coal at around 4mph (6.4 km/h). Pursuing his interest in steam-powered locomotion, Stephenson went on to design and build several historically significant steam locomotives, including *Locomotion* and, in 1829, *Rocket*. In many respects the age of steam locomotion might truly be said to have begun with the building of *Rocket*.

For the remainder of his life, Stephenson continue to be one of the most important figures in railroad design and construction. He died on August 12, 1848, in Derbyshire, England.

PEOPLE

James Watt had studied the Newcomen engine in detail while working as a scientific instrument maker at the University of Glasgow. He devised a way of making the engine much cheaper to run, and at the same time increased its power output by adding an airtight cover to the cylinder and driving the piston by a combination of the downward force of atmospheric pressure as well as steam pressure.

Watt moved to Birmingham, England, in 1774. There, in 1775, he formed a business partnership with manufacturer Matthew Boulton (1728–1809), in whose factory he began to produce his new design. Over the next ten years their steam engine became the choice of mine owners and factory owners alike. Boulton stated at the time: "I sell here, sir, what all the world desires to have—power." It was only a

matter of time before steam power, the driving force behind the industrial revolution, was applied to moving goods and passengers along railroads.

The world's first steam locomotive

It was yet another Cornishman, Richard Trevithick (1771–1833), who constructed the world's first steam-driven railroad locomotive. Against the advice of many of his peers, including James Watt, Trevithick constructed a highly pressurized steam engine that was lighter, more powerful, and even more efficient than the one designed by Watt, who favored a less powerful but safer low-pressure design. In March 1802, Trevithick filed a patent for a high-pressure steam engine that could be used in a fixed location (to drive drainage pumps) or equally be used to drive a locomotive. Having already demonstrated the engine in London, where he had attached it to a carriage and driven through the city's streets, he built his pioneering stream-driven railroad locomotive at the Penydarren Ironworks in south Wales.

A demonstration of Trevithick's steam locomotive was given on February 21, 1804, when he used it to transport 70 ironworkers and 10 tons (9 tonnes) of iron along 10 miles (16 km) of track extending out from the Penydarren Ironworks. A year later he built a similar locomotive at Gateshead in northeast England, and in 1808 he demonstrated yet another steam-driven locomotive, the *Catch-Me-Who-Can*, on a circular track in London. Such was the size and weight of Trevithick's locomotives, however, that they eventually shattered the brittle cast-iron rails on which they ran. Disheartened by this, Trevithick abandoned railroads altogether and eventually left England for Peru to pursue other interests.

Birth of the railroad

Around the time of Trevithick's departure, the chief mechanic at Killingworth colliery in northern England, George Stephenson (1781–1848), was looking at ways of improving the design of the steam engine. By introducing the steam blast, a technique for increasing the air intake to the steam engine's furnace, Stephenson was able to improve its power output. In 1821, he took his designs to industrialist Edward Pease, who was building a railroad between the English towns of Darlington and Stockton. Pease had intended to use horses to pull railroad cars along the track, but he was so impressed by Stephenson's ideas (and his claim that his locomotive could provide 50 times the pulling power of a team of horses) that he commissioned him to build a steam locomotive for use on the new railroad.

September 27, 1825, was the day that the modern railroad began in earnest. On this day Stephenson's locomotive, the *Active*—which was later renamed *Locomotion*—traveled from Darlington to Stockton, pulling enough carriages to accommodate 450 passengers at an average speed of 15 mph (24 km/h). The event excited great interest and Stephenson was approached to build a railroad line between the rapidly expanding industrial cities of

Manchester and Liverpool. In 1829, a competition was held to find the best possible locomotives for the new route. Not surprisingly, Stephenson's latest locomotive, *Rocket*, which his son Robert (1803–1859) helped him to design, beat all other rivals. When the Liverpool–Manchester railroad opened on September 15, 1830, all eight of its locomotives had been designed and built by Stephenson.

Stephenson's achievement proved to the world that the steam locomotive was a practical proposition and provided the spark that caused an explosion of railroad building all over Europe and North America. By 1841, over 1300 miles (2100 km) of railroad track had been laid in the United Kingdom alone to carry the new steam locomotives and their accompanying passengers and freight.

Railroads in the United States

The chronology of the development of railroads in the United States is similar to that of the British railroads. Around the start of the 19th century, plateways had been built for moving blocks of stone on horse-drawn cars in quarries and at construction sites. In 1826, the first track with raised rails was built to carry stone for the construction of the Bunker Hill monument. Then, in the same year that Stephenson built the *Rocket* (1829), a British-built locomotive—the *Stourbridge Lion*—was imported by the Delaware and Hudson Canal Company and tested at Honesdale, Pennsylvania.

The first U.S.-designed locomotive was the *Tom Thumb*, which was built in 1830 by Peter Cooper of New York City for the Baltimore and Ohio Railroad Company—the first U.S. railroad. (Work began on this historic route between Baltimore and the Ohio River on July 4, 1828.)

Early U.S. locomotive designs were very similar to the original British designs. However, the designs in the two countries soon diverged: British locomotives continued to be compact and more suited to short runs over relatively even terrain; U.S. locomotives tended to be larger, more robust, and more powerful to cope with greater distances, rougher terrain, and steeper grades (see RAILROAD LOCOMOTIVE).

Engineers on the Baltimore-to-Ohio line developed more powerful steam locomotives and leveling rods to improve stability. They also added a pivoted truck, or wheel assembly, to the front of locomotives that could swivel on tight bends. The function of this truck was to help to keep the train on the track by guiding it around bends. An enormous improvement in track design came shortly afterward when U.S. civil engineer Robert L. Stevens (1787–1856) introduced the inverted-T rail for the Camden and Amboy railroad (see RAILROAD CONSTRUCTION AND TRACK). The flat bottom of the inverted-T format made the rails mechanically strong, so that heavier trains could be supported by lighter rails. The rails were laid on ties (blocks of wood that stretched across the track) and held in place by spikes that were driven into the ties on either side of the rails so that the spikes' heads would grip the rails' flat bottoms.

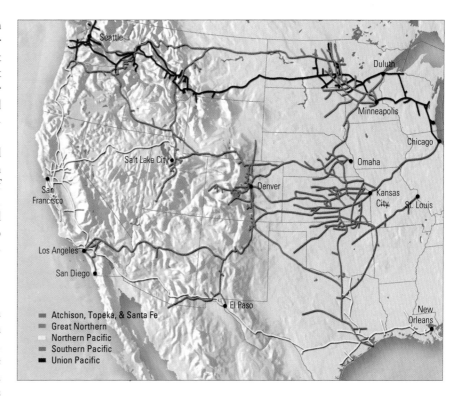

A map of the more than 40,000 miles (64,000 km) of railroad that crossed the West by 1893.

Not all railroad building was done with the intention of conquering the vast wildernesses. The world's first rail hub (where several lines fan out from a central point) was established in Boston by 1835. It was formed from three different railroads: the Boston and Lowell, Boston and Providence, and Boston and Worcester, all of which were begun in 1830. Although each line originally had a metropolitan station (in Boston), these were eventually consolidated into the North Union Station and the South Station. An elevated line across the city linking the two principal stations.

Boston's principle contribution to the expansion of the U.S. railroad was, however, in the area of finance. Having been involved at the start, Boston merchants soon acquired an enthusiasm for railroad building that saw most of New England linked to Boston by the 1840s. When the New York legislature blocked plans to link their city with Boston, the merchants simply looked farther afield, investing heavily in the Michigan Central Railroad and the Chicago, Burlington, and Quincy Railroad before going on to fund much of the building of the Union Pacific Railroad and the Santa Fe Railroad.

Controlling rail traffic

As the railroad expanded and locomotives became heavier and faster, it became increasingly apparent that some formal system for controlling rail traffic was needed if serious accidents were to be avoided. The first of these necessary safety measures involved placing a signalman at stations along the track. Using hand signals or signal flags, the signalman would inform the locomotive driver about any dangers (such as another train) he might face farther up the line. The signal flags were eventually replaced with colored boards (in daylight) or colored lights. Also introduced around this time was the time-interval

This railroad signalman from 1925 controls the signal arms and lights in his block, or length of track.

system, whereby trains were spaced at predetermined safe distances along the track to prevent crashes should a train break down.

An unfortunate drawback of this system was that there was no way of warning drivers when the train ahead broke down or the track became blocked in some way. This problem was largely overcome with the introduction of the electric rail telegraph in 1837, which allowed signaling from set points along the track. Signalmen were assigned sections of track, known as blocks, and given the responsibility of insuring that it was safe for trains to enter or leave their particular section. Although this system appeared sound in principle, it was prone to causing delays as individual signalmen tended to be overcautious when issuing instructions to proceed to the next section of track.

A more efficient system was introduced with the development of semaphore arm signals (see RAILROAD OPERATION AND SIGNALING). Operated remotely by wires and levers from a signal box, the angle of the semaphore arm could be changed to convey any necessary information about the state of the track ahead. At night, colored lenses and a lamp were used for the same purpose (red for stop, green for go).

Twentieth-century railroads

Railroads continued to spread across the face of the earth, bringing with them enormous improvements in communication and, especially in the case of North America, opening up areas for cultivation and trade that previously would have been inaccessible for commercial purposes. New towns and cities sprang up along the length of the expanding railroad (usually around goods depots and passengers stations), and it soon became the economic lifeline for much of the country. By the early years of the 20th century, there were around one million miles (1.6 million km) of functioning railroad distributed across the world. Of these one million miles,

approximately 350,000 miles (560,000 km)—nearly a quarter of the total worldwide—were situated in the United States and Canada.

The major technical innovation to have made an appearance by the beginning of the century was the introduction of electrification. Although electrically powered locomotives were in use from this time, it was not until the middle of the century that diesel and electric locomotives began to replace steam-powered locomotives to any significant extent. Even today, steam engines are a common site in some parts of Asia, especially China.

Although new track was still being laid, by the second half of the 20th century the spread of the railroad had slowed almost to a halt. The railroad began to fight for its share of the transport market against privately owned automobiles, cheap and flexible road haulage, and fast domestic air travel. Recognizing the need to improve to survive in an increasingly competitive marketplace, railroad companies—often in tandem with governments—looked to improvements in speed in the hope of preserving their market share.

Japan opened its first high-speed railroad in 1964. Traveling between Tokyo and Osaka, the new service of so-called bullet trains was able to achieve speeds of between 130 and 160 mph (209 and 257 km/h). This trend toward greater speed is also reflected in late-20th-century developments in Europe. France led the way with the building of the lines for the TGV (*train á grande vitesse*—high-speed train) and high-speed rail links between cities such as Paris and Lyon, where the train can travel at 168 mph (270 km/h). Similar developments are also to be found in Spain, Italy, and Germany, and eventually all Europe will be linked by these high-speed routes.

The North American railroad continues to suffer as a result of the very thing that made it so successful in the first place: the sheer scale of the country. During the 19th century, no other available means of transport could possible have offered practical and realistic competition to the railroad. By covering vast distances at previously unimagined speeds, the railroad was able to beat all competitors. The development of the airplane and the advent of cheap domestic flights have made the North American railroad a less popular mode of passenger transport for long-distance journeys. Nevertheless, the economy of freight haulage by railroad maintains its popularity for heavy goods such as coal and mineral ores.

M. FLYNN

See also: MASS TRANSIT SYSTEM; MONORAIL; MOUNTAIN RAILROAD AND FUNICULAR; RAILROAD CAR; STREETCAR AND TROLLEY; SUBWAY SYSTEM.

Further reading:

Blumberg, R. *Full Steam Ahead: The Race to Build a Transcontinental Railroad*. Washington, D.C.: National Geographic Society, 1996.
Nice, D. *Amtrak: The History and Politics of a National Railroad*. Boulder, Colorado: Lynne Reinner, 1998.

REFRIGERATION

Refrigeration is a method of cooling food, medical supplies, and other items to extend their lives

Throughout history, people have used many different methods to keep produce from spoiling, such as curing, pickling, and smoking, but it is the technology of refrigeration that has provided the most reliable way to keep food fresh.

The word *refrigeration* comes from the Latin word *frigidus,* which means "cold." The technique of preserving things by keeping them at low temperatures has been known since at least 1000 B.C.E. Chinese people of the T'ang dynasty (618–907 C.E.) stored perishables in underground ice pits. The Romans enjoyed ice in their drinks; Emperor Elagabalus (218 C.E.) reputedly ordered a snow mountain to be built in his garden for cooling in summer. From the early 1800s until the 1920s, it was common for Americans to keep perishables in insulated wooden boxes kept cold by daily deliveries from the iceman.

The first refrigerator to use vapor (a gas that can be liquefied by compression) was designed, but not actually built, by pioneering American engineer Oliver Evans (1755–1819) in 1805. A modern-style refrigerator that was cooled by compressing a vapor was developed in 1834 by American inventor Jacob Perkins (1766–1849). The first domestic refrigerator, the Domelre, was sold in Chicago from 1913, and refrigerators became widespread in the 1920s.

Freezers are essentially low-temperature refrigerators: typical food freezers keep their contents at approximately 0°F (−18°C), whereas typical household refrigerators keep contents at 40°F (4°C). The same refrigeration mechanisms can be used but a freezer's thermostat is set to a lower temperature.

The physics of refrigeration

Refrigeration is based on the physics of heat, particularly the laws of thermodynamics. The first law of thermodynamics (also known as the conservation of energy) states that energy, including heat (thermal energy), can be moved from place to place or converted from one form into another, but it cannot be created or destroyed (see ENERGY RESOURCES; HEAT, PRINCIPLES OF). The second law of thermodynamics states that heat energy will only transfer from a hot

An iceman sprays ice into a refrigeration truck.

object to a colder one; to move heat from a cold object to a hotter one requires an input of energy from outside. Together these laws suggest that a refrigerator could move heat from warm food to a low-temperature cooling compartment, and then transport it to the higher-temperature surroundings outside. The second part of this law (the transfer of heat from a low temperature to a higher one) requires an input of energy, which is typically supplied by electricity.

How does a machine pick up and move heat? When water boils to produce water vapor (steam), it stays at the same temperature, 212°F (100°C), even though heat is being absorbed constantly. The energy needed to boil water, known as the latent heat of vaporization, breaks the bonds between water molecules, turning liquid into gas. In other words, when water turns to steam, it absorbs heat; when steam turns back to water, the same amount of heat is released to the surroundings. This phenomenon is the basis of a simple refrigerator. The coolant, a substance that can be a liquid or a vapor, flows in a closed loop from the inside of the cooling compartment to the heat fins outside the refrigerator and back inside again, moving heat from the cool inside to the warm outside (see HEAT EXCHANGER).

CORE FACTS

- The ancient Chinese preserved food in underground ice pits as early as the seventh century C.E.
- Most domestic refrigerators work by alternately compressing and expanding a coolant, changing it from a vapor to a liquid and back again.
- Coolants include ammonia, water, carbon dioxide, and chlorofluorocarbons (CFCs).
- Thermoelectric refrigerators cool their compartments not by circulating a coolant, but by using an electrical phenomenon known as the Peltier effect.

CONNECTIONS

- The **FUELS AND PROPELLANTS** used by a **ROCKET ENGINE** must be kept in refrigerated storage.

- In **ARTIFICIAL INSEMINATION AND FERTILITY TREATMENT**, embryos can be frozen for future implantation.

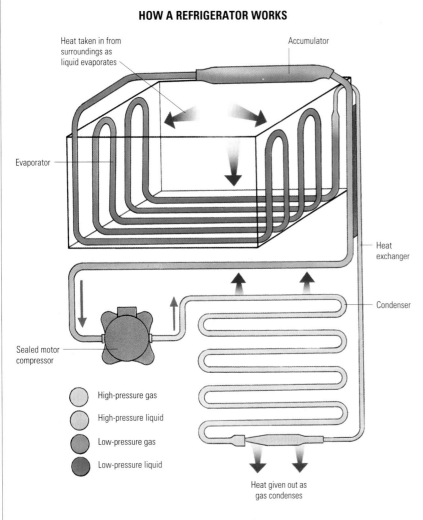

HOW A REFRIGERATOR WORKS

Heat taken in from surroundings as liquid evaporates

Accumulator

Evaporator

Heat exchanger

Condenser

Sealed motor compressor

High-pressure gas

High-pressure liquid

Low-pressure gas

Low-pressure liquid

Heat given out as gas condenses

A diagram showing the processes through which the coolant goes in a refrigeration system. The coolant undergoes evaporation, compression, and condensation in order to take heat from inside the appliance and dissipate it to the surrounding air.

CRYOGENICS

Absolute zero, which is –459.67°F (–273.15°C), is the lowest theoretically possible temperature—the temperature at which all thermal vibrations of the atoms in a material stop. Cryogenics is the science of cooling materials to temperatures between room temperature and absolute zero. Most cryogenic research is carried out using the gases nitrogen and helium, which are cooled using compressors to such low temperatures that they become liquids.

Liquid nitrogen, which boils at –321°F (–196°C), and liquid air have a variety of uses. One of the main applications is in the fast freezing of foods, which seals in more flavor than conventional refrigeration. Another is in shrink fitting, in which an axle is cooled to a low temperature to fit tightly inside a wheel.

Liquid helium boils at –452°F (–269°C) and is used to investigate superconductivity, the phenomenon by which the electrical resistance of metals disappears. The applications of superconductivity include very efficient power transmission, high-speed computers, and trains that float on superconducting magnets (see ELECTRICITY AND MAGNETISM; LINEAR MOTOR).

Cryogenics includes cryonics, the process of freezing the bodies of people after death in the hope that advances in medical science will make it possible to restore them sometime in the future.

A CLOSER LOOK

Inside a refrigerator

Most domestic refrigerators work by alternately compressing and expanding the coolant, changing it from vapor to liquid and back again, which absorbs and releases heat. The coolant, with a boiling point close to the desired refrigerator temperature, starts off as a liquid at high pressure. As it enters the refrigerator compartment, it is pushed through a small nozzle, which reduces the pressure of the liquid as it passes into a large, coiled pipe known as the evaporator. Reducing the pressure of a substance reduces its boiling point. As the liquid coolant boils, it becomes a gas and absorbs heat from the refrigerator compartment and reduces its temperature.

The coolant, now a low-pressure gas, flows through the evaporator coil to the outside of the refrigerator until it reaches a compressor (see PUMP AND COMPRESSOR). This compressor pressurizes and warms the gas in the way that a bicycle pump warms the air inside it. The hot, pressurized gas then enters the condenser (a coiled pipe connected to a set of heat-dissipating fins on the back of the refrigerator). The pressure is such that the boiling point of the refrigerant is above room temperature, so the gas liquefies and gives up its latent heat of vaporization to the atmosphere. The liquid coolant then flows toward the expansion valve and the cycle is repeated.

Coolants

Refrigerator coolants include water, air, carbon dioxide, sulfur dioxide, and ammonia. Ammonia—a toxic, corrosive gas—was used in many early refrigerators but was dangerous when it escaped. In the 1930s, this led the DuPont chemical company to develop chlorofluorocarbons (CFCs), which were found to work well as refrigerants. However, it was discovered in the 1970s that escaped CFCs from old refrigerators played a part in destroying the atmospheric ozone layer (see POLLUTION AND ITS CONTROL). An ozone-friendly coolant using a mixture of isobutane and propane is now used.

Other types of refrigerators

Most domestic refrigerators work by compression, but there are other technologies. Steam-jet refrigeration, common in industrial plants and breweries, uses the expansion of a high-pressure jet of steam to cool objects to temperatures no lower than 32°F (0°C). Thermoelectric refrigeration uses thermocouples (junctions between two dissimilar metals across which a current flows). One hundred thermocouples produce a cooling effect of 50°F (10°C). Gas refrigerators are also common. A gas flame is used to vaporize liquid ammonia, the coolant.

C. WOODFORD

See also: AIR CONDITIONING AND VENTILATION; FOOD PRESERVATION.

Further reading:
Corinchock, J. *Technician's Guide to Refrigeration Systems.* New York: McGraw Hill, 1997.

RESISTOR, CAPACITOR, AND INDUCTOR

Resistors, capacitors, and inductors are electrical elements that are used to control electric potential and current

Electricity is used for an extraordinary range of applications, from huge electric motors that provide air-conditioning in multistory buildings to miniaturized circuits in cellular phones and miniature radio receivers. For some applications the electricity must be provided at constant voltage, while in other applications the voltage must change from positive to negative millions of times each second. To transport electrical power from its source to the many places and into the many forms in which it is needed, components known as resistors, capacitors, and inductors are used.

Resistors and their uses

When electric charge flows through a conductor such as a metal wire, an electric current is said to flow through the wire. To cause the current to flow, an electric potential difference, or voltage, must exist between the ends of the wire. The ratio of the potential difference (measured in volts) to the amount of current flow (measured in amps) is called the *resistance*. Resistance is measured in ohms and is calculated as volts per amp. For many materials the ratio of current to potential difference is constant for all voltages. However, some substances, such as silicon, are called semiconductors because their resistance changes as the voltage changes.

When a potential difference is placed between the ends of a conductor, an electric field results that causes electrons (negatively charged particles) to move along the conductor from its negative end to its positive end. The flow of electrons within the conductor is impeded by their collisions with atoms in the wire. This is the origin of electrical resistance.

As well as the type of material that the wire is made from (see MATERIALS SCIENCE), the resistance of any wire depends on its length and cross-sectional area. How readily electrons can pass through a particular material is indicated by its resistivity, for which all substances have a unique value. Materials with low values of resistivity are called conductors; materials with high values of resistivity are insulators (see the table on page 1108).

Electrical wires are often formed from copper, which combines low resistivity, ease of extrusion into wires, and low cost. When a significant

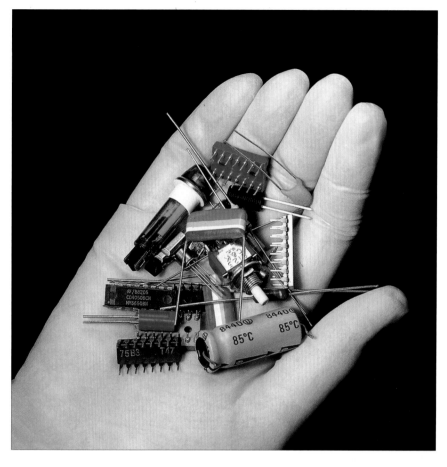

A handful of electrical components, including resistors, capacitors, and inductors, are pictured above.

resistance is desired in a circuit, resistors made from carbon components or long thin wires are used. Both types can be made with resistance values that range from a few ohms to many hundreds of megaohms.

In addition to the resistance value, an important parameter that characterizes resistors is their power rating. When an electric current passes through a resistor, the collisions with atoms in the resistor that cause the resistance also set those atoms vibrating: the resistor becomes hotter (see HEAT, PRINCIPLES OF). The rate at which heat can be dissipated—the power rating of the resistor—is measured in watts (W).

Modern carbon resistors are formed by depositing a thin film of graphite (a form of carbon that conducts electricity) between two contact wires on an insulating base. Carbon film resistors come in a variety of power ratings, from 0.125 W to 2.000 W. When greater power dissipation is needed, wire resistors are used. Wire-wound resistors are formed using long strands of thin wire. The wire is wound into long continuous coils around a hollow, insulating ceramic core. Such ceramic resistors can dissipate heat with a power of up to 50 W.

Electric space heaters commonly used for home heating are essentially large resistors that dissipate many kilowatts of electrical energy as heat. Similarly, the filaments of lightbulbs are heated by a current in order to glow brightly.

CORE FACTS

- Resistors are electrical components that are used to impede the flow of current in a circuit.
- Capacitors are devices that store electrical charge on large conducting plates. These plates are separated by a very small gap.
- Inductors are coils of wire that create magnetic fields to slow the rate of change of a current.

CONNECTIONS

● Resistors, capacitors, and inductors are often used in **ELECTRONIC** machines such as **COMPUTERS** and **RADIO RECEIVERS**.

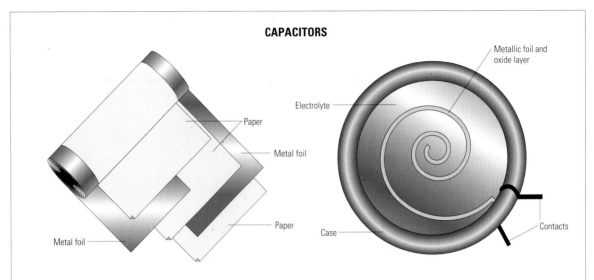

CAPACITORS

Metallic foil and oxide layer

Electrolyte

Paper

Metal foil

Paper

Case

Contacts

Metal foil

The cylindrical capacitor (at left) has paper separating its rolled-up plates. The electrolytic capacitor (at right) has a roll of metallic foil coated with oxide and surrounded by an electrolytic substance inside a case.

For some applications variable resistors are required. In the case of wire-wound resistors, this is accomplished by leaving one side of the wire coil exposed. A sliding contact is then allowed to move along the exposed wire. The resistance between the sliding contact and one end of the resistor wire varies as the slider is moved, changing the length of the coil in the circuit. When used to control large currents, such as the power supply of a large motor, these devices are called rheostats. Miniature rheostats called potentiometers are used as television volume controls and in other low-current applications. They are formed by allowing a sliding contact to move over a thin film of carbon.

The resistance of metals decreases as their temperature decreases. If the temperature is reduced sufficiently, the metal can lose all resistance, a state known as superconductivity. Superconductors have a power rating of zero and so generate no heat when a current flows through them. Usually the change of resistance with temperature is an undesirable effect in electric circuits. The resistance of semiconductors is particularly sensitive to temperature.

Contrary to the behavior of metals, semiconductor resistivity goes down with increasing temperature (see SEMICONDUCTOR AND SEMICONDUCTOR DEVICE). This effect is exploited by manufacturing temperature-sensitive resistors (called thermistors) from semiconducting materials. The resistance of semiconducting materials also decreases when they are exposed to light. This property is exploited in the construction of photocells and phototransistors (see PHOTOCELL; THERMOMETRY).

Capacitors and their uses

Capacitors are devices used to store electric charge. They consist of two facing plates made of conducting material that are separated by a thin gap. The gap is often filled with an insulating material called the dielectric. The measure of the capacitor's ability to hold charge is called the capacitance. Capacitance is measured in farads (F) and is calculated as charge (measured in coulombs) per volt. The capacitance depends on the area of the plates, their distance apart, and the permittivity (ability to store a charge) of the substance filling the gap between the plates.

When a vacuum occupies the space between the plates, its permittivity is 8.85×10^{-12} farads per meter (F/m). The permittivity of other materials is often expressed relative to the value for a vacuum and is called their dielectric constant. Dielectric constants for commercially used dielectrics vary from 1.0 for air and 2.0 for mica to 11 for tantalum oxide.

The largest capacitors used in electronic circuits are called electrolytic capacitors. They are constructed from layers of aluminum foil separated by a conducting paste and rolled into a cylinder. During manufacture, a direct-current (DC) voltage is applied across these capacitors, creating a very thin layer of aluminum oxide (an insulator) on one surface. Because this layer is very thin, the capacitance can be made quite high. The capacitors are then sealed to prevent the dielectric paste from drying out. The disadvantage of electrolytic capacitors is

RESISTIVITY OF SOME COMMON MATERIALS

Material	Resistivity	Classification
Silver	1.62×10^{-8}	Good conductor
Copper	1.72×10^{-8}	Good conductor
Carbon (graphite)	$c.100 \times 10^{-8}$	Conductor
Germanium	0.45	Semiconductor
Silicon	640	Semiconductor
Glass	1010–1014	Insulator
Rubber	1013–1016m	Insulator

Resistivity is measured in ohm meters (Ωm). These are measured at a temperature of 68°F (20°C).

that they must always be connected in the circuit with the same electric polarity as was used when the oxide layer was formed. If they are connected with the opposite polarity, the oxide will be chemically reduced and convert back into its constituent parts, thereby releasing oxygen gas into the sealed capacitor and very likely causing an explosion.

Capacitors are used for several important applications. They are commonly used in digital circuits so that information stored in computer memories is not lost during a momentary electric power failure. The electrical energy stored by the capacitors is used to provide a current to maintain the data during the temporary loss of power. Capacitors also function as electrical "shock-absorbers" by filtering out electric surges and thereby prevent damage to sensitive components and circuits. The charge accumulated during the peak slowly discharges into the circuit.

When used with alternating current (AC), capacitors act similar to frequency-dependent resistors. Since it takes time for electric charge to accumulate on the capacitor plates and create a potential difference between them, the capacitor voltage lags behind the alternating current by a quarter of a wavelength. This behavior is exploited for radio and television tuning circuits (see ELECTRONICS; RADIO RECEIVER).

Inductors

An inductor is a long coil of wire wound around a central core in the shape of a cylinder or donut. When a current passes through the coil, a magnetic field is created inside the core. If the current changes, the strength of the magnetic field inside the core changes. The change in the magnetic field within the core induces another electric field in the wire of the coil itself (see ELECTRICITY AND MAGNETISM). This induced field is in a direction that is in opposition to the direction of the changing in current that created it and therefore slows the rate of change.

The result of this is that a potential difference exists between each end of an inductor whenever the current through the inductor changes. The magnitude of the inductance, measured in henrys, is proportional to the square of the number of turns of the coil and to its cross-sectional area.

Components in combination

When two or more electrical elements are connected in a string with only two elements connected at each junction, the elements are said to be connected in series. The total resistance for a number of resistors in series is the sum of the individual resistances (R): total resistance = $R_1 + R_2 + R_3$. A similar rule applies to inductors in series. When capacitors are connected in series, the reciprocal of the total capacitance is found by adding the reciprocals of their capacitances: $1/$total capacitance $= 1/C_1 + 1/C_2$.

When electrical elements are combined by joining both ends of the elements together so that they experience the same potential difference, the elements are said to be in parallel. The total resistance of resistors in parallel is given by the equation

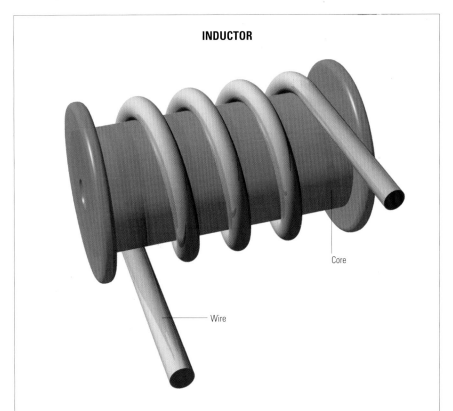

INDUCTOR

An inductor is made up of a wire coiled around a core. The inductance value of an inductor depends on the number of turns in the coil and its cross-sectional area.

$1/$total resistance $= 1/R_1 + 1/R_2$; a similar rule applies to inductances. Capacitors in parallel obey the simple addition rule: total capacitance $= C_1 + C_2 + C_3$.

A. WESTERN

See also: ELECTRICITY TRANSMISSION AND SUPPLY; ELECTRIC MOTOR AND GENERATOR; ELECTROMECHANICAL DEVICES; INSULATION.

Further reading:
Principles of Electronic Instrumentation. Edited by D. james and B. Holden. Philadelphia: W. B. Saunders, 1997.

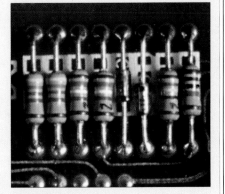

RESISTOR COLOR CODE

Black	0	Green	5
Brown	1	Blue	6
Red	2	Violet	7
Orange	3	Gray	8
Yellow	4	White	9

The first two bands indicate two digits of the resistance value. The third band indicates the exponent in a power of ten multiplier. For example, green, brown, and red is $51 \times 10^2 = 5100$. The fourth band indicates the precision of the resistance value.

A CLOSER LOOK

RETAIL INDUSTRY TECHNOLOGY

Retail industry technology encompasses the processes used in the sale of goods and services

The scanning of bar codes printed on product packaging has completely changed stocktaking and the way in which goods are sold in stores.

Retailing is the sale of goods, in relatively small quantities, directly to the consumer. In the early stages of the history of retailing, the part played by technology was small and was limited to the construction of fixed or mobile booths in streets or fairs on which goods could be displayed and from which they could be sold. However, as retailing premises expanded from booth to village shop, department store, supermarket, and even larger combinations, technology has played an increasingly important role. In recent years, it has become a determining factor in the success of retailing enterprise.

Point-of-sale technology

The point of sale (POS) is the location at which a transaction occurs and the ownership of goods is transferred to the buyer. For almost a century, from around 1880, POS technology was represented almost solely by the cash register. Initially, this was a mechanical device that displayed the cost of the transaction and opened a secure drawer into which cash was placed and from which change could be given. With the advent of the electric cash register, the facilities of totaling and recording each sale on a roll of paper were added. (U.S. engineer Charles Kettering (1876–1958) invented the first electric cash register in 1905.)

With the development of microelectronics in the 1960s and 1970s, cash registers were greatly improved, and some incorporated a weighing facil-

ity so that the cost of goods sold by weight could be automatically calculated. Prior to the development of central computing in stores, isolated cash registers could perform many functions. They were able to print the full details of the sale and provide a copy for the customer; maintain a record of each sale with a note of the POS location in the store; calculate change; and record whether the sale was a cash transaction or was to be charged to the customer's account. Electronic cash registers of this kind are still widely used in the smaller retail outlets and are commonly accompanied by machines that allow credit card or immediate debit transactions.

Larger stores are now almost always run on the basis of central computing technology. This is a system in which all POS locations are connected by a local area network (LAN) to a main computer (see COMMUNICATION NETWORK). The commercial

CONNECTIONS

● Both **COMPUTER** technology and **MONEY AND BANKING TECHNOLOGY** have revolutionized the way the retail industry conducts business.

CORE FACTS

■ Technology, especially at the point of sale, has revolutionized retailing in moderate-to-large stores.

■ The simple cash register has developed into a highly sophisticated machine.

■ A single pass by a laser bar-code reader at the point of sale can check and record prices, adjust store stock figures, and lead to automatic reordering of stock when inventories fall below a predetermined level.

emphasis is on the most rapid possible throughput of customers, so time must not be wasted in checking and recording the price of each item. This is done quickly by reading the details on a bar code using a low-power laser scanner (see the box at right). In some stores, customers can keep a running total of their purchases by scanning each item as it is placed in the shopping cart by using a handheld scanner.

The central computing system automatically carries out all the functions of the most advanced individual cash register but also checks the customer's credit if a credit card is being used, provides a detailed printed list of all items bought with prices, and offers cash-back facilities with debit cards for the customer's convenience and to reduce the amount of cash held in the store. More importantly, it automates stocktaking and reordering.

The other familiar POS technological application is the moving-top surface at checkout counters, used to bring merchandise within easy reach of the checkout operator. This involves a simple electric conveyor belt that is controlled by a foot-operated switch or by an electronic eye (see CONVEYOR).

Stocktaking and reprovisioning

Stocktaking is now the principal function of central store computing. As the bar code on each item is scanned, the central computer is informed that the total store stock of that item has been depleted by one. It is also informed that one of these items has been removed from the shelves. This information is essential for stockroom organization and for the organization of shelf restacking. It also provides the data for automatic reordering of items to be supplied by truck from central warehouses. In this way the whole process of flow from warehouse to customer is largely automated and more efficient. These efficiency gains cut down on wastage of perishable products and have reduced the need for retail companies to have large storage facilities. Furthermore, electronic stock control has eliminated the need to close stores on a regular basis to take inventory.

Essential to the whole process is the use of bar codes. These were introduced in the 1970s and are now almost universal. In the United States, the code system most often used in food stores is known as the Universal Product Code. In this code, the five digits on the left indicate the manufacturer, and the five digits on the right identify the item or make of product. At the checkout counter, the bar code is scanned either by passing it across a laser beam or by passing the beam across the code with a handheld scanner. The store computer instantly calls up the appropriate information and passes the price of the item to the cash register, where it is added to the customer's bill (see INFORMATION THEORY).

R. YOUNGSON

See also: COMMUNICATION NETWORK; CONTROL SYSTEMS AND CONTROL THEORY; CONVEYOR; LASER AND MASER; PACKAGING INDUSTRY; PRODUCTION ENGINEERING AND PROCESS CONTROL.

BAR CODES

Bar codes are a familiar means of representing data in a form that can be read by a machine quickly and efficiently. They consist of a number of narrow vertical black bars of different width, below which there are usually numbers.

A single bar code can represent a considerable amount of information about a product, including its manufacturer, nature, variety, content, weight, price, expiration date, and even the amount of stock left in the store. It can, if necessary, represent a whole page of data about an item. However, none of this information is actually contained in the code, which merely indicates the stock number (printed under the code). Instead, it identifies a record of data held in a large database, and this record can have as many different fields as is required. When the scanner reads the bar code, the unique record in the database is instantly retrieved and the information required can be abstracted. In the event of failure of the laser scanner for any reason, such as a damaged or obscured bar code, the number can be entered manually.

A CLOSER LOOK

Further reading:
Barr, V. *Designing to Sell: A Complete Guide to Retail Store Planning and Design.* 2nd edition. New York: McGraw-Hill, 1990.

RETAILING ON THE INTERNET

The Internet allows customers to view, order, and pay for products.

Shopping by computer from home is currently one of the most rapidly expanding areas of retailing. A wide range of products, from books and compact discs through groceries, can be described or illustrated on screen and ordered with a few keystrokes. Amazon.com, currently the largest bookshop in the world, conducts all its business via the Internet. A number of supermarket chains are extending into home computer-ordering of groceries and other items supplied by a free home-delivery facility. Retailing of other products, such as tickets for shows and transportation, is also growing rapidly. Elaborate security systems have been evolved to ensure that credit card numbers can be entered and sent via the Internet service provider (ISP) without too much risk of loss to the customer (see INTERNET).

WIDER IMPACT

ROAD BUILDING

Road building is the production of durable, safe, cost-effective surfaces for efficient ground transportation

The Decumanus is a paved Roman road that leads to the Arch of Trajan in Timgad, Algeria.

CONNECTIONS

● **TRACKED VEHICLES** are usually used on difficult road-building sites. Technology for building a **TUNNEL** or **BRIDGE** is also often required.

● **SAFETY SYSTEMS** must be in place during road building to avoid underground **PIPELINE** damage.

The first roads were simple tracks between settlements, some of which developed into trade routes, such as the famous silk routes between China and Persia. The ancient Egyptians were the first to surface their roads, using polished stone. The relatively smooth surfaces were needed to help transport heavy stone blocks used in building the pyramids. In Mesopotamia, special roads reserved for religious processions were built using bricks set in mortar, topped with limestone flags. But the masters of early road building were the ancient Romans.

Roman roads

One of the earliest, most famous Roman roads is the Appian Way, started in c.312 B.C.E., which extends south from the city of Rome to the heel of Italy. Another stretched from Rome to Constantinople. Because major Roman roads were mainly intended to move legions of infantry, they were paved to provide a firm footing no matter what the weather. The roads were built on raised embankments, which kept them out of the mud and snow and improved visibility of rival armies. Some had unpaved paths alongside with softer surfaces that were easier on the hooves of horses. Secondary roads were often graveled. The high, hard surfaces of Roman roads preserved them, so many can still be traced today by the ridges that remain. By contrast, heavily traveled, unpaved roads,

such as those used by the Gauls, were worn down ever deeper, and some remain as ditches today.

Roman engineers often placed roads in depressions and built large arched stone bridges across valleys and rivers. They tended to go over, rather than around, hills and mountains, and they preferred not to make cuttings that might make their armies vulnerable to floods, mud slides, and avalanches or block their line of sight. As a consequence, some of their roads had grades as steep as 20 percent, which were difficult to negotiate safely in an era before the invention of brakes.

The Roman road was built up in layers from a trench dug several feet deep. The specific materials used in the layers varied according to the purpose of the road and the resources at hand. Major roads in Italy generally consisted of several layers: a bottom layer of sand, mortar, or a combination of both; stone blocks set in cement or mortar; gravel set in clay or concrete; a layer of concrete alone; and a polished pavement surface of large stones set in concrete. The structure was about 4 ft (1.2 m) thick (from the base of the sand layer to the top of the polished pavement surface) and up to 20 ft (6 m) wide; this type of construction would last for up to a century before needing major maintenance. The Appian Way can still be driven on today; occasional gaps in the asphalt reveal original Roman flagstones.

The path to modernization

The Middle Ages saw the stagnation of the road system in Europe. King Charlemagne (724–814 C.E.) launched a project to restore some old Roman roads and build new ones, but the effort did not long outlast his reign. The constant threat of skirmishes between feudal overlords prompted some townspeople to destroy roads leading into their communities. Often the paving stones were carried off to be used as building materials. It was not until the 12th century that city streets began to be paved, and the job was still incomplete in the 1700s. Part of the problem was that the efficient public works infrastructure of the Romans, with taxes paying for municipal projects, was absent. Instead, laws were passed that

---

CORE FACTS

■ The ancient Romans built many fine paved roads for military transportation.

■ In the United States, road building was driven by commerce and the opening of the West.

■ Paved roads are built in layers of foundation and surface materials.

■ 2.27 million miles (3.63 million km) of the 3.90 million miles (6.24 million km) of roads in the United States are paved; 90 percent of these are surfaced in asphalt.

required building owners to pave outside their establishments, and often these laws were simply ignored.

Increased trade and manufacturing finally created a demand for all-weather paved road systems to accommodate the more frequent passage of heavier vehicles. French civil engineer Pierre-Marie-Jérôme Trésaguet (1716–1796), appointed inspector general of the French road system in 1775, was the first to put into place a program of routine road maintenance. In England, John Metcalf (1717–1810) introduced the concept of adequate drainage to road design. In the United States, many of the early turnpikes were surfaced with split logs or tree trunks. The Cumberland Road, financed by the federal government and begun in 1811, ran from Maryland to Missouri, providing a gateway to the American West.

PREPARING TO BUILD A ROAD

Planning for traffic needs
The U.S. highway system includes many classes of roads. Some 2.27 million miles (3.63 million km) of the 3.90 million miles (6.24 million km) of roads in the United States are paved; the rest are dirt or gravel. Paved roads include county and state routes and limited access highways, which have grade-separated (multilevel) intersections to increase efficiency and safety. Parkways are high-volume highways that are landscaped to ameliorate their visual impact on national or state parks or other scenic areas. The Interstate Highway System, developed as an element of the national defense, provided major arteries and beltways all across the country.

Many factors must be considered when choosing the alignment (path) of a new highway. Traffic desire lines are determined by studying the route traffic would follow given a free choice. Topography is important, since it affects the feasibility of a given alignment, its cost to build, and the appearance and functionality of the finished highway. Economy is also important, but more than just the construction costs must be accounted for. In built-up areas, the cost and difficulty of obtaining a right-of-way is significant, because it may involve purchasing and demolishing many homes and commercial buildings. In any case, it might be preferable to bypass congested built-up areas. The authorization and funding of a new road is a political process, and if those affected by a project are numerous, influential, or angry enough, it may be canceled. Therefore it is in the best interest of the transportation planner to site the road to minimize any negative impact on the citizenry.

Civil engineers and transportation planners get the information they need from aerial photographs, topographical maps, municipal planning and zoning maps, and ground surveys (see SURVEYING). The soil must be tested to ensure that it can support the weight of the road without collapsing. The largest vehicle expected to travel on the road is considered when determining the height of overpasses and the width of lanes, which is normally 12 ft (3.7 m). Expected traffic flow is determined by traffic counts

on existing roads, mail surveys, and interviews. Research has shown, however, that new roads and road improvements encourage more people to start using their cars, which is a problem if the road is intended to relieve existing traffic congestion.

Designing intersections
Where roads intersect, there are many different ways to route the traffic. The traditional configurations were simple forks, T intersections, and crossroads. Rotaries (traffic circles) keep all entrances and exits on the right, thereby eliminating some of the lane switches that can lead to accidents. However, rotaries cannot accommodate very much traffic, and they often induce confusion about where to get off and who has the right of way. The cloverleaf interchange was first used in Woodbridge, New Jersey, in 1928. It also has the advantage of entrances and exits on the right, but it is suitable for limited-access high-

Heavy construction machinery is used to move soil and level the ground on sites where roads are to be built.

THE PAN-AMERICAN HIGHWAY

The Pan-American Highway system stretches from Alaska down to Santiago, Chile. Originally envisioned as a single road, the system has expanded to include alternative routes in some areas, for a total of nearly 16,000 miles (25,700 km). There is only one stretch where there is no highway—the Darien Gap. This 100-mile (160-km) stretch between Panama and Colombia can be crossed by car ferry.

The concept of a transport link joining the Americas arose in the 1880s, when the vehicle of choice was the train. But the proposed railroad project never took hold. In the 1920s, it was abandoned in favor of a highway project, and the Pan-American Highway Congress was formed. This entity still exists, as a branch of the Organization of American States, and it meets every four years.

In the majority of cases, the highways designated as part of the Pan-American Highway system have other names within their own countries. Each country decided which of its roads were to be part of the system. The 1523-mile (2451-km) Alaska Highway, the 3400-mile (5470-km) Inter-American Highway between Nuevo Laredo, Mexico, and Panama City, and parts of the U.S. Interstate Highway System all belong to the Pan-American Highway.

A CLOSER LOOK

ways with high volumes of traffic. Its major disadvantage, particularly in built-up areas, is the amount of space it requires.

Earthworks

Before a highway can be built, its path must be cleared of rocks, old pavement, plants, and debris, and it must be excavated so that the layered road construction will come out level. In many cases, large quantities of rock must be blasted out. Ordinary excavation is accomplished using construction equipment such as backhoes to break up large chunks of material, front-end loaders to scoop up dirt, and dump trucks to haul everything away. Where practical, the excavated material will not be moved very far: as much of it as possible will be used to build up any embankments or similar constructions that are included in the design of the new road (see CONSTRUCTION AND EARTHMOVING MACHINERY). Samples of topsoil are analyzed in a soil laboratory to determine their ability to support loads. This property is stated as a Californian bearing ratio (CBR).

When building a city street, underground infrastructure—such as sewer and water pipes—must be accommodated, and holes must be built for regular maintenance access. In any road construction,

drainage is an important consideration. This includes surface drainage of the rain that falls on the road itself and of runoff from surrounding areas, as well as subsurface drainage from below the road in swampy areas. Drainage from the surface is usually provided by a crowned surface. This is highest in the middle and sloping at the edges, and it sheds the water to the side of the road into ditches, paved gutters, or culverts (wide drain pipes laid under the pavement). In urban areas, a system of storm sewer pipes that is separate from the city's sanitary sewer system carries the runoff to a nearby river or sea. Subsurface drainage is provided by porous material within the layered pavement structure.

To obtain a surface upon which pavement can be applied, a grader—a tractor with a heavy steel blade underneath—is used to smooth out the dirt. The grader is followed by a compactor, which has a heavy roller instead of front wheels. The roller weighs around 5.5 tons (5 tonnes) and can vibrate, which gives it the effect of a 18-ton (16.3-tonne) force.

Before a road is paved, curbs and gutters are made from a concrete—a mixture of sand, gravel, cement, and water prepared in a cement mixer (see CEMENT AND CONCRETE). The concrete is poured from the mixer into a curb-and-gutter machine, which pours out a continuous formed curb as it moves forward. The alignment of the road is marked out with taut string; sensing rods on the curb-and-gutter machine detect the position of the string and guide the machine accordingly. Rough spots are smoothed out by hand before the concrete hardens.

PAVEMENT CONSTRUCTION METHODS

Choice of pavement depends on traffic volume, road speed, drainage needs, climate, and budget, among other factors. Asphalt (blacktop) pavements are flexible and have little tendency to crack; they may, however, become soft and sticky in hot weather. Concrete decks are durable but more likely to crack than flexible pavement.

Roads that will be lightly trafficked can be made simply and inexpensively by compacting dirt and covering it with gravel, cinders, shells, or other materials that are available locally.

Flexible pavement

Flexible pavement, or blacktop, covers 90 percent of the length of paved roads in the United States. It comprises four layers (see the diagram at left).

The subbase. The subbase is a layer of granular crushed concrete or rock. It has a typical thickness of at least 6 inch (15 cm) and is composed of lumps of 1.4–3 inch (3.5–7.5 cm) diameter. The function of the subbase is to spread the weight of passing traffic. Soils that do not support loads well—those with low CBR values—require thicker subbase layers.

The roadbase. The roadbase is poured onto the subbase. It is typically a 6-inch (15-cm) layer of lean concrete: a mixture of 0.8–1.6-inch (2.0–4.0-cm) gravel and 5–6 percent by weight cement. The roadbase increases the overall strength of the road.

STRUCTURE OF A FLEXIBLE PAVEMENT

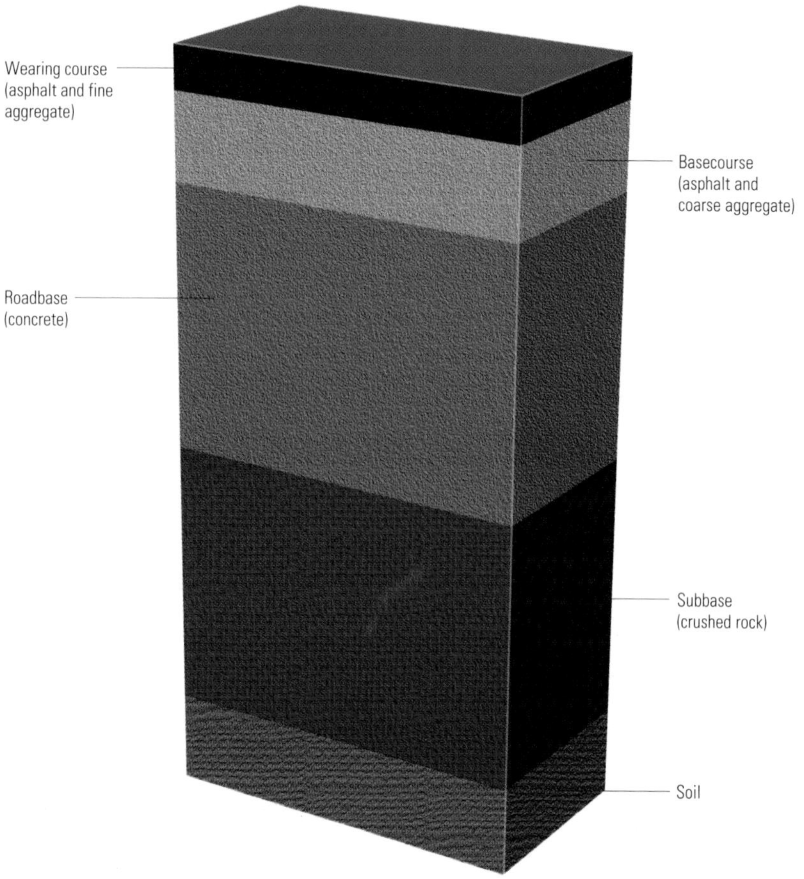

Wearing course (asphalt and fine aggregate)

Basecourse (asphalt and coarse aggregate)

Roadbase (concrete)

Subbase (crushed rock)

Soil

The four layers of a blacktop, or flexible pavement, are the wearing course, the basecourse, the roadbase, and the subbase. The overall thickness of the three layers is at least 15 inches (37.5 cm).

The basecourse. The basecourse lies directly below the surface layer. It is a 2-inch (5-cm) layer of 0.8-inch (2.0-cm) rock chippings mixed with asphalt (a residue from petroleum distillation; see OIL REFINING). The mixture is usually produced at 400°F (200°F) in a hot-mix plant, transported hot to the construction site, and loaded at 225°F (107°C) into a dump truck that feeds the hopper of a paving machine as it progresses. Softened by the heat, the asphalt spreads easily across the ground, and is compressed by the paving machine into an even surface.

The wearing course. The wearing course, is a 1-inch (2.5-cm) layer of a 0.4-inch (1.0-cm) aggregate and asphalt that is prepared and applied in the same way as the basecourse. Its function is to provide an even surface to which vehicles' tires can adhere well.

Rigid pavement

Rigid pavement is the most commonly used road type after blacktop. As with blacktop, a subbase of coarse aggregate is laid to spread the weight of the road and passing traffic. The road surface is then formed by pouring a layer of Portland-cement concrete to a depth that depends on the anticipated traffic loading. A slip-form machine allows the concrete to be poured without setting up forms (molds) at the edges of the pavement.

More basic concrete roads have regular gaps that allow the concrete in the deck to expand and contract without cracking as the ambient temperature changes. The gaps must be filled with an elastic sealant to prevent water from penetrating the subbase and washing it away. Alternatively, concrete with continuous reinforcing bars can be used, which eliminates the necessity for the expansion joints.

FINISHING AND MAINTENANCE

Before a road or highway can be put in service, it must be fitted with the signs and signals that provide drivers with information about directions, right of way, weather and traffic conditions, and potential hazards. Markings often contain tiny glass beads to make them reflective and more visible in the light of headlamps at night. Cat's-eyes—reflective glass spheres mounted in flexible rubber sockets—are often used to supplement lane markings. Overhead lighting columns are installed on many major roads.

Highway maintenance

Maintenance of minor defects in road surfaces is important, because cracks and other breaks make roads deteriorate quickly under the barrage of heavy traffic. Dirt roads require regular scraping and leveling with a grader. Gravel surfaces need periodic shaping, which is done by a drag (a frame of heavy timbers) pulled over the road. Asphalt and macadam can be patched and resealed. For concrete surfaces, maintenance consists mainly of filling in cracks with asphalt. Pavements can be completely refurbished by stripping away the layers of pavement and relaying them. The original materials are often reused in the new pavement and the thicknesses of the layers can be increased to cater to heavier traffic loadings. In many cases, however, the pavement can be restored adequately by overlaying existing concrete or blacktop with a new basecourse and wearing course. The old pavement must first be roughened to provide a surface to which the new layers can bond. Road maintenance also includes shaping the shoulders, tending the landscaping, clearing ditches and drains, removing litter, and repainting traffic stripes. Plowing and treating surfaces for snow and ice is also a winter necessity in most areas of the United States.

S. CALVO

See also: ROAD SYSTEMS AND TRAFFIC CONTROL.

Further reading:
Bituminous Mixtures in Road Construction. Edited by R. Hunter. London: Thomas Telford, 1994.

ROAD SYSTEMS AND TRAFFIC CONTROL

Modern road systems are designed to integrate roads with different purposes and volumes of traffic

Heavy rush-hour traffic builds up on Interstate 5 in Seattle, Washington.

As vehicles have become faster throughout history, better engineered roads on which to drive safely have become increasingly important. Since the late 20th century, the great number of people in highly developed, industrialized countries who own vehicles has required modern road systems to be built to handle both high speeds and heavy volumes of traffic. Highway engineers classify roads into four types, according to their particular functions and characteristics: access roads, collector roads, arterial roads, and freeways. For maximum comfort and safety, each type of road is designed to be driven at a specific speed. Roads often change their purpose over time, because the factories, shopping centers, or communities that they serve shift location. Engineers therefore try to design roads to cater to expected use 20 years after they are built.

General road design

When designing or upgrading a road, engineers have the difficult task of estimating the average traffic volumes expected in 20 years' time, in each direction, and at different times of the day, week, and year. The basic factor in designing for traffic volume is the number of traffic lanes. Where it is not possible, or not practical, to have a wide street—in a crowded, urban area, for example—traffic volume may be coped with by turning two streets into one-way roads in opposite directions. Rush-hour problems, with inbound and outbound traffic jams occurring at different times of day, can sometimes be solved

with reverse-flow traffic lanes. These are lanes that change their direction of travel according to the direction of the greatest volume of traffic. They are usually marked by special electric signs and hand-placed traffic cones that channel vehicles in and out of the lanes in the proper direction. Overhead signs may indicate the hours when traffic goes in different directions. This arrangement saves building extra lanes that are only used at certain times.

In most climates, drainage of water from rain or snow must also be considered when designing roads. Pooled water can splash and obscure a driver's vision, or may cause hydroplaning, in which the vehicle's tires lose contact with the road and skid or float over the water. To avoid this, roads are sloped slightly downward on each side of a central crown (high point). Water is then carried away by storm drains in the city, by channels or culverts (transverse drains) in rural areas, or by special chutes or pipes on elevated roads. In cities that receive a lot of snow,

CORE FACTS

■ Roads are classified into four types according to their particular functions and characteristics: access roads, collector roads, arterial roads, and freeways.
■ Different road types are deliberately designed to be driven at different speeds.
■ To prevent accidents, different design considerations must be taken into account for each road type.

storage space for snow plowed from the streets is generally provided to avoid potentially hazardous mounds of snow at the sides of roads.

Roads designed for especially large trucks have wider lanes, wider turning spaces, higher bridge clearances, and provision for deceleration (slowing down) on grades. Highways are designed for the largest possible vehicles, whereas access roads are usually designed for cars and delivery trucks.

Designing for speed

There are several ways to design for driving speed on particular roads. One way is to select the right superelevation (tilt on curves) for the intended road speed. Where practical, road curves are tilted upward toward the outside, which reduces the pressure the driver needs to put on the steering wheel in order to turn the vehicle. Highway engineers can calculate the precise amount of superelevation that will move the average automobile, going at a certain speed, into a circular path. Ideally, a driver traveling at exactly this speed would not have to steer at all on curves, since the vehicle would turn of its own accord. Although imperfections in the design and building of roads mean this never happens in practice, superelevated curves are much easier and safer to negotiate as long as the driver stays near the speed for which they were intended. If the speed is too high, the car may skid outward and off the road. If the speed is too low, the driver must steer up the slope, away from the curve, to turn effectively.

Another method engineers use to design roads for particular speeds is to allow enough sight distance (visible road ahead) for drivers to be able to react to upcoming changes, such as intersections, railroad crossings, signs, or lanes leaving the road. On roads where passing must be done in the opposite-direction lane, passing areas should be provided at intervals that allow enough sight distance for safe passing at the road's intended speed. On high-speed roads, signs should be widely spaced so that they do not interfere with each other. Signs that are placed so that drivers must make several decisions at once slow the decision-making process. For this reason, commercial signs are severely restricted on many fast roads. Highway engineers have access to a great deal of data, such as stopping distances for different vehicles at different speeds under a variety of weather conditions and driver response times. Such information helps road design engineers to calculate and design safe sight distances for roads of different speeds. One danger of driving faster than the intended speed of a particular road is that sight distances before stops will not be long enough for the driver to stop in time.

Designing steep grades in such a way that heavy trucks do not impede traffic going at the designed speed is another important consideration (see TRUCK). This is of particular concern with roads that have only one lane in each direction, in that traffic may be tempted to pass slow trucks dangerously. Using extensive data on different trucks, grades, and

A cluster of road signs indicates directions at an intersection in the southern United States.

speeds, engineers can estimate the point at which trucks' slowness will create an intolerable situation for following automobiles. In cases where a grade presents a serious problem, it is either leveled or a truck lane (slow lane) is added on the uphill side so that fast-moving automobiles will be able to pass slow-moving trucks in safety. In cases where this is impractical, turnouts on shoulders are widened and made safe for large vehicles to pull off and let others pass. If there is inadequate sight distance in each

THE SCHOHARIE CREEK BRIDGE DISASTER

The American Association of State Highway Transport Officials, known as AASHTO (see the box on page 1118) sets rigorous standards for width, clearance, weight-bearing capacity, and other characteristics of bridges built in the United States. But each situation presents problems, beyond the standard guidelines. The case of a bridge that carried the New York State Thruway (a tollway incorporated into Interstate 90) over the Schoharie Creek in New York State offers a dramatic example. When building the bridge in 1953–1954, engineers drove two of the four supporting piers into the creek bed, instead of placing them all well away from the path of the water. Ignoring warnings from local people that the normally modest-flowing Schoharie Creek, which follows a steep path from its source in the Catskill Mountains, can build into a fierce torrent during spring runoffs, engineers placed riprap (large stones and concrete blocks) at the bases of the piers. This protected the piers from mild erosion but not from extensive water damage. The tollway managers then failed to make underwater inspections of the piers, even though the riprap had to be replaced after 30 years.

On May 4, 1987, during an unusually high runoff, hydrologists measured the flow in the Schoharie at 65,000 cubic ft (1840 m^3) per second, which is 15,000 cubic ft (425 m^3) per second faster than the average flow over Niagara Falls. The thruway commission was notified, but did not realize the need to close the highway. The following day, the center span of the bridge collapsed, plunging a heavy tractor trailer and four automobiles 80 feet (24 m) into the creek and killing 10 people. This tragedy devastated the local economy, especially factories depending on last-minute shipments of raw materials, and the tollway lost $7 million in revenue. It was two months before a local bridge was reinforced to provide an alternative route, and this was too weak to carry tractor trailers.

A CLOSER LOOK

THE U.S. INTERSTATE HIGHWAY SYSTEM

Route 163 traverses the sparsely populated Navajo Indian Reservation in Monument Valley on the Utah-Arizona border.

Before the middle of the 20th century, road building and maintenance in the United States served largely local needs and was almost entirely managed by individuals or local political units. Before 1923, when the Lincoln Highway from New York to San Francisco (now Interstate 80) was built with private funds, there were no roads other than dirt tracks going west beyond Nebraska. As private automobiles became more popular, pressure to build highways grew. In 1921, Congress passed an act that contributed money to the building of federal highways, but left the choice of routes and the actual building to individual states, many of which failed to follow through. Originally founded in 1914, a group known as AASHO, which later changed its name to AASHTO (The American Association of State Highway Transport Officials), was a broad-based and widely respected organization comprising almost all highway specialists in the country. AASHO lobbied state and local officials to build more highways and appointed committees to draw up specifications for road and bridge design and standardization of traffic signs.

However, it was not until 1956 that Congress passed a stronger bill authorizing the building of the National System of Interstate and Defense Highways. This was a grid of modern freeways laid systematically across the entire country. Following AASHO guidelines, the highways covered many stretches of road that local money could never have financed, such as those through sparsely populated mountains and deserts, and complicated, expensive urban expressways and intersections.

Unlike highway systems in some countries, which tend to converge on national capitals, the U.S. system has been designed to emphasize decentralization of political and economic power, with a grid that serves all areas. One justification for this was the potential need to evacuate cities and move military troops and supplies quickly in times of war (as with the German autobahn system that it imitates). But the chief effect of the highway system has been to stimulate the economy, helping to open new regions of the country to trade and economic development, notably the deserts of the Southwest. The system also provides ordinary citizens with the opportunity to spend vacations in wilderness areas, hundreds of miles from their homes. Today, AASHTO committees advise on effective national highway policy, keep abreast of discoveries and inventions, and maintain the authoritative *A Policy on Geometric Design of Highways and Streets* and other publications.

HISTORY OF TECHNOLOGY

direction for turnouts to be safe, or if the shoulder is not wide enough, then the speed limits on the road may have to be reduced.

Engineers try to design roads to allow enough space for vehicles to recover from mistakes. Wider lanes, wider shoulders, paved shoulders, and wider recovery areas beyond the shoulders all help cars that leave the highway at high speeds to recover control safely. Because a stalled car is much more dangerous on a high-speed road than on a low-speed road, there are often paved shoulders on the grassy median (center) strips of fast divided highways as well as on the right-hand, slow-lane sides of the road (see ACCIDENTS AND DISASTERS).

Designing access roads
Access roads are small roads or streets that lead directly to destinations, such as homes, farms, businesses, or parking areas. Since their primary and sometimes only function is to give access, they are designed for low speeds, with ample space for parking and turning. A major concern in designing access roads in city residential areas is to create a pleasant environment, often with median (center) strips, wide borders and sidewalks, and curving streets. In commercial areas, adequate parking and space for trucks are central considerations. There are specifications for widths, numbers of lanes, and other details for different types of access roads.

Designing collector roads
Collector roads carry vehicles to and from access roads and have mixed functions, which makes designing them more difficult. Some vehicles use them for access alone, while others use them to travel quickly between different neighborhoods. This creates conflict between slow traffic that is parking or turning and fast vehicles, giving collector roads a high potential for accidents. To combat this, collector roads in cities usually have extra parking lanes in

addition to two, and sometimes four, lanes of moving traffic. Where there is sufficient space, extra left-turn lanes are often added for safety. A left-turn lane down the middle of the entire street permits left turns into driveways without slowing traffic. Median left-turn lanes are clearly marked by paint on the road. In most cases, traffic from only one side of the street can use them at any one point.

Where there is not enough space for a middle lane, a divider such as a concrete barrier or an island helps to prevent head-on collisions of vehicles attempting to go around slower traffic. Another safety feature for busy collector streets is a city law prohibiting left turns in the middle of the block. The American Association of State Highway Transport Officials (see the box on page 1118) provides detailed guidelines for the design of collector streets of different types in the United States, but engineers often have to invent solutions for specific problems resulting from local landscapes and traffic volumes.

Designing arterial roads

Arterial roads include rural highways and major traffic arteries in cities. They are designed for higher speeds than collector roads and usually for a large volume of long-distance traffic. Many arterial roads are also required to allow access to driveways, parking lots, and intersections. A major challenge in designing these roads, as with collector roads, is to prevent the access functions from slowing the rapid traffic. Similar methods as those used on collector roads are also used to separate fast traffic from slow traffic on arterial roads. In addition, parking and left turns at intersections are often prohibited, and alternative bypass arterial roads are sometimes created around especially congested city areas. An effective way of handling the access problem is to turn the streets on each side of an arterial road into frontage roads, which offer access to businesses or homes not accessible from the arterial road itself. These frontage roads then join the arterial road via a network of cross streets.

Channelizing intersections, which means providing them with raised islands that separate and channel streams of traffic, reduces accidents and makes driving more comfortable. Channelized three-way intersections that direct traffic safely into right and left turns are common. The islands also provide safe refuges for pedestrians. Sophisticated traffic signaling at intersections, including concurrent left turns from opposing directions and the timing of successive signals to allow free traffic flow, can also help to reduce congestion. At points where intersecting streets are less heavily traveled than the arterial road, traffic lights are set to favor the traffic on the arterial road, or even to stay green until there is a vehicle waiting on the cross street.

In rural areas, it is important that arterial roads serve all major destinations. Networks of rural highways are therefore planned so that all developed areas of the state are within reasonable distance of a fast road. All urban areas that have a population of over

50,000, and a large majority of towns with a population of over 25,000, are linked directly to each other by arterial roads.

Designing freeways

Freeways are arterial roads that are designed for uninterrupted high speeds. Access to freeways is completely controlled by interchanges (exit and entrance ramps that do not interfere with traffic flow). Both the fatigue of long-distance travel and the separation of the driver from surrounding countryside can cause inattention to driving. To combat this, slight curves are usually built into freeways to keep drivers more alert. Rest areas with rest rooms, drinking water, road information, and telephones allow motorists to rest and are located at intervals along the freeway, often in scenic spots. Designs for interchanges depend on traffic needs and topography (the physical features of the landscape), and some are

Instructions and arrows painted on busy arterial roads help drivers maneuver without congesting traffic.

ROTARY

An urban rotary helps traffic flow in central Barcelona, Spain.

A rotary (or traffic circle) is a form of channelization widely used in many countries, including the United States. The rotary is a large circular island in the middle of an intersection that forces all vehicles into the same circular path, whether they are going straight through the intersection or making a turn. In circles that do not have traffic signals, vehicles wait for an opening to enter the circle, in a similar way as vehicles enter a freeway, and turn off when they reach the road they want.

Rotaries are intended to prevent head-on collisions of crossing traffic, and head-to-side collisions with cars that are turning. They are also highly useful in simplifying turning at intersections that have more than four roads.

Another advantage is that many of them are self-regulating, since vehicles can enter the circle immediately if traffic permits, rather than stopping for traffic lights or stop signs. However, vehicles from low-volume roads can be at a disadvantage when entering the circle where there are also high-volume roads, as are less aggressive drivers. In circles where there are no stop signs or signals, pedestrians wishing to cross the roads are at a disadvantage.

A CLOSER LOOK

ingeniously designed to fit in with the environment. The cloverleaf interchange, where loop roads lead traffic from one freeway to another, is the most common arrangement where two freeways meet. Interchange ramps must be long enough so that waiting automobiles do not back up on the road from which they are exiting. Extra lanes before exits and after entrances give vehicles more space to aim toward and away from the ramps without slowing and creating congestion for other traffic.

Where a freeway runs through a city, it must be related to the streets of the city in some way. The most widely used system in the United States is a beltway (circular freeway) at the edge of the city, which allows through traffic to reach freeway exits without having to enter the city itself. City-bound vehicles can take arterial roads from the beltway into the heart of the city. Another pattern is for freeways to be elevated over the town, with cross streets running beneath them, or depressed, so that cross streets run on bridges over them. Depressed freeways are generally preferred, because they are less conspicuous, noise and emissions are more contained, and the slopes below retaining walls can be planted with foliage. Where land is not available for the required number of lanes, elevated freeways with two or three levels are sometimes built through cities, but these are not popular with the public. The space underneath elevated freeways is usually lost for business, residential, or recreational purposes, and it is difficult to blend them successfully into the environment. Sometimes a city street is sacrificed to

DESIGNING ROADS FOR BICYCLES AND PEDESTRIANS

A lane reserved for cyclists runs along the seafront road at Hove on the southern coast of England.

Since road systems are designed primarily for vehicles, special efforts have to be made to protect other road users, such as cyclists and pedestrians. Bicycles are generally expected to behave like motor vehicles on streets, staying within lanes and taking up the space of an automobile. However, slow bicycles can congest traffic, tempting vehicles to pass in the same lane, and fast bicycles may distract drivers. Cyclists sometimes endanger themselves by darting through narrow spaces between automobiles, turning illegally, or riding on the wrong side of the street. Increasingly, the solution is to create narrow bicycle lanes, located inside turn lanes, bus lanes, and parking lanes and outside regular traffic lanes. These isolate bicycle activity and make it more predictable, but they still leave cyclists in the vicinity of larger vehicles. Where space is available, special bicycle paths are often built off the road, parallel to sidewalks. On roads without wide shoulders, paved sidewalks for both bicycles and pedestrians are sometimes created.

Wide sidewalks and crosswalks in areas of high pedestrian density, special traffic signals for pedestrian movement, and special walkways on freeways are widely used. Although elevated walkways and underground tunnels for crossing streets are efficient ways to separate pedestrians from high-speed traffic, these are seldom used by the public. Pedestrians often prefer to jaywalk directly to their destinations rather than use the crosswalks. Where practical, some cities try to bar all vehicular traffic from some business areas.

Handicapped and elderly pedestrians can be especially ill-served by current road systems, since they often do not have the speed, vision, or hearing to cross busy streets safely. Solutions to benefit all pedestrians include longer walking traffic signal phases, refuge islands at wide intersections, bright paint on crosswalks and other pavement changes, large lettering on signs, and enhanced lighting at night (SEE ERGONOMICS; LIGHTING).

A CLOSER LOOK

become the city leg of a freeway. In this case, parallel streets acting as frontage roads give access to buildings. Freeways in cities may have special turnouts where buses can be boarded, and in some places, rail transit lines run in the median splits between freeway roads.

M. COBERLEY

See also: AUTOMOBILE, HISTORY OF; BUS; MASS TRANSIT SYSTEMS; RAILROAD OPERATION AND SIGNALING; ROAD BUILDING; ROAD TRANSPORT, HISTORY OF.

Further reading:
Hokanson, D. *The Lincoln Highway: Main Street Across America.* Iowa City: University of Iowa Press, 1988.
Lewis, T. *Divided Highways: Building the Interstate Highways, Transforming American Life.* New York: Viking, 1997.

ROAD TRANSPORT, HISTORY OF

Throughout history, roads have improved communication and trade and have carried armies into war

The wide roller wheels on this 19th-century Conestoga wagon gave the smoothest possible passage over difficult roads, having been designed to be easier on the road surface than earlier, narrower wheels.

CONNECTIONS

● As the number of cars on highways increases, new technologies to monitor **ROAD SYSTEMS AND TRAFFIC CONTROL** have been developed to prevent **ACCIDENTS AND DISASTERS**.

● Nearly all road vehicles now use **GASOLINE** to run **INTERNAL COMBUSTION ENGINES**.

The invention of wheeled vehicles spurred early road construction, with ancient empires building roads to carry messengers. When the empires broke up into small feudal states, roads fell into neglect. Not until the rise of new empires many years later and the invention of new forms of transport, such as the gasoline-powered automobile, did modern road building begin.

Natural trails

All land animals leave trails. Human trail use probably goes back to prehistory, with animals and humans tending to use the same sets of trails to move around their habitats. Being the most convenient routes, trails became worn and well established. Traditional human trails would cross rivers at shallow fords, avoid swamps and dense forests for high ground (which provided safety from ambush as well as good drainage), and favor hillsides that lost snow and dried out quickly. Travelers would maintain the trail and make improvements by removing fallen boulders or trees, laying logs over wet areas, shoring up slopes, or finding alternative paths around obstacles. Then, as now, signs were used to help show the way. Signs ranged from piles of stones to images or words displayed on trees or rocks. The natural fords over rivers, where land transport and river transport met, frequently evolved into main market centers.

Ancient civilizations

When wheeled vehicles spread from the Eurasian steppe peoples to the great civilizations of the ancient world, from c.3000 B.C.E. onward, the construction of roads by these rich, powerful cultures improved dramatically. Unlike people and animals, who walk more comfortably in soft dirt than on pavements, and who can use narrow paths, chariots and wagons needed wide, hard, smooth surfaces to travel safely at their best speeds. Before wheeled vehicles, humans and animals either carried loads or dragged them on sleds. The first vehicles seem to have been two-wheeled war chariots with solid wheels, pulled by oxen. Later, spoked wheels and then metal wheels made the chariots lighter, and they could be drawn by faster animals, such as mules, then horses. Four-wheeled wagons were used for heavier loads. These were cumbersome and had to be dragged around corners. Because of this, roads were built as straight as possible. Heavy loads were pulled by oxen, harnessed at the shoulders, because harnesses for the faster-moving horses pressed against their windpipes, severely limiting the weights they could pull (see ANIMAL TRANSPORT; HORSE-DRAWN TRANSPORT).

CORE FACTS

■ Before the advent of wheeled vehicles, travelers walked or rode along ancient trails. These trails tended to be through clear, high ground and avoided swamps and forests.

■ Roads were first built for moving large, wheeled vehicles that carried heavy loads. These wagons could not turn corners easily, so roads tended to be built as straight as possible.

■ Roads that were originally built for kings and their armies stimulated the economy by carrying raw materials and finished goods to and from cities.

■ The invention of the automobile has driven the development of modern highway systems.

The best roads for large vehicles were built by the Minoans (from Crete), Etruscans (from northern Italy), and Romans (from central Italy), who not only constructed carefully surveyed, wide, well-drained stone roads and bridges, but also stone-paved city streets with well-planned drainage systems, curbs, and raised sidewalks. The Indus Valley civilization of ancient India also had extensive, well-designed urban drainage systems and streets paved with sun-baked brick. The Inca people, in what is now Peru, did not use draft animals. They built stone-paved roads, stone bridges, and ingenious rope bridges.

The world's first civilizations, based in Persia, Mesopotamia, Syria, and Palestine, had few sources of stone, and the soft Mesopotamian brick did not hold up well under heavy wheels or rain, so these civilizations relied on dirt roads and fords or ferries over streams. Greece and Egypt, using mostly water transport, put little effort into paving streets, but Greek mountain roads sometimes included stone steps or grooves cut into dirt or rock to hold chariot or wagon wheels steady. All these cultures, however, constructed elaborate, decorated brick or stone roads for their ceremonial processions. Most early civilizations show little evidence of town planning, but the Indus Valley cities and colonial Etruscan, Roman, and Hellenistic towns were laid out according to a standard square grid pattern. Farm boundaries and rural roads often paralleled this grid.

The power of roads

An important use for roads in ancient civilizations was to assure communication for rulers throughout the kingdom. Powerful centralized empires of the ancient world—China, Egypt, Assyria, Persia, Rome, and the Inca empire—had roads radiating from their capitals. The roads were used by the kings, messengers, tax collectors, and other envoys. They typically had rest houses to break journeys, with inns, changes of horses, and perhaps soldiers, inspectors, and other state officials. In the desert, wells were dug at intervals along the roads. River crossings had bridges or ferries. The roads were as straight and level as possible, designed for speed, and often had stone or wooden milestones that marked distances. In the Persian royal service, a message could be carried 1500 miles (2400 km) in ten days; horses would be changed at regular post stations. Inca relay runners, passing oral messages in full stride to their replacements after two-mile runs, are thought to have taken a message 1200 miles (1900 km) in seven days.

Good roads were important in war in order to move troops and supplies quickly. Sargon of Assyria (c.2300 B.C.E.) boasted that he cut a road through the impenetrable mountain forests of Uartu, widened a pass to allow foot soldiers through, and hauled his chariots over it with ropes. The Assyrian, Persian, and Roman Empires, and also Macedonian conqueror Alexander the Great (356–323 B.C.E.), had road-building specialists as part of their armies. Alexander was famous for his army's lightning construction of roads over mountains, often catching enemies by surprise. Roman and Inca armies never advanced without establishing a direct, defended line of communication back to their base. The Roman Empire had about 50,000 miles (80,000 km) of major roads (more than the U.S. Interstate Highway System) and about 200,000 miles (322,000 km) of secondary roads throughout Europe, North Africa, Greece, Turkey, Arabia, and Mesopotamia.

Moving people and goods

Although imperial roads were constructed for the needs of kings and their armies, they were also used by other citizens, to the benefit of general trade and communication. Excellent roads stimulated the economy, carrying raw materials from the countryside back to the cities, and returning finished goods.

ANCIENT TRADING ROADS

This map shows Venetian merchant Marco Polo traveling on the silk road to China.

Before modern transportation, the overland trade routes of the world were ancient, natural dirt trails, often stretching thousands of miles through wild country. Ancient traders followed the amber routes, from the North and Baltic Seas to the Mediterranean, bringing amber and tin to Mediterranean civilizations and taking jewelry and pottery northward.

Another famous route, known as the spice roads, carried incense and aromatic gums, aloes, balsam, cinnamon, and myrrh from East Africa, through the deserts of southern Arabia, to Egypt and ports on the Mediterranean. From Syrian ports, they were shipped as far away as India and China.

By far the longest and most difficult trading trails were the silk roads, on which caravans brought silk from China and intermediate points and brought back glassware, gold, spices, and incense. The silk routes stretched from China to the Aral Sea in central Asia, from where local trading routes to the Mediterranean were well established. They were only open for their whole length during part of the Han dynasty, from c.200 B.C.E.–200 C.E., when China made attempts to garrison and protect the road. The silk roads were still in use when Venetian adventurer Marco Polo (1254–1323) set out for China in 1271.

HISTORY OF TECHNOLOGY

Scottish civil engineer John Loudon McAdam (1756–1836) greatly improved roads with his invention of a surface consisting of broken granite bound with gravel and raised for drainage.

U.S. ROAD PLANNING BEFORE THE 20TH CENTURY

Before the middle of the 20th century, the United States lagged far behind European countries in road planning and development. Dutch and British settlers had brought with them the European custom of holding local landowners responsible for the building and maintenance of roads that crossed their estates. This did not change in the United States in the same way that it did in Europe. Attempts to authorize government-funded systems of roads invariably failed at a political level. Roads remained locally funded, often not connecting with any other roads, seldom crossed state boundaries, and were almost never paved or otherwise maintained. In 18th-century America, the important cities were accessible by sea, which offered less expensive, faster transport than land.

In the 19th century, enthusiasm for canals (funded by cities to promote their trade) and railroads (motivated by profit) superseded any interest in road building. By the end of the 19th century, railroads were the main means of medium- and long-distance travel and transport, while roads remained of the same quality as at the time of the revolution. Despite competition from other forms of transport, a notable achievement in the 19th century was the construction of the National Road—also called the Cumberland Road—between 1811 and 1852. Crossing almost 800 miles (1300 km) between Cumberland, Maryland, and Vandalia, Illinois, the National Road was vital to the development of the West and Southwest: it provided a line of communication and supply for settlers from the East.

Nevertheless, it was only after the introduction of private automobiles and truck travel in the 20th century that the planning and construction of roads started to acquire a greater degree of importance to Americans.

HISTORY OF TECHNOLOGY

Roads in Europe after the Roman Empire

As the Roman Empire fell apart after barbarian invasions, communities organized themselves to repel marauders. The resulting compartmentalized feudal system discouraged communication and trade. Most of these small states could not afford to maintain the Roman roads. Even though they were able to charge tolls to travelers, the roads eventually deteriorated from natural causes and from robbery of the stones. At this time, only the Moors and Turks were building roads through North Africa, Spain, and the Balkans.

A positive development in the early Middle Ages was the adoption of the horse collar, used to harness horses to carts, which had been known for some centuries to the Chinese. The horse collar was particularly well suited to use in combination with a pivoting wagon axle, an axle that could be turned to face the direction of travel and thereby increase the ease of turning. The pivoting axle had long been used by the Celts of Britain and Ireland.

After c.1000 C.E., as political stability, economic specialization, and trade increased in Europe, pilgrimages and travel to local markets and great annual fairs also increased. The Christian Church—a powerful authority in Europe at that time—issued orders to improve roads and bridges along the routes of pilgrimages to aid the passage of pilgrims. A series of inventions and improvements in carriage design, harnessing methods, and road surface construction allowed Europe to move ahead of China and other countries in the technology of road transport.

France, a powerful kingdom at the close of the Middle Ages, was the first country to lay out a national system of roads designed for fast travel as well as freighting. Other countries followed its example as their degrees of wealth and centralization of power permitted. The French also took the lead, in the 17th and 18th centuries, in improving construction of highways from the Roman model, draining the subsoil of roads, and constructing compact foundations with graded sizes of stones in layers. In 1830, when Scottish civil engineer John McAdam invented flexible asphalt-mortar pavement, roads in Europe surpassed the quality of Minoan roads of c.3500 years earlier. With the invention of steam-powered vehicles in the 19th century, most transport investment was directed toward railroads (see RAILROADS, HISTORY OF). However, with the spread of the gasoline-powered automobile in the 20th century, modern high-speed highways were built. The first highways—large roads designed for vehicles to cruise at high speed over long distances—were built in Nazi Germany in the 1930s.

M. COBERLEY

See also: AUTOMOBILE, HISTORY OF; ROAD SYSTEMS AND TRAFFIC CONTROL; STEAM-POWERED ROAD VEHICLES; STREETCAR AND TROLLEY; TRUCK.

Further reading:
Advanced Technology for Road Transport. Edited by I. Catling. Boston: Artech House, 1994.

ROBOTICS

Robotics is the science of engineering machines to emulate the manipulative tasks performed by living organisms

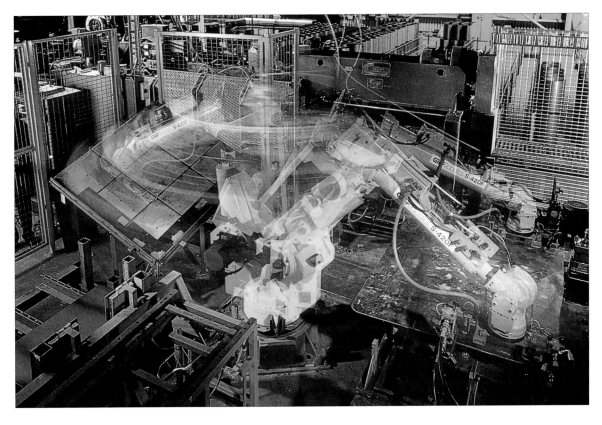

These huge robots are essential to production at an energy plant. They work more efficiently than the humans they replaced.

The word *robot* is associated in the popular imagination with autonomous machines made to look and act at least something like humans. In fact, typical robots bear no resemblance to the human form: their shape is suited to the tasks they perform.

Humans are the ultimate generalists, with a form designed by millions of years of evolution to respond to a very wide variety of circumstances. The science and technology of robotics is usually concerned with building machines to perform a much smaller number of tasks within a specific set of problems, such as inspecting or assembling parts on production lines. Such robots generally have a much simpler form—they often consist of a jointed arm with a gripper or other device that works like a hand and a microprocessor that functions like a brain. They have

become commonplace in industry, and many other applications are being discovered for them, such as in medical technology and mail delivery.

Robotic programming

The key feature of a robot that makes it different from other machines is its adaptability to new situations, either by learning or by programming. Many machines today include microprocessors: computer chips have been incorporated into cash-dispensing automated teller machines (ATMs), video cameras, microwave ovens, and washing machines. But these devices, which combine complex mechanical components with electronic control, perform only one basic task (see MECHATRONICS). A washing machine cannot be trained to dry clothes, and an ATM cannot be taught to sell lottery tickets (much less wash clothes). But mass-produced robotic arms can be fitted with the appropriate manipulator device and programmed to weld, spray paint, assemble delicate components, or pack products into a box.

Incorporation of ideas

Robotics draws on many different disciplines of science and engineering. As programmable machines, robots certainly benefit from all the advances in computer science, particularly in the field of artificial intelligence (see ARTIFICIAL INTELLIGENCE). The study of control systems (methods of organizing and controlling behavior), both in organisms and in the machines that to some degree

CORE FACTS

- Programmable robot arms are used for many tasks in factories and other industrial settings.
- Sensors of various types allow robots to take in information so that they respond appropriately to a particular situation.
- Advanced robotics research is concerned with machines that can handle a wide range of circumstances and "learn" from their experiences.
- Robotics design seeks to make machine behavior more intelligent and complex. Some robots may be programmed by "teaching" them desired movements.

CONNECTIONS

- The use of robots eliminates the need for humans to work in the radioactive areas of **NUCLEAR POWER** stations.

- Robots interest researchers who work in the field of **ARTIFICIAL INTELLIGENCE**.

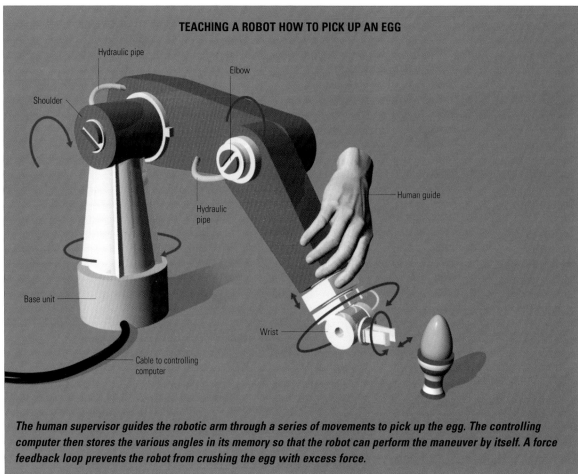

TEACHING A ROBOT HOW TO PICK UP AN EGG

Hydraulic pipe

Elbow

Shoulder

Hydraulic pipe

Human guide

Base unit

Wrist

Cable to controlling computer

The human supervisor guides the robotic arm through a series of movements to pick up the egg. The controlling computer then stores the various angles in its memory so that the robot can perform the maneuver by itself. A force feedback loop prevents the robot from crushing the egg with excess force.

emulate them, is called cybernetics (see CONTROL SYSTEMS AND CONTROL THEORY). And industrial processes and other potential application areas must be studied extremely carefully in order to make robots that have the ability to solve particular problems (see MECHANICAL HANDLING; PRODUCTION ENGINEERING AND PROCESS CONTROL).

FRANKENSTEIN'S GRANDCHILDREN

Myths and legends from many civilizations include stories of inanimate objects that come to life. There was the Greek myth of the statue of Aphrodite, which was awakened by the love of Pygmalion; the Jewish legend of the Golem, risen from clay in response to magical incantations; and Mary Shelley's famous 1818 novel *Frankenstein*. In the 1700s, clockmakers and other craftsmen actually built complex mechanical automata that could play instruments or write letters. The music they performed or the passages they wrote could be changed by some mechanism, such as replaceable perforated metal disks.

Playwright Karel Čapek (1890-1938) coined the term *robot* from the Czech word for forced labor and popularized it in his 1920 drama *R.U.R.*, which stood for Rossum's Universal Robots. Today the metal men of his vision would be called androids. Shortly after World War II, human-controlled teleoperators, which could manipulate objects at a distance, began to be used. At about the same time, the first general-purpose computers were built. These were room-sized machines that could never move around as people imagined robots should, but that began to make thinking machines a reality. When computers were miniaturized, the two technologies were combined.

HISTORY OF TECHNOLOGY

Theory of robotics

A robot is required to take commands, analyze its situation, move to its point of operation, and perform complex manipulations with a minimum of human intervention. Advanced robotics research concentrates on the ability of a robot to act more autonomously, so that it can be used in a wider range of applications. This requires that the robot have some sort of world model of the environment in which it is operating and that it know how to avoid collisions and similar mishaps.

Humans and animals use their senses to provide feedback to the brain, which then determines an appropriate course of action. An important area of robotics research involves simulating these senses. A robot might need something corresponding to a sense of touch so that it will not keep trying to push a square peg into a round hole. This may be implemented with a force feedback loop. The manipulator hand detects the amount of force it is exerting on the peg, and this value is supplied to the computer brain. If the force is too large, it means the part does not fit, and the manipulator is withdrawn. The same criteria can be applied to the force with which a robot grips something so that it will not destroy the object. Robot manipulators have been programmed to pick up eggs without breaking them.

Providing a sense of sight to a robot is a more complex problem. It isn't providing the picture that is the difficulty; there are video cameras and other imaging technology devices that can digitize all the visual information a robot might come across (see IMAGING TECHNOLOGY). The challenge is getting the robot to respond appropriately to the information. Images are full of information: a single black-and-white television frame contains 8 million bits (binary digits of information), and a standard television transmits 30 of these frames every second. A robot could spend most of its time processing images, taking in a great deal of information irrelevant to its task, and have very little time left to do anything else.

Machine vision applications rarely attempt to resolve complete images. Instead, they attempt to distinguish those objects that are relevant to a task that is to be performed from those that are not (see PATTERN RECOGNITION). A robot used on an assembly line may recognize the part it needs to attach by its shape and size. It might be able to compute its orientation from the visual information and apply its grippers accordingly. If the object it "sees" does not meet its correctness criteria, it may be programmed to ignore it or to sweep it into a discard bin.

Robots are called upon to perceive system problems and shut down without catastrophe. They might also be required to coordinate their operations with other machinery, including perhaps other robots. To these ends they may employ expert systems (computerized knowledge databases), which have rules as to what to do under various conditions. An advanced capability, of interest to many researchers in the field of artificial intelligence, is the application of heuristic techniques. This means learning lessons from a situation and applying that knowledge in the same or similar circumstances, just as humans do.

Practical robots

About 40 percent of today's industrial robots are used in the automobile industry for assembly line tasks. Most of these robots are mounted at a particular spot on the line and consist of a single arm with five or six joints. Each of these joints may have a number of possible directions of motion, which are known as degrees of freedom. The hand on this arm may consist of grippers that simulate some of the movements of the human hand, or a suction cup that can pick up parts. Alternatively, if the robot is dedicated to performing a single task, the hand may be replaced by a spray painter, a welder, or another tool.

In early robotic arms, the joints were made to work by oil or air pressure with flexible tubes running through the robot's works (see HYDRAULICS AND PNEUMATICS). These provided a great deal of power but were not easily controlled with high precision. Hydraulic or pneumatic joints are still used for heavy lifting, but for other applications, smaller, lighter, and more easily controlled electric motors at each joint are preferred. Stepper motors, which can rotate a number of degrees at a time, are better at making precise movements, but the weight of the motors tends to slow the operation of the joints (see ELECTRIC MOTOR AND GENERATOR).

Programming a simple industrial robot consists of an operator running it through the movements

WHERE HUMANS FEAR TO TREAD

Cleo, a microrobot, was designed as a prototype for possible future surgical robots.

In radioactive areas of nuclear power plants, robots provide a means of getting work done safely without exposing humans to radiation. The robots are usually designed to be inserted through pipes and into reactor vessels, where they perform tasks such as operating a camera for inspection, taking ultrasound measurements, clearing channels, and replacing machine parts.

Mining is another dangerous occupation in which automation could reduce the risk of fatal accidents and long-term health problems (see MINING AND QUARRYING). However, robotic mining has been slow to take off because the constantly changing environment of a mine makes programming a challenge. Areas that are being considered for robotic implementation include removing dirt and other unwanted material covering coal deposits and controlling the hydraulic booms used in underground hard-rock mines.

Robotic explorers have been used to take pictures and acquire soil samples in the hostile environments of Mars and the Moon, as well as in volcanoes on Earth. Curiosity and the desire for adventure is part of human nature, and there will always be explorers who yearn to walk on other worlds. But for pure scientific investigation, human presence in space is not particularly cost-effective. Astronauts require larger spacecraft, expensive life-support equipment, and complex risk-reduction measures. Their random movements also tend to destabilize the spacecraft and jostle delicate equipment more than a well-designed robot would. A balanced space program therefore includes robotic explorers to increase human knowledge about the Solar System faster than would be possible with human spaceflight alone (see SPACE TRAVEL AND TECHNOLOGY).

WIDER IMPACT

involved in the task it is to perform, which are recorded in the memory of the robot. Some robots have a teach mode. When robots are functioning in this setting, they are able to memorize the sequence of movements that the operator puts them through manually. In many cases, the operator will hold the robot's hand and lead it through each step in turn. Other systems include a teach box, which can be plugged in and used to record the position of each joint at the termination of a particular movement. The process is repeated for each movement; this method consumes less time than step-by-step programming instructions.

This robotic vehicle samples the composition of a large Martian rock. The vehicle incorporates a high-resolution camera and X-ray spectrometer. It is powered by a solar panel.

The perfect worker?

In the 1980s, 50 robot welders installed at a Chrysler plant replaced 200 employees with a 20 percent increase in production. Robots work without spending time socializing, going out for coffee, or taking lunch breaks. Their work pace is consistent. They are exempt from occupational safety regulations on temperature and hazardous materials. They do occasionally break down, but they do not call in "broken down" so that they can go fishing. Altogether their down time is about 5 percent, versus 25 percent for human workers. They provided the means for American automobile producers to compete with those in other countries.

This was convenient and profitable for the automakers, but the overall costs to society still need to be considered. The workers who were displaced by robots needed to find some other means to support themselves and their families. Structural unemployment is defined as joblessness that occurs when the economy or technologies change in such a way that a particular type of work is no longer required. Sometimes it can be addressed by retraining affected employees so that they can transfer to different types of jobs. However, not every worker can be retrained or redeployed, and there is often a hidden human cost.

However, robots do not just compete for jobs that people do not want to give up. They can be used to handle work that is far too monotonous for human employees. For example, inspecting the quality of small electronic diodes can be very stressful on the eyes, and humans can only perform the operation for a few hours before they experience headaches and eyestrain. The repetitive movements of assembly line work such as the packing of boxes can induce fatigue, dangerous inattention, and work-related disorders such as repetitive strain injury.

Other robots go where humans simply cannot fit. In Japan, an experimental snakelike robot was built that crawled through machinery, looking for particular parts that needed repair. Tiny microrobots might someday be able to perform surgery from the interior of the human body; nanorobots may even be able to interact with certain individual cells (see NANOTECHNOLOGY AND MICROMACHINES). In hazardous places such as mine shafts, volcano craters, outer space, or even the fuel chambers in nuclear power plants, robots can help to reduce the risk of serious accidents for humans (see the box on page 1127).

In some of these highly dangerous places, the tasks required are too complex to be performed autonomously by the robot. In such cases, the robot can be integrated into a virtual reality system and supplied with instructions by a human operator. This requires sophisticated sensory feedback from the robot to the operator, as well as equally advanced control devices.

The goal of the sensory feedback is to make the operators feel that they are actually in the position of the robot. The system uses stereo sound, vision headgear, and a glove that receives tactile information. Commands for motion of the robot are generated by foot-operated sensors, head position tracking, and the movement of gloves.

S. CALVO

See also: ARTIFICIAL INTELLIGENCE; COMPUTER; MECHATRONICS; PATTERN RECOGNITION; SOFTWARE AND PROGRAMMING.

Further reading:

DeAlmeida, A. *Autonomous Robotic Systems*. London: Springer-Verlag, 1998.
Gray, J. *Advanced Robotics and Intelligent Machines*. London: Institution of Electrical Engineers, 1996.

ROCKET ENGINE

A rocket engine generates thrust by the principle of action and reaction

Rocket engines have a variety of uses but are best known for their use in space exploration, for which they provide the propulsion for launch vehicles. The rocket is a unique type of engine because it works well both within the atmosphere and in the vacuum of outer space; it can also generate the huge forces needed to overcome gravity.

Rocket principles

The rocket works by the simple principle of action and reaction that was defined by British physicist Sir Isaac Newton (1642–1727) in 1687. Newton's third law of motion states: For every action there is an equal and opposite reaction. A rocket works by expelling material (propellant) from one end at high speed (usually by an explosive chemical reaction), and this generates a force that pushes the rocket in the other direction, in the same way as a cannon recoiling when it fires a cannonball. Because of this propulsion method, a rocket can travel through a vacuum. In contrast, a propeller works by pushing against air and so cannot work in a vacuum. Unlike jets, which use oxygen from the air to burn their fuel to produce a high-speed exhaust, rockets carry their propellant with them (see MECHANICS; PROPELLER).

The force generated by a rocket is known as thrust. If a rocket is to lift off the ground, the thrust it generates must be greater than its weight (the downward force caused by gravity). Traditional rockets use a chemical reaction called combustion to generate thrust. Combustion occurs when two propellants—a fuel and an oxidizer—are mixed together and ignited. Burning a match is one type of combustion reaction: the wood (or the carbon within it) is the fuel, and oxygen in the air is the oxidizer. Normal burning is a slow and steady form of combustion, but rocket fuels combust with far more energy, releasing gases that expand at high speed.

Some rockets use only one propellant, stored either as a compressed gas or liquid, that provides a gentle thrust as it escapes through the nozzle. This type of rocket has a simple design and is particularly well suited to maneuvers in space.

A Vulcain liquid-propellant engine is assembled in Vernon, France. It will be used in the European Space Agency's Ariane 5 launch vehicle.

Solid-propellant rockets

Modern solid rocket propellants are divided into three basic types: double-base, in which the fuel and oxidizer elements are chemically bonded in each propellant molecule (as in explosives such as nitroglycerin); composite, in which the fuel and oxidizer are two separate chemical compounds mixed and bound together in a resin; and composite/double-base, a combination of both.

A solid rocket consists of a casing with an electronically controlled igniter and a rocket nozzle at the bottom (see the diagram on page 1130). The rest of the casing is filled with solid propellant. The propellant is usually cast as a cylinder with a hole through the middle. To start the rocket, the igniter triggers combustion. The reaction spreads across the inner surface of the propellant cylinder, and the combustion products are forced down through the rocket and out of the nozzle, producing thrust.

Solid rockets have several drawbacks. Once they are ignited, they cannot be stopped and restarted. In addition, they still produce comparatively low thrusts. However, they are reliable, cheap, and easy

CORE FACTS

- A rocket is a vehicle that carries its propellant on board and can travel through a vacuum.
- In most chemical rockets a fuel and oxidizer are combined and the mixture is combusted; the force of the expanding gases creates a reaction in the rocket.
- Solid-fuel rockets are like giant fireworks: they are comparatively simple but limited in their applications.
- Liquid-fuel rockets often contain complex pumps and fuel recycling systems. They are more versatile but also more expensive and prone to failure.

CONNECTIONS

● Gunpowder, a weak **EXPLOSIVE**, was the first rocket propellant.

● A wide range of **FUELS AND PROPELLANTS** is used in rockets.

Solid-propellant rocket engine

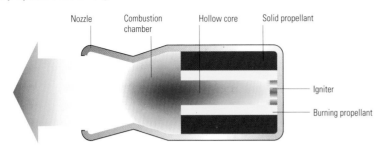

In a solid-propellant rocket, the propellant burns from the inside out and the combustion products are forced out of the nozzle, causing an opposing thrust force.

Liquid-propellant rocket engine

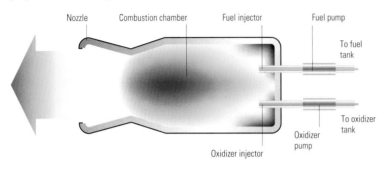

Liquid-propellant rockets also generate thrust by expelling combustion gases. The amount of thrust can be controlled by adjusting the fuel and propellant flows.

ALTERNATIVE ROCKETS

As well as chemical rockets, there are several other designs of rockets that use the same principle of action and reaction for propulsion. The most successful of these alternative rockets is the ion engine, used for satellite attitude corrections and for propulsion of the experimental NASA space probe *Deep Space 1*. Ion engines work by firing a beam of electrons into a gas such as xenon. The beam knocks more electrons off the xenon atoms, turning them into positively charged ions, which are then repelled through a negatively charged grid until they move at very high speeds. The thrust generated by *Deep Space 1's* ion engines is minute—roughly equivalent to the force a single sheet of paper exerts on the table below it. However, because the rocket is powered by electricity from solar panels and uses the xenon propellant very efficiently (delivering ten times more thrust per pound of propellant than a chemical rocket), it can keep going for long periods, constantly accelerating the craft. Ion engines cannot provide the thrust necessary to escape Earth's gravity (see PARTICLE ACCELERATOR).

The ion engine is just one of several different electric rocket designs. Another type is the electrochemical rocket (also called an arc jet), which uses solar cells to generate electricity, creating an electric arc that heats the propellant and causes it to expand rapidly to produce a force.

Electromagnetic rockets generate a "neutral plasma"—a mix of charged particles in gas form that has no overall electrical charge—and expel this through a magnetic field. Electric rockets of various types are used for stabilizing and correction motors on many satellites.

In the 1960s, NASA developed a prototype nuclear rocket called NERVA (*n*uclear *e*ngine for *r*ocket *v*ehicle *a*pplication). This rocket carried a small nuclear reactor on board, which heated a liquid hydrogen fuel, causing it to boil and expand in the same way as the combusting fuel in a chemical rocket.

A CLOSER LOOK

to store for long periods in space or on Earth. Their main use today is as booster rockets for the early stages of launch vehicles, although they are also sometimes used for other stages of launch vehicles or to propel crafts in space (see LAUNCH VEHICLE).

Liquid-propellant rockets

Rockets that use liquid propellants are a recent innovation: the first one flew in 1926. However, because liquid propellants are more versatile and can generate greater thrusts than solid propellants, they have become the focus of a great deal of research. Liquid-propellant rockets are generally more complicated than solid ones. The fuel and oxidizer are stored in separate tanks and are fed, usually under pressure, into a combustion chamber at the base of the rocket. There they are ignited and the combustion products escape through the rocket nozzle.

A wide range of different liquid fuels and oxidizers has been used throughout the development of the rocket engine, and many are still used today. Fuels vary from the complex molecule unsymmetrical dimethylhydrazine (UDMH) through gasoline mixtures to liquid hydrogen.

Liquid oxygen is the most common oxidizer. Some experiments have used liquid fluorine, which gives greater thrust but is itself highly toxic and leads to toxic combustion products.

The most complex liquid-propellant engines used today are the space shuttle main engines that power each space shuttle orbiter. These engines burn hydrogen and oxygen. During ignition, the liquid hydrogen is pumped through a jacket around the engine nozzle, where it acts to cool the engine. Both liquids are then pumped into preburners where, ignited by spark plugs, a small proportion of the oxygen is burned with the hydrogen, producing a mixture of hydrogen and steam. Some of this mixture is then tapped off and used to drive the engine's turbopumps, but most is allowed to continue to the hot gas manifold, where it mixes with a much higher proportion of oxygen. From there it is pumped into the combustion chamber. The main combustion reaction is triggered there by a second igniter, and the explosive gases are forced out of the nozzle.

Liquid-propellant rocket engines have a number of advantages over solid-propellant rocket engines. The amount of propellant reaching the combustion chamber can be throttled to control the amount of thrust, or even cut off entirely and reignited later. They can produce more thrust than solid propellants, but they are more complex, expensive, and prone to technical difficulties.

G. SPARROW

See also: ROCKETRY; SPACE FLIGHT; SPACE PROBES; SPACE TRAVEL AND TECHNOLOGY.

Further reading:
Sutton, G. *Rocket Propulsion Elements: An Introduction to the Engineering of Rockets.* New York: John Wiley & Sons, 1992.

ROCKETRY

Rocketry is the development of flying missiles and space vehicles that carry their propellants within them

The rocket is a great symbol of the contribution of technology to society. It brought the means to put human beings into space and send probes to other worlds. The principle of the rocket has been known for hundreds of years, but its importance in the modern world can be traced to just a few pioneering scientists.

Invention of the rocket

Although there is no written record of the rocket's invention, it probably developed soon after the invention of black powder, the first explosive, around 1044 during the Sung dynasty in China. Black powder is a mixture of charcoal, sulfur, and saltpeter (potassium nitrate) that explodes when ignited.

Once a workable explosive was known, the idea of using it to propel a rocket would have been a natural development. Historians think that references to the defenders of the besieged city of Kaifeng using flying bombs against the invading Mongols in 1232 may be the first written reference to rockets. Even if rockets were used, though, they did not stop the conquest of China, and the Mongols themselves were using rockets in battle by 1241.

As the Mongols swept west from China in the 13th century under the leadership of Genghis Khan, they brought many Chinese inventions with them. Around 1250, English scholar Roger Bacon (1220–1292) became the first European to give a recipe for black powder (he wrote the instructions in code to prevent this information from falling into the wrong hands). By 1288 the Arab forces that invaded Spain and Portugal were using rockets against the city of Valencia. The first European picture of a rocket is in *Bellifortis*, a military manual written by engineer Konrad Kyeser von Eichstädt around 1400.

Early rockets

Most early pictures of rockets show them as tubes of explosive attached to a long spear. The tube was made of cardboard or some other suitable light-

A European Space Agency Ariane 5 rocket blasts off from a launch site in French Guiana.

weight material, and the explosive was lit at the base by a simple fuse. As it burned its way up the tube, the explosive force produced a shower of sparks from the back and pushed the rocket forward. (A rocket is essentially any vehicle that works by the principle of action and reaction: the backward force of hot gas expelled through a rocket's exhaust creates an equal and opposite thrust that propels the rocket forward; see MECHANICS). The spear acted as a stabilizer and allowed the rocket to be roughly aimed by placing it on a launcher with a hole for the spear. Rocket makers soon discovered that a short rocket was difficult to aim and could easily be blown off course.

Throughout the Middle Ages (500–1500 C.E.), Europeans continued to use the rocket as a weapon. In China, where Mongol rule was replaced by the less belligerent Ming dynasty, rockets were developed for peaceful purposes, chiefly as fireworks.

Rockets continued to be an important weapon well into the 17th century. Around 1650, the military manuals of Polish artillery engineer Kazimierz Siemienowicz showed rockets with a wide range of

CORE FACTS

- Solid-fuel rockets, powered by exploding black powder, were invented in China by the 13th century.
- William Congreve turned the rocket into a weapon system by encasing it in metal. From 1806, Congreve rockets were an important weapon of war.
- Russian schoolteacher Konstantin Tsiolkovsky from the 1880s and U.S. physicist Robert Goddard from the 1900s both realized liquid propellant was needed to escape Earth's gravity.
- The forerunner of many of today's missiles and space rockets was the V-2, developed by Wernher von Braun in Germany during World War II.

CONNECTIONS

● Most rockets launched into space are **UNPILOTED VEHICLES AND AIRCRAFT**.

● Rockets are often part of **STRATEGIC DEFENSE SYSTEMS**.

A Chinese rocket (in the man's hand) and a launcher on a tripod. This weapons system was very inaccurate but was still used in battle by the Chinese in the 1900s.

sophisticated adaptations. These included fins to make the rocket's flight more stable, and even multistage rockets, in which several rockets were joined together so that they fired in parallel or in sequence to carry the projectile further.

In 1715, in his new capital at St. Petersburg, Russian czar Peter the Great (1672–1725) opened the world's first military rocket factory. However, the limitations of inaccurate and short-range rockets were becoming more apparent at a time when artillery was becoming more precise and far-reaching (see ARTILLERY).

Metal rockets

Although rockets had fallen out of favor in the West, they were still used in the thousands by the warring princes of India. In the mid-18th century Hyder Ali (1722–82), ruler of Mysore in southern India, ordered the construction of a new type of rocket that had an iron casing in place of the traditional cardboard one. Trapping the powder within a rigid container meant that all the explosive force it produced would be directed out through the exhaust, and none could escape by burning through the sides. With the much heavier casing, the increased thrust gave these new rockets ranges of just over half a mile (approximately 1 km).

Hyder Ali's son, Tippu Sultan, put these rockets into mass production and equipped his army with a division of 5000 rocket launchers. The new technology enabled him to inflict heavy casualties on the British forces at the sieges of Seringapatam in 1792 and 1799, although they could not save him from eventual defeat.

Several captured Indian rockets were taken to England, which at that time was also embroiled in the Napoleonic Wars against France. The rockets may well have inspired Sir William Congreve (1772–1828), a British army officer who revolutionized the military use of rockets.

Congreve's rockets

Although Congreve may have copied the idea of a metal casing from Tippu Sultan's rockets, he made several breakthroughs of his own. Probably the most important of these was the splitting of the black powder into separate propellant and explosive charges. The propellant charge launched the rocket toward its target, while the explosive charge was only detonated when the target was reached. Congreve's explosive charges were the first warheads.

Once the problem of the rocket's short range had been solved, Congreve recognized that the rocket had an important advantage over artillery of similar range: its portability. He designed eight different models of rockets, the heaviest of which weighed 300 pounds (135 kg) and had a range of 0.6–1.8 miles (1–3 km). These rockets still had stabilizing sticks, and they were launched from a platform with a ladder that could be cranked to different angles for different ranges. The rockets were used to destroy Napoléon's invasion fleet at the French port of Boulogne in 1806 and gave the alliance against France an important advantage through the rest of the war.

Although the Napoleonic Wars came to an end with the Battle of Waterloo in 1815, Congreve continued to improve his rockets. He replaced the single exhaust hole of his early rockets with a ring of five smaller outlets that provided greater stability. He also built the first launch tubes, which he made from copper, that helped improve the range and accuracy of the rockets. Although they were still of limited accuracy, Congreve's rockets were widely copied and developed further.

Rockets in the 19th century

Rockets were used for a wide range of applications throughout the 19th century. Weapons development continued and gave rise to some innovations, such as the delta wing design, that had a lasting effect on later military rockets and missiles. In 1844, British engineer William Hale finally found that it was possible to dispose of the cumbersome stabilizing stick by making the rocket spin like an artillery shell and therefore be more stable in flight. To do this, Hale tilted the exhaust outlets at a slight angle, so they spun the rocket and pushed it forward.

Meanwhile, other uses were being found for rockets. In 1808, Englishman Henry Trengrouse invented a lifesaving rocket that could carry a cable to a ship in difficulties, and these soon became a vital part of coast guard equipment, saving countless lives around the world. In 1821, U.S. inventor Thomas Roys devised a rocket harpoon for use in whaling. The lifesaving flare—a type of firework that produced a brilliant light, visible for miles, that could be set off in the case of an emergency to attract help—was also introduced around this time.

Possibly the first experiments in manned rocket flight were carried out as early as 1830 by French inventor Claude Ruggieri, who used rockets to launch rats and mice in cages to high altitudes. The cages then gently floated back to Earth on parachutes, and Ruggieri studied the effects of the journey on their occupants. Ruggieri even had plans to launch a child on a larger rocket, but he was stopped by the police.

Improvements in artillery and continuing problems with accuracy meant that rockets once again became obsolete as weapons of war by the late 19th century. However, another revolution in rocketry was approaching.

Science fiction and science fact

The industrial society of the late 19th century saw the birth of science fiction, as writers such as Englishman H. G. Wells (1866–1946) and Frenchman Jules Verne (1828–1905) began to speculate on new uses of technology. One of the most popular subjects was space travel (which has been a subject for fantasists since Roman times). French

writer Savinien de Cyrano de Bergerac (1619–1655) suggested using rockets to reach the Moon in books published in the 1650s. In *From Earth to the Moon* (1865), Verne's heroes were fired into space in a huge artillery shell; in *First Men in the Moon* (1901),

U.S. physicist Robert Goddard displays his first liquid-fueled rocket in 1926.

WERNHER VON BRAUN

Wernher von Braun (1912–1977) is often called the father of the U.S. space program. A member of the German Society for Space Travel (VfR) from 1930, von Braun soon distinguished himself in Nazi Germany's military rocket program and became technical director at the Peenemünde site, which opened in May 1938; there he masterminded the V-2 project during World War II (1939–1945).

At the end of the war, von Braun and the leading scientists of the V-2 team surrendered to U.S. troops. Von Braun worked at White Sands Missile Range in New Mexico, then the team transferred to the Redstone Arsenal, Alabama, where it developed the first U.S. intercontinental ballistic missile (ICBM).

With the successful launch of the *Explorer 1* satellite in 1958, von Braun joined the newly formed NASA space agency. There he masterminded the development of the Saturn V rockets for the Apollo project before quitting in 1972, when funding for more ambitious human missions was suspended.

PEOPLE

Two men take a test flight on the Bell Pogo, a prototype rocket-powered transport vehicle. Designed for air travel on Earth, the Bell Pogo was developed in 1967.

eventually reach a speed at which gravity could never pull it back. He calculated—correctly—that this speed, known as Earth's escape velocity, was approximately 25,000 mph (40,000 km/h).

In order to reach these speeds with conventional powder or any other solid propellants, huge amounts of it would be needed, but the rocket would then be held back by this additional weight. Tsiolkovsky suggested that liquid propellants (which generate a much higher thrust per unit weight) could be the answer. Because weight was such a crucial factor in reaching space, he also suggested using rocket trains, which were multistage rockets that jettisoned tanks and engines once they were exhausted.

Tsiolkovsky never built a practical rocket, and many of his ideas went unpublished until the 1920s; however, he laid the groundwork for the development of the large and powerful rockets that followed.

Liquid-fueled rockets

Although solid-fuel rockets were obsolete as bombardment weapons by World War I (1914–1918), they did find several other uses. As well as for flares, Allied troops used rockets for sending messages to and from the front line. After 1917, some aircraft were also equipped with rockets for shooting down military observation balloons.

However, one man had bigger ideas. Like Tsiolkovsky, U.S. physicist Robert Goddard (see the box on page 1132) was convinced that liquid-fuel rockets were the way into space (see ROCKET ENGINE). Unlike Tsiolkovsky, however, Goddard was a practical experimenter. Although Goddard began his work during World War I, it was not until 1926 that his first gasoline/liquid-oxygen rocket took off from Auburn, Massachusetts, reaching an altitude of 41 feet (12.5 m) in its 2.5-second-long flight.

Goddard continued his work into the 1930s and beyond, refining his rocket until by 1937 it was able to reach an altitude of 1.8 miles (3 km). He also pioneered many of the other systems needed for space rockets, in particular developing a guidance system controlled by gyroscopes linked to steering vanes that directed the exhaust stream. As the ideas of Goddard and Tsiolkovsky circulated more widely, spaceflight societies were formed in many countries, including the United States and the Soviet Union.

The most important of these societies was the German Society for Space Travel, or VfR. German interest in space travel had been aroused by a book called *The Rocket into Planetary Space* by Hermann Oberth (1894–1989) published in 1923. Oberth was a theoretician rather than a rocket-builder, but he was a great popularizer of space travel. In 1929 he acted as consultant on Fritz Lang's popular film *Frau Im Mond* (*The Woman in the Moon*).

The VfR attracted many of the finest young scientists in Germany, and by 1930 they were conducting their first rocket tests. At around this time, they caught the attention of the German government, which was looking for ways of rearming without breaching the terms of their 1918

Wells invented a spaceship built of a substance that blocked out the effects of gravity. Neither of these ideas is practical, but they were read by a new generation of children who were inspired with ideas for making space travel a reality.

The first person to seriously consider the practical problems of using rockets to reach space was a Russian schoolteacher, Konstantin Tsiolkovsky (1857–1935), whom many regard as the founder of spaceflight as we know it.

Tsiolkovsky applied the laws of physics established by English mathematician Sir Isaac Newton (1642–1727) to the problem of spaceflight. He recognized that a spacecraft would need to produce thrust while in the vacuum of space, and most known methods of thrust relied on pushing against a surrounding medium (the atmosphere). He was the first person to figure out how a rocket actually works. He proved that a rocket would work in a vacuum, since the thrust force was a reaction to the force of the exhaust leaving the rocket.

In order to reach space, the rocket would have to overcome Earth's gravity. Tsiolkovsky realized that if it could travel fast enough, the rocket would surrender agreement (the Treaty of Versailles). This treaty said nothing about rockets, so Captain Walter Robert Dornberger (1895–1980) was put in charge of developing a military rocket system.

The VfR closed down in 1933 after the Nazis came to power, but many of its members, including Wernher von Braun (see the box on page 1133), transferred to the military rocket program in Kummersdorf, near Berlin. The liquid-fuel rocket was set to become a devastating weapon of war.

The V-2 program

In 1938, the German rocket program relocated to Peenemünde on the coast of the Baltic Sea, where von Braun and his team developed a wide variety of rocket weapons throughout World War II (1939–1945; see the box at right). The largest of these was a rocket called the *Aggregat 4*, or A-4, which could carry a 1.1-ton (1-tonne) warhead for several hundred miles. Over the next five years, the A-4 was transformed into *Vergeltungswaffe 2* (vengeance weapon 2), or V-2—the precursor of most modern space rockets.

The V-2 made its first test flights from Peenemünde in 1943, and the first of nearly 3000 launches against British, French, and Dutch targets took place in 1944. Shortly before the new weapon started falling on their cities, the Allies obtained parts from several crashed V-2s and began to piece together its secrets.

The V-2 was a single-stage rocket, 46 ft (14 m) tall and weighing 14 tons (12.8 tonnes). Most of the rocket was made of sheet steel, with aluminum tanks for ethyl alcohol (the fuel) and liquid oxygen (the oxidizer). The rocket engines burned only for the first few seconds of flight:they cut out at an altitude of 17 miles (27 km). From there, the rocket rose to 50 miles (80 km) before falling in a ballistic curve onto a target several hundred miles away. The rocket's flight path was controlled by gyroscopes linked to graphite steering vanes that directed the exhaust, and to flaps on top of the fins. The settings of the gyroscopes were adjusted throughout the flight by a timer (see GYROSCOPE).

The Germans perfected the art of hit-and-run attacks. The V-2 could be transported by road or rail, and a number of rockets and launchers could be moved into an area and fired in just a couple of days. The support vehicles could be well away from the scene before the Allies could react. The V-2 was an impressive and terrifying weapon—traveling faster than the speed of sound, it arrived in total silence—but with its limited accuracy, the V-2 could only be used against city-sized targets. Nevertheless, von Braun continued work on larger rockets, including a two-stage weapon that could have reached the United States from German-occupied territory.

The secrets of the V-2 team were a valuable prize to whoever captured them, and von Braun realized this. In the closing weeks of the war, as Soviet troops closed in on Peenemünde, the project's chief scientists moved to Bavaria, taking parts for 100 V-2s with

ROCKETS OF WORLD WAR II

The Me 163 Komet was a German rocket-powered fighter aircraft.

The V-2 was the most famous in an arsenal of German rocket weapons during World War II. Other rocket-powered missiles included the Henschel HS 293 air-to-ground missile, which burned for 10 seconds after release from a bomber. During this time, the bombardier could steer the rocket toward its target by radio control. The impact, at 500 mph (800 km/h), was devastating, but guidance problems and vulnerability to radio jamming meant the HS 293 did not have a meaningful effect on the outcome of the war.

Another rocket missile was the X-4. Designed for use in air-to-air combat, the X-4 got around the problems of radio jamming because it stayed physically linked to the bomber aircraft by two long control wires.

Perhaps the most advanced of all the German rocket weapons, though, was the Messerschmitt Me 163 rocket-propelled fighter aircraft. Although rocket units had been used to assist aircraft during takeoff in some U.S. experiments, the Me 163 was revolutionary. After takeoff, the delta-wing aircraft jettisoned its wheels, and climbed steeply for ten minutes until its engines burned out. It then swooped down onto Allied bombers with devastating results before gliding back to the airfield, where it landed on a cart. However, like most of these early rocket weapons, the Me163 had its drawbacks: its range was limited and its toxic propellant had to be handled carefully. In addition, many pilots found it hard to engage with enemy aircraft because the rocket planes flew so much faster.

A CLOSER LOOK

them. There they awaited capture by U.S. troops. The Soviets, meanwhile, captured the V-2 factories and many junior personnel. The United States and the Soviet Union did not remain allies for long, however, and rockets were to become an important part of cold-war rivalry.

ICBMs and the space race

The United States was the first nation to demonstrate nuclear technology in war when it dropped nuclear bombs on Hiroshima and Nagasaki in Japan in 1945. The Soviet Union conducted its first nuclear test in 1949 (see NUCLEAR WEAPONS). At the time, nuclear weapons could be delivered only by bombers, but there were two other possibilities: the intercontinental ballistic missile (ICBM), a long-range rocket missile; or the cruise missile, a delivery system similar to a pilotless airplane (see MISSILE).

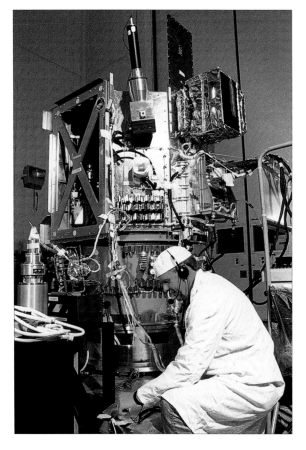

NASA's Deep Space 1 spacecraft undergoing tests before its launch in 1998. The craft is equipped with a revolutionary ion-propulsion rocket engine used for steering during spaceflight.

In the late 1940s, von Braun's team started work on huge rockets that would be capable of launching the heavy nuclear weapons of the 1950s against the Soviet Union. These rockets would also be able to reach space, and it seemed possible that the United States would be able to launch a satellite by 1951.

However, the United States switched the emphasis of its missile program in the early 1950s. With a much lighter version of the hydrogen bomb in development, they decided to concentrate on cruise missiles instead. This decision was to give the Soviets an edge in rocket development.

The Soviet rocket program was led by two men who had been founding members of the first Soviet spaceflight societies in the 1930s, Valentin Glushko and Sergey Korolyov. They had been involved in the design of the first Soviet liquid-fueled rockets, and they led the efforts to understand the V-2 and develop a rocket-powered ICBM. The resulting vehicle, the R-7, had a central core surrounded by four booster engines, each burning kerosene and liquid oxygen. The R-7 also used a new control system: instead of steering vanes, a series of small rockets were spaced around it whose direction could be adjusted remotely to alter the missile's course.

In 1954, the U.S. Air Force, concerned by the threat of Soviet superiority in ICBMs, decided to their own ICBM development program extremely high priority. At the same time, both the United States and the Soviet Union announced they would be launching satellites for International Geophysical Year 1958. U.S. interest in the exploitation of space was increasing, having been rekindled by a proposal for a lightweight scientific satellite called MOUSE

(Minimum Orbital Unmanned Satellite of Earth). Wernher von Braun was convinced that a MOUSE-type satellite could be launched with the Redstone ICBM he had been developing for the U.S. Army, but it was decided to back a U.S. Navy scientific project called Vanguard instead, since it was felt that the Vanguard lacked the military overtones of an ICBM.

While the U.S. scientists raced to build their rocket in the glare of publicity, the Soviet promise to launch a satellite had been all but forgotten. Then, on October 4, 1957, the Soviet Union announced the launch of a 184-lb (84-kg) satellite called *Sputnik*, which used an adapted R-7 ICBM as a launch vehicle (see LAUNCH VEHICLE; SATELLITE). Americans were shocked and felt threatened to have been overtaken in the space race, but the U.S. team were surprised by the weight of the Soviet satellite—their own Explorer satellite weighed only 31 lb (14 kg). Shock turned to humiliation when the first Vanguard rocket crashed on launch in December 1957. Von Braun was immediately authorized to restart his Redstone-based Project Orbiter, which finally launched *Explorer 1* on January 31, 1958.

New types of rockets

From these early beginnings, the space race grew to dominate the 1960s, both politically and technologically. Nearly all the rockets used by the U.S. and Soviet (later Russian) space programs to this day are modifications of ICBM designs from the 1960s. Notable exceptions are the giant Saturn V rocket that took U.S. astronauts to the Moon, and the Soviet Energiya. These pioneered the use of the highly efficient mixture of liquid hydrogen and liquid oxygen, which was first suggested by Tsiolkovsky in 1903. The space shuttle main engines also use this mixture.

Although rocket technology is still dominated today by liquid-fuel rockets (often with solid-fuel boosters), various other types of rockets are possible. A nuclear rocket called NERVA was developed and tested by NASA in the 1960s. It consisted of a nuclear reactor that was used to heat a propellant fluid (liquid hydrogen) so that it boiled, evaporated, and expanded through the rocket exhaust. Since the late 1990s, ion engines, which work by expelling an electrically charged gas, have been used for steering satellites and to propel the experimental NASA Deep Space 1 probe. None of these alternatives is suitable for generating the enormous thrust needed to reach orbit, but new adaptations of conventional rocket technology may lower the cost of access into space in the next few decades.

G. SPARROW

See also: SPACE FLIGHT; SPACE PROBES; SPACE STATION; SPACE TRAVEL AND TECHNOLOGY.

Further reading:

Baker, D. *Spaceflight and Rocketry: A Chronology.* New York: Facts on File, 1996.
Breuer, W. *Race to the Moon: America's Duel with the Soviets.* Westport, Connecticut: Praeger, 1993.

ROTATIONAL MOTION

The principles of rotational motion govern all rotating objects, from tiny toy motors to huge galaxies in space

The forces generated by rotational motion and gravity hold people in their seats on this amusement park ride.

Rotational motion is important in many fields of science and technology. Planets revolve on their axes and orbit around the Sun. The invention of the wheel was one of the most important developments in human civilization. Most of the engines, motors, generators, and turbines that are used to provide us with mechanical energy use rotational motion. All of these rotating bodies move in accordance with the same basic principles (see ENGINE; GAS TURBINE; INTERNAL COMBUSTION ENGINE; TURBINE).

Angular velocity and acceleration

Linear motion is motion in a straight line. One familiar example is a car traveling along a street. If the front left fender travels three blocks north, the front right fender must also travel the same three blocks

north, and consequently the entire car moves as a single unit. The velocity of the car is a measure of its speed in a particular direction. Quantities such as velocity that are described by both an amount, or magnitude (such as miles per hour), and a direction (such as north) are called vectors. Often vectors are drawn as arrows pointing in the appropriate direction. Quantities such as speed, which have magnitude but no direction, are called scalars.

The linear velocity—motion in a straight line—is the same for all parts of the car's body. However, if we look at one of the rotating wheels of the car, we find that the different parts of the wheel do not have the same velocity. If a wheel is rotating about a fixed axis, points near the center will move much less than points on the rim. Both points will have rotated the full 360 degrees that make up a complete circle for each revolution. If one point on the wheel rotates forward one revolution per second, all the points on the wheel will have exactly the same angular velocity. In the same way that a change in linear velocity per unit time is called linear acceleration, a change in the angular velocity per unit time of a rotating object is called the angular acceleration.

By convention, the vector for angular velocity is drawn as an arrow that points along the axis of rotation. The correct direction of the arrow can be figured out using the right-hand rule: imagine a right hand with the fingers curled around a pen and the pad of the thumb resting on the pen (the pen represents the axis of rotation). By moving the hand

CORE FACTS

- Many terms used to explain the motion of a rotating object, such as *angular velocity* and *moment of inertia*, are analogous to terms that explain motion in a straight line, such as *linear velocity* and *mass*.
- All points on a rigid rotating object have the same angular velocity.
- Centrifugal force, the apparent force that a person feels when cornering sharply in a car, is a result of an object's tendency to continue moving in a straight line.
- The way in which mass is distributed in an object is important in determining the way it rotates.

CONNECTIONS

- **SPACE STATIONS** of the future may use rotational motion to create the sensation of gravity for the crew inside.

- Rotational motion can be converted by **MECHANICAL TRANSMISSION** systems into linear motion, and vice versa.

THE FORCE OF CIRCULAR MOVEMENT

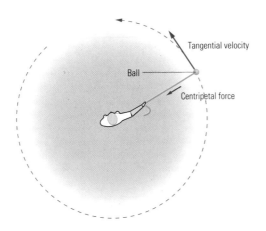

The person exerts a centripetal force on the rock by pulling on the string, forcing the object to move in a circular path.

CENTRIPETAL ACCELERATION

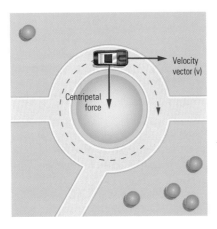

A car moving with constant speed along the circular path undergoes a centripetal acceleration because the direction of its velocity vector (v) changes as it moves.

around so that the fingers curl round from knuckle to nail in the direction of spin, the thumb then points in the direction of the angular momentum vector.

Unlike the angular velocity, the linear or tangential speeds of the various points on the wheel are not all the same. The tangential velocity relative to the axis is equal to the angular velocity multiplied by the radius (or distance from the axis) at the tangent point. Although the angular velocity is constant throughout the wheel, the speed is at a maximum at the edge of the wheel and zero at the wheel's axle.

Centripetal force

Imagine a person tying a string onto a ball and swinging the ball in a circle. If a snapshot of the ball is taken at any time, an arrow that corresponds to the exact magnitude and direction of the velocity vector can be drawn on the photograph. This vector is a straight line in the direction that the ball is moving at that particular instant: at a tangent to the circle.

If the person swinging the ball lets go of the string, the ball will not keep going around in circles. Newton's first law of motion tells us that objects moving in a straight line will continue to do so unless an external force acts on them (see MECHANICS). While the person is holding the string, the string's inward pull constrains the motion of the ball and forces it to move in a circle rather than a straight line (see the diagram at left). This is an example of a centripetal (inward) force, which is supplied by the string. The apparent outward (centrifugal) force, which most people have experienced when turning a sharp corner in a car, is a consequence of mass tending to proceed in a straight line. This behavior is real enough: it is exploited in equipment such as the centrifuge (see CENTRIFUGE). Rotational motion requires imposing a centripetal force on a mass—the mass must be pulled toward the rotational axis.

Kinetic energy of rotating bodies

Kinetic energy is the energy of motion. An object that is standing still has no kinetic energy. If movement occurs in a straight line, its kinetic energy (K.E.) is half its mass (*m*) multiplied by the square of its velocity (*v*):

$$K.E. = \tfrac{1}{2}mv^2$$

A rotating object also has kinetic energy. In this case, the kinetic energy is half the angular velocity squared, multiplied by a quantity called the moment of inertia (*I*). This can be shown by the following equation, where ω is the angular velocity:

$$K.E. = \tfrac{1}{2}I\omega^2$$

The moment of inertia is the equivalent of mass for determining the motion of a rotating body. Such a quantity is necessary because the mass is not concentrated at a single point, and each point is not moving in the same direction at any given time. The moment of inertia expresses the way the mass of the rotating object, distributed along its radius, opposes angular acceleration.

Objects of different shapes have different moments of inertia. For a uniform disk rotating on its axis, the moment of inertia is one half the mass multiplied by the square of the radius (*r*):

$$I = \tfrac{1}{2}\,mr^2$$

A flywheel, which has almost all its mass near its edge, has a greater moment of inertia than a uniform disk and stores more kinetic energy for a given mass and angular velocity (see the box on page 1139).

Conservation of angular momentum

The angular momentum of a rotating object is the product of its angular velocity and its moment of inertia. Angular momentum is a conserved quantity. This means that unless some torque is applied to the object, its angular momentum will remain the same.

The conservation of angular momentum can be demonstrated by a figure skater doing a spin on the ice. With arms outstretched, the skater spins slowly. However, when the skater's arms move in toward his or her body, the spin becomes faster. This is because more of the skater's mass is at a smaller radius from the axis of rotation, and so the skater's moment of inertia becomes a lot smaller. The angular velocity must therefore increase to maintain a constant angular momentum, so the skater spins faster without the application of any external torque.

Angular momentum only changes when a torque is applied to a rotating object. A gyroscope is a device that spins like a top (see GYROSCOPE). It is often used in determining the orientation of spacecraft in the absence of gravity: provided that no external torques are applied to a gyroscope, it will remain pointing in the same direction in space.

Orbits in space

Not all rotational motion is circular. In fact, the motion of planets as they revolve around the Sun is elliptical. An ellipse is an oval shape: it does not have a constant diameter or a single center like a circle. Instead it has two foci. An object moving in an ellipse is at distances from each focus that always add up to the same amount. A circle is a special type of ellipse, in which the two foci are in the same place.

There is relationship between the period of an orbit (the duration of one round trip) and the distance from the central object: the square of the period is proportional to the cube of the mean distance of the satellite from the central object (see SATELLITE). Earth-orbiting satellites are sometimes placed at the specific altitude where their period lasts one day, matching the rotation of Earth. These orbits, at 22,000 miles (35,000 km) above Earth's surface, are described as geostationary—any satellite at that altitude will remain positioned above a fixed area on Earth. Most telecommunications satellites occupy geostationary orbits to simplify contact with their users on Earth (see GROUND STATION).

Other cases of rotational motion

An understanding of rotational motion is essential to engineers in a variety of fields. Automobiles and railroad track and rolling stock must all be designed to provide a safe and comfortable ride during turns. Centrifuges are used to separate water from clothes, juice from pulp, and radioactive waste from water (see HAZARDOUS WASTE); the pieces of equipment used in all these processes behave according to the principles of rotational motion.

S. CALVO

See also: GEAR; HELICOPTER; PROPELLER; WHEEL.

Further reading:
Feynman, R. *The Character of Physical Law*. New York: Modern Library, 1994.
Tipler, P. *Physics for Scientists and Engineers*. New York: Worth Publishers, 1991.

HOW A SATELLITE STAYS IN ORBIT

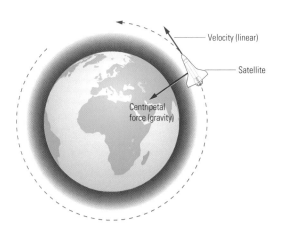

Velocity (linear)

Satellite

Centripetal force (gravity)

A satellite moving in a circular path with a constant speed around Earth is held in orbit by the gravitational force acting between the satellite and Earth.

FLYWHEELS

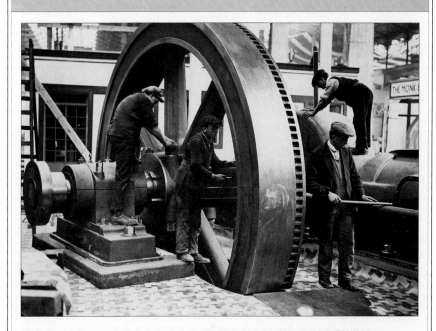

This 23-ton (20.8-tonne) flywheel was displayed at the 1924 British Exhibition.

Flywheels are heavy cylinders with large moments of inertia that can be used to store enormous amounts of kinetic energy as they spin. In their early uses, flywheels would typically be connected to rotating shafts driven by steam engines (see STEAM ENGINE). A steam engine only generates mechanical power while steam is expanding against a piston—this is when the flywheel starts to turn faster. The flywheel then continues to spin and some of its energy is used to push the piston back into the cylinder for the next cycle. Through doing this, the flywheel slows only slightly and the speed of rotation of the shaft can be kept almost constant.

Flywheels also help internal combustion engines to keep running smoothly. Furthermore, when a load is applied to an engine-and-flywheel combination, the flywheel prevents the system from stalling until the engine's power has increased to match the load. Used in combination with gears and clutches, flywheels can absorb the energy of a vehicle as it brakes and then return the energy through a lower gear for acceleration, thereby improving fuel economy.

A CLOSER LOOK

RUBBER

Natural and synthetic rubbers are tough, elastic materials that have a variety of industrial and domestic uses

Raw rubber is stored at a wholesaler's in Thailand.

CONNECTIONS

● The main use of rubber is in the manufacture of tires for **AUTOMOBILES** and other vehicles.

● An early use of rubber was in waterproof **CLOTHING MANUFACTURE**.

Natural rubber first arrived in Europe in 1736, when it was sent to France by French naturalist and mathematician Charles-Marie de La Condamine (1701–1774) by his expedition party in South America. By 1823, British chemist and inventor Charles Macintosh (1766–1843) had patented a method for making waterproof material by binding sheets of fabric together with rubber latex. The waterproof coats made from this material became known as macintoshes, or macs. Then, in 1888, Scottish manufacturer John Boyd Dunlop (1840–1921) patented an pneumatic (inflatable) tire made of rubber. With the development of the automobile industry from the late 19th century, demand for rubber soared. In 1872, British explorer Sir Henry Wickham (1846–1928) smuggled *Hevea brasiliensis* seeds from Brazil and used them to establish new plantations in Southeast Asia. Today, Malaysia is the world's largest natural rubber producer, contributing 1.5 million tons (1.3 million tonnes) to a total global output of 4.9 million tons (4.4 million tonnes) each year.

Natural rubber is composed of repeating isoprene units (2-methyl-1,3-butadiene, $CH_2=C(CH_3)-CH=CH_2$). However, attempts to make a synthetic polymer from isoprene failed, and research concentrated on producing alternative synthetic polymers based on butadiene ($CH_2=CH-CH=CH_2$), which is a product of oil refining (see OIL REFINING). One of the first synthetic rubbers to be developed, in 1931, was neoprene: a polymer of 2-chloro-1,3-butadiene ($CH_2=CCl-CH=CH_2$). Neoprene is a good all-around replacement for natural rubber and has better resistance to solvents than natural rubber. Other synthetic rubbers include Buna, which is made by polymerizing butadiene in the presence of a sodium (Na) catalyst; Buna–N, which is a copolymer of butadiene with acrylonitrile ($CH_2=CH-CN$); and styrene-butadiene rubber (SBR), which is used in large quantities because it is relatively cheap.

Natural rubber and its synthetic counterparts belong to a class of materials called elastomers. These substances are elastic: they can be stretched or deformed under stress and quickly recover their original shape when the stress is released. One of the main uses of rubber is in the manufacture of tires for cars and other vehicles.

The history of rubber

Natural rubber is derived from latex, a milky fluid that exudes from cuts in the bark of *Hevea brasiliensis*, a tree native to Brazil. While this is not the only plant that makes latex, it is by far the most important economically. The potential of rubber for waterproofing clothes was first discovered by the civilizations of South and Central America and noted by Italian navigator and explorer Christopher Columbus (1451–1506) on his voyage in 1498.

The properties of rubber

Synthetic and natural rubbers consist of long-chain molecules that are joined together at intervals along their lengths by chemical bonds known as cross-links. In the unstretched state, the molecules are a loosely tangled mass. When rubber is stretched, the

> ### CORE FACTS
>
> ■ Rubber is reversibly elastic: it returns to its original size and shape after stretching.
> ■ Natural rubber is produced from the sap of *Hevea brasiliensis*, a tree native to Brazil.
> ■ Natural rubber and synthetic rubber are examples of highly elastic materials known as elastomers.

molecules straighten out and line up together. The material extends, but as soon as the stretching force is removed, the cross-links pull the molecules back into their original form. The material therefore resumes its original shape. Rubber can be stretched reversibly to over six times its original length.

If rubber is overstretched, it undergoes a permanent extension known as creep, which is a result of the rupture of cross-links and the polymer chains' slipping over one another. Natural rubber tends to be soft and sticky at high temperatures and hard and brittle at low temperatures. These drawbacks limit the usefulness of rubber. The addition of sulfur followed by heating under pressure creates additional cross-links that strengthen the material and prevents creep. U.S. inventor Charles Goodyear (1800–1860) discovered the process, which he called vulcanization, in 1839 (see the box at right). If too much sulfur is used, too many cross-links form, reducing the elasticity of the rubber.

The uses of rubber

About three-quarters of all natural rubber is used in the manufacture of tires. The heavier the load the vehicle has to support, the more natural rubber must be used in its tires. This is because natural rubber is stronger and builds up less heat during stress than synthetic rubber. Many aircraft require 100 percent natural-rubber tires to withstand the huge pressures that arise during takeoff and landing. Space shuttles and off-road land vehicles, such as large-tired earthmovers, also use all natural rubber. Large vehicles such as buses and trucks will use up to 75 percent natural rubber in their tires; the rest is SBR. Automobiles, which bear a lighter load, are made of a mixture that contains less natural rubber. Some subway trains in Canada, France, Mexico, and Japan run on wheels with rubber tires, which reduce running noise (see. TIRE).

Many other parts of a car are made of rubber, including the watertight seals around the doors and windows, radiator hoses, and floor mats. The engine is mounted on rubber to cut down vibration and noise, as are many small components hidden under the hood of the car.

As well as its major use in car tires, SBR is also found in motorcycle and bicycle tires, the soles and heels of footwear, floor tiles, and carpet backing. Neoprene is valued for its strength and weather resistance. The main uses of neoprene are in wet suits, wire and cable coatings, gloves, industrial hoses and belting, and adhesives.

Rubber is also valued for its adhesive properties: mixed with substances such as rosin—a natural resin that makes it sticky—rubber is found in fabric-backed adhesive strips for wounds, for example.

The manufacture of rubber

Latex is removed from the rubber tree by tapping; in this process, cuts are made in the bark and the liquid that oozes out is collected. Acid is then added to the liquid to make the rubber particles clump

CHARLES GOODYEAR

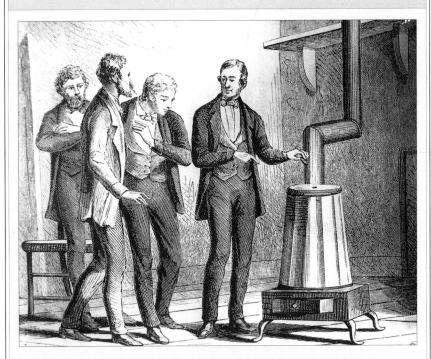

U.S. inventor Charles Goodyear demonstrates his dry-heat vulcanization process.

Inventor Charles Goodyear was born in New Haven, Connecticut, in 1800. He became interested in finding a chemical treatment to improve the properties of India rubber (as it was then known), and discovered vulcanization when he accidentally dropped a mixture of rubber and sulfur on a hot stove. Goodyear developed the vulcanization process in 1839 and patented it in 1844. He subsequently displayed articles made of vulcanized rubber to the British public in the Great Exhibition of 1851. However, most of his business dealings failed, and, even though his discovery was to make the large-scale use of rubber a practical possibility, he died in debt in 1860.

PEOPLE

together (coagulate). The coagulated particles are separated from the liquid, then they can be pressed into sheets and dried. Alternatively, castor oil is added to the mixture to form crumb rubber, which can be pressed into bales and dried. After drying, various additives may be mixed in before vulcanization. These additives include filler materials, such as carbon black, which enhance the strength and stiffness of the rubber. Objects are then shaped by pressing the rubber into molds.

S. ALDRIDGE

See also: ADHESIVE; COMPOSITE; MATERIALS SCIENCE; PLASTICS.

Further reading:
Barlow, C. *The World Rubber Industry*. New York: Routledge, 1994.
Brown, R. *Physical Testing of Rubber*. New York: Chapman & Hall, 1996.
Engineering with Rubber: How to Design Rubber Components. Edited by A. Gent. New York: Oxford University Press, 1992.

RUDDER

A rudder is a plate, usually of metal or wood, that is hinged to the rear of a boat or airplane and used for steering

The rudder of a ship at Hamburg Maritime Museum in Germany.

CONNECTIONS

● The shape and positioning of a rudder are important considerations in both **AIRCRAFT DESIGN AND CONSTRUCTION** and **BOATBUILDING AND SHIPBUILDING**.

Ever since people have used vessels to travel through the water or the air, they have needed a method of steering on the correct course. The earliest form of rudder was a simple oar that was used to force the stern of a boat sideways. Later, an oar was secured to the side of the ship and a lever was added at the upper end of its handle—this lever was called a tiller. By the 12th century, vertical rudders were attached to a post at the stern of the vessel.

Scientific principles

When a ship passes through water there is a flow of water across both surfaces of the rudder. The ship will travel in a straight line as long as the rudder is aligned along the centerline of the ship (from bow to stern) and the propulsion on either side of the ship is equal. If, for example, the rudder is turned right, the flow of water across its right-hand surface will be slowed and the water pressure will increase; at the same time, the flow across the left-hand surface becomes faster and the water pressure drops. These pressure changes are manifestations of the Bernoulli effect that generates lift when an aircraft wing moves through air (see AERODYNAMICS); the pressure difference creates a force that pushes the stern to the left while the bow swings to the right.

The rudder also deflects passing water to the right, which creates a reaction force that pushes the stern to the left (see MECHANICS). However, the rudder can stall if it is angled too steeply: the flow of water behind the rudder becomes turbulent and the turning force becomes negligible compared to the drag caused by turbulence.

Airplanes rudders function in air by the same principles. The main difference is that airplanes move in three dimensions, whereas ships move in two. Airplanes always bank (lean to one side) as they turn, and turns involve a plane's ailerons and elevators—control surfaces that modify lift on either side of the plane—as well as its rudder, which provides the basic turning force.

Rudder mechanics

A number of different arrangements are used to support the rudder and allow it to turn, with most using a fixed vertical rod supported by bearings. In some cases all the support is provided by the upper bearing on the ship's hull, and in others there is a lower bearing beneath the rudder. The turning motion is provided by the rudder stock, which is made from steel and bolted to the rudder. The upper end of the stock passes into the ship's hull through a watertight seal and is connected to the steering mechanism.

The largest ships have rudders up to 40 ft (12 m) deep. A large ship's rudder is moved by hydraulic rams supplied with oil from electric pumps and controlled from the bridge of the ship.

Aircraft controls

Conventional flight rudder control consists of rudder pedals through a system of cables or rods. In many modern aircraft, there is no direct mechanical linkage between the pilot and the control surfaces; instead, signals from the pilot's controls actuate electric motors that move the control surfaces. The term for this is *fly-by-wire*. In addition, the controls are often boosted hydraulically or pneumatically. In both fly-by-wire and boosted controls, the feel of the control action, fed back to the pilot, is simulated.

R. BROWNLIE

See also: AIRCRAFT DESIGN AND CONSTRUCTION; FLIGHT, PRINCIPLES OF; SAILING; SHIP AND BOAT.

Further reading:

Mott, L. *The Development of the Rudder: a Technological Tale*. London: Chatham, 1996.

SAFETY SYSTEMS

Safety systems are measures designed to protect people from hazards at work, at home, or while traveling

In many ways, technology has made the world a more dangerous place. For centuries, accidents were regarded as hazards of everyday life or, in some places, as retribution for committing acts that displeased the gods. With the dawn of the Industrial Revolution in the late 18th century, it became clear that power-driven machinery and industrialized workplaces were posing new threats to human life.

In the early years of industrialization, dangers arose from the location and design of the workplace and from poor operating conditions (see the box on page 1144). Industrialized countries gradually developed legislation to ensure that safety devices and systems were installed, used, and maintained to provide reliable protection. In the United States, this involved groups such as the American Society of Safety Engineers and the world's largest safety organization, the National Safety Council.

Today, accidents cause more deaths in industrialized societies than major infectious diseases, with people under 35 still more likely to die in an accident than for any other reason.

Safety systems at work

In industries such as mining and quarrying, which have always had high accident rates because of the nature of the work, safety systems were brought in at an early stage. Risk of explosions was minimized by the introduction of safer, more predictable explosives and detonators. New routines were set up to insure that detonation could only take place when no one was close enough to be injured, either by the explosion itself or by the masses of material loosened by the shock (see MINING AND QUARRYING).

To prevent falls from elevated worksites, quarry workers were provided with safety harnesses that were flexible enough to allow them to work freely but would support them if they lost their footing. Roof falls in mines became less common as stronger, more reliable propping systems were introduced, including hydraulic pit props that were used in areas where a working face was being extended.

A fire escape provides an exit in an emergency.

Coal miners were issued with a metal token as they went down the shaft so that all workers could be accounted for in an emergency. A major hazard in early coal-mining operations was the presence of pockets of methane gas, which were easily ignited by the candles used for illumination. The Davy safety lamp, invented by British chemist Humphrey Davy (1778–1829), provided the first safe light. It had a fine wire gauze cylinder that absorbed the heat of the flame before it reached the gas. Because the appearance of the flame changed when gas was present, the Davy lamp was also the first gas detector.

Specialized clothing insulates workers from dangerous chemicals, high voltages and temperatures, or radiation (see BODY PROTECTION). Miners and quarrymen are also susceptible to long-term hazards, such as silicosis or asbestosis, which are diseases caused by breathing in dust particles. Mine workers now wear masks to filter out harmful dust particles.

CORE FACTS

- In industrialized societies, people under 35 are more likely to die in accidents than for any other reason.
- Used in coal mines, the Davy safety lamp was the first gas detector, with its changing flame alerting miners to pockets of methane gas.
- In the United States, six times as many people are injured each year in nonfatal home accidents than in nonfatal motor vehicle accidents.
- Special sensors called smart pigs can be sent down pipelines to locate corrosion or possible flaws so that repairs can be made before breakdown occurs.

CONNECTIONS

- **ACCIDENTS AND DISASTERS** could often be avoided by the provision of proper safety systems.

- The **AIR BAG** has been included in many **AUTOMOBILE** designs as a safety measure.

SAFETY LEGISLATION

Horrific accidents often provided the spur for early safety legislation on the location and design of the workplace. One such accident happened at 4:45 P.M. on Saturday, March 25, 1911, when a fire broke out in the workshops of the Triangle Shirtwaist Company on the eighth, ninth, and tenth floors of the Asch Building, in New York. The company employed 500 people, mainly young immigrant women, with the working floors so crowded that people could not move easily. Paper patterns and piles of fabric scattered between the machines fueled the fire and helped it spread.

In all, 146 people died, many because escape doors had been locked to prevent employees from stealing cloth. Elevators failed, and the building's only fire escape collapsed under the weight of people climbing to safety. Firemen's ladders failed to reach the burning floors, and people jumping from the windows broke right through lifesaving nets. Just 18 months earlier, the Triangle workers had gone on strike, demanding, among other things, unlocked safety doors and adequate fire escapes, but the management had refused to meet their demands. The victims' mass funeral created a huge public outcry, and the disaster led directly to the creation of fire regulations and laws governing improved health and safety provisions in the workplace.

HISTORY OF TECHNOLOGY

In general industry, machinery presents the greatest dangers to workers. To prevent the trapping and crushing of limbs and fingers in industrial machines, engineers designed safety guards linked to the power supply. These insure that the machine only functions when the person operating it is safely out of the way. Machine tools have safety covers that must be lowered over the workpiece in order to complete an electrical circuit and allow the machine to be switched on. Power presses can only be started by buttons that insure the operator is out of reach of the press (see ERGONOMICS; MACHINE TOOL).

In the nuclear, chemical, and oil-refining industries, computerized safety systems control whole processes that could endanger workers on a large scale (see PRODUCTION ENGINEERING AND PROCESS CONTROL). These systems sample a wide range of data and respond to changing conditions by taking corrective action where necessary. If a hazardous situation worsens, the computerized system will trigger automatic safety measures.

Safety systems in the home

In the United States, six times as many people are injured each year in nonfatal home accidents than in nonfatal motor vehicle accidents. Although people in general tend to spend more time in the home, this statistic points to a low perception of risk in the apparently nonthreatening environment of the home.

Today, many kinds of labor-saving devices are powered by electricity (see HOUSEHOLD APPLIANCES). However, electrical supply and equipment can be dangerous or faulty, and several different safety systems are required.

The fuse box is one such system, in which electricity is led through standardized fuses to supply circuits in different parts of the house or apartment. Each fuse has gapped metal contacts, bridged by a fuse wire of specified thickness. If a fault occurs, a circuit's resistance may fall sharply and the electrical current increase, heating or melting wires and components, which could then catch fire. For this reason, the fuse wire is deliberately made to be the weak link, so that if the current increases because of a fault, the fuse wire will melt, isolating the faulty circuit before any damage is done. The fuse wire must be replaced once the fault is rectified.

Circuit breakers are a convenient alternative to fuses. Basic circuit breakers interrupt the supply to a circuit if it starts to draw a current in excess of a nominal value. Ground-leakage circuit breakers provide yet greater protection by interrupting the supply if even the slightest current is detected in the ground circuit (this is a symptom of a fault). Once the fault has been rectified, the breaker can be reset by pushing a button or flicking a switch.

Early power sockets were dangerous in that the user's fingers could make contact with the current-carrying pins as the plug was inserted in or removed from the socket. Engineers modified the design of the plug to insure that power is not supplied to the pins unless the plug is fully in the socket.

House fires account for many accidents in the home, particularly at night. When people are sleeping, they are vulnerable to suffocation from smoke before the fire reaches them. Smoke detectors that react even to a lighted match are used to produce an alarm loud enough to wake the heaviest sleepers. Modern security systems against home burglary use door contacts, floor pressure pads, and infrared movement detectors to give warning of intruders.

Smoke detectors provide a lifesaving warning in case of fire. Battery-operated detectors should be tested regularly for battery life; devices wired to the power supply emit a warning signal if the supply is interrupted.

LIFEBOATS, LIFE JACKETS, AND LIFE RAFTS

Students at the Royal Naval College in Dartmouth, England, practice lifesaving techniques.

Lifeboats, life jackets, and life rafts are all safety aids designed to protect survivors of maritime disasters until they can be rescued. The traditional life jacket can keep an individual afloat indefinitely, with buoyancy provided by air-filled pockets of material. It needs no inflating, is difficult to damage, and is usually a legal requirement on passenger ships.

Less cumbersome and restrictive is the kind of inflatable buoyancy aid worn by many boating enthusiasts, which was developed from an inflatable vest called the Mae West, worn by World War II fighter pilots. Many of these vests are inflated by blowing through a tube, but others are inflated by an internal gas cylinder, activated either automatically on impact with water or by pulling a ripcord.

Longer-term survival at sea depends on adequate provision of lifeboats. Many people who drowned in the *Titanic* disaster in 1912, when the ship sank after hitting an iceberg, died because there were not enough lifeboats on the ship.

Lifeboats are often equipped with sails and inboard motors, food and water, medical supplies, and signaling equipment, but they are heavy and cumbersome to launch, particularly in rough weather. The modern life raft, when deflated, is the size of a small suitcase; it is automatically inflated by gas when it is thrown overboard. Life rafts contain emergency supplies and a radio beacon; its roof protects occupants from sun, high waves, and bad weather, thereby improving the chances of survival.

A CLOSER LOOK

Safety while traveling

The motor vehicle is now the primary cause of accidental death on a worldwide scale. Accordingly, a whole series of safety systems has been developed both to prevent auto accidents and to make them more survivable when they do occur.

Active safety (making accidents less likely) has been improved by modern suspension systems, which allow more reliable turning, and by disk brakes and antilock braking systems, which make it possible to stop in shorter distances. Halogen headlights and fog lights have made it easier to see the road ahead when visibility is poor. Road surfaces have been developed to provide better grip, and highways

with crash barriers and improved junction layouts help to reduce the number of accidents (see ROAD SYSTEMS AND TRAFFIC CONTROL).

Passive safety (making accidents more survivable) has been greatly aided by the invention of the seat belt, which holds occupants in place during an impact. The first seat belt patent was granted to U.S. inventor E. J. Claghorn, in 1885, and was first used on a U.S. Army airplane in 1910. Seat belts were not fitted to automobiles until much later. Automobiles were made safer by structures that crumple progressively under impact, leaving the passenger compartment intact, and by the use of safety glass, better door locks, and collapsible steering columns.

All new automobiles are fitted with rear safety belts for passenger safety. When properly installed, this booster seat can reduce the risk of a child being thrown around the passenger compartment in the event of an accident.

The railroad remains one of the safest ways to travel, thanks to centralized traffic control, effective signaling, and powerful braking systems (see RAIL-ROAD OPERATION AND SIGNALING). Locomotives increasingly use a control handle, called a dead man's handle, that regulates speed and upon which the driver must maintain constant pressure in order to operate the train. Any relaxation of pressure, caused by the driver collapsing, for example, turns off the power and brings the train to a halt. Railroad cars in the United States now have conductor-operated central locking that prevents passengers from opening doors until the train has stopped in the station.

Airplanes are generally so safe that the most dangerous part of air travel is usually the drive to and from the airport. However, the heights and speeds at which airplanes operate make efficient safety systems essential, and much aviation technology is devoted to giving the pilot a greater degree of control over how the aircraft behaves and to providing early warning of potential faults. The principal advance in safety systems beyond individual aircraft has been the development of air traffic control, whereby airplane positions are monitored on radar. This enables planes to be guided through crowded airspace and helped to a safe landing in inclement weather. Military pilots who abandon their aircraft because of accident or combat damage can rely on the combination of ejection seat and parachute to return them safely to the ground, at all speeds and from all altitudes (see EJECTION SEAT; PARACHUTE).

Maritime safety systems began with the Plimsoll line, which was a line painted on the side of cargo ships that acted as a safeguard against overloading. More recently, the division of ships into watertight compartments has helped keep them afloat even when badly damaged, and collision danger has been almost eliminated through the use of radar and sonar (see RADAR). Better communications technology has allowed vessels in difficulty to transmit the international mayday signal (from *m'aidez*, French for "help me") in order to bring lifeboats or helicopters to the scene. The law has also helped maritime safety in the form of legal requirements for the carrying of lifeboats, life rafts, and life jackets (see the box on page 1145). Ashore, safety has been improved by the spread of containerization, which has eliminated the danger of cargo falls and of crush injuries for dockers unloading the goods (see MECHANICAL HANDLING).

Pipelines are one of the safest methods of transporting fluids (see PIPELINE). Reliable information on the location of underground pipelines increasingly prevents accidental damage by excavation or construction gangs. Corrosion-inhibiting chemicals, such as hydrazine and sodium sulfite, are used to reduce corrosion in water pipes by removing dissolved oxygen. Computers are used to warn of leakages by reacting to abnormal increases in flow rates. Smart pigs (rubber spheres fitted with sensors) can be sent through a pipe to detect sites of corrosion and flaws, allowing preventative repairs to be done.

D. OWEN

SAFETY AND SOCIETY

Sometimes human nature prevents safety systems from being effective in reducing accidents. When seat belts were made compulsory on automobiles in the 1960s, many drivers refused to wear them. Engineers fitted warning lights and dashboard reminders to try to persuade people to buckle their belts, and many countries eventually introduced legislation to make it mandatory to wear seat belts while driving. However, so many drivers and passengers ignored the law in the United States that automobile manufacturers developed the air bag as a passive safety restraint that operates automatically in an accident (see AIR BAG).

Unfortunately, air bags have drawbacks and are not intended to replace seat belts. Owners have no way of testing whether they still work correctly after years of inactivity. It has also been known for passengers to suffer injuries on deployment of the air bag, including a number of cases of tinnitus (ringing in the ears). These injuries, however, are generally much less severe than those people may have suffered without the air bag.

In some cases, safety systems work against safety. Evidence shows that more effective automobile braking systems lead to drivers braking later in emergencies, and that vehicles that handle better tempt drivers to take corners more quickly. The number of accidents has therefore not dropped as rapidly as expected. In some industries, it has been found that machinery safety guards that can cut output have been tampered with so that the machines run without them. This often occurs when workers are paid for the number of parts they produce.

A CLOSER LOOK

See also: FIREFIGHTING AND FIRE PROTECTION; HYDRAULICS AND PNEUMATICS.

Further reading:

Bryant, P. *A Review of the Potential for Vehicle On-board Diagnostic Safety Systems*. Warrendale, Pennsylvania: Society of Automotive Engineers, 1992.
Cox, S. and Cox, T. *Safety, Systems and People*. Boston: Butterworth-Heinemann, 1996.

SAILING

Sailing is traveling on water, using vertical sails to harness the wind as an energy source to propel the vehicle forward

These sailboats use large triangular sails called spinnakers to power them across the water during a race in the Caribbean.

Tens of thousands of years ago, when people first attempted water travel on logs and rafts made from bundles of reeds or branches, sailing was possible only where water currents or simple paddles allowed. However, it soon became obvious that the wind, which often forced the craft to drift in the wrong direction, could be harnessed to the sailor's advantage—a fact illustrated in Egyptian vase paintings and clay models dating from between 7000 and 11,000 years ago. Certainly by 3000 B.C.E., controlled drifting (downwind sailing) using large, square-shaped sails was a firmly established seagoing technique for the transport of people and goods. From the details of reliefs depicting these ancient vessels, we can deduce that the sails were hung from a horizontal length of wood called a spar, which could be set at different angles to the wind by means of ropes attached to one end.

Working with the wind

Depending on the direction of the wind relative to the intended direction of travel, sailboats can harness the wind in three different ways to drive themselves forward: by running, reaching, or beating.

Running. A sailboat is running when it is sailing in the direction of the wind. The amount of drive depends on the strength of the wind and the cross-sectional area of sail presented to the wind. Early sailboats were only capable of sailing with the wind direction or at a slight angle to it.

Reaching. A sailboat is reaching when it sails at around 90 degrees to the wind direction. The sails are angled so that they deflect air backward over the boat (see the diagram on page 1148). The momentum of the backward-deflected air creates a reaction force on the sail that acts forward and sideward in the direction of the wind. The forward component of this force drives the boat forward and the sideward component must be counteracted to prevent the boat from drifting to the side or overbalancing. Modern yachts use a retractable centerboard—a vertical fin that projects into the water from the bottom of the hull—to counteract the sideward force.

Reaching was particularly important for mariners who wanted to make ocean crossings: since large-scale air-circulation patterns over oceans are

CORE FACTS

- Sailing has been practiced by humans for around 11,000 years, and early sailing vessels were depicted in Egyptian vase paintings and clay models.
- There are three main points to sailing: running is sailing downwind, with the wind pushing the sails forward; reaching is sailing across the wind at a 90-degree angle; beating is sailing into the wind.
- When a boat is reaching or beating, there are two forces acting on the hull and the sails: the drag force and the side force.
- Running, or downwind sailing, is the easiest but most dangerous form of sailing.

CONNECTIONS

● The early history of **BOATBUILDING AND SHIPBUILDING** centered on the campaign to harness **WIND POWER** for traveling on water. Today, sailboats are mainly used for recreational purposes.

relatively stable, the wind directions at the ocean surface tend to be fairly constant. This makes large sections of oceans inaccessible by downwind sailing alone. Before boats were designed to be able to reach, sailors would have to dismount the sails to reduce wind resistance and then row with a side wind or, worse, into a head wind.

Beating. A sailboat is beating when it sails at around 45 degrees into the wind, that is, when the wind strikes its bow (front end) at an angle of around 45 degrees to the centerline from the front to the back (stern) of the boat. When a sailboat is beating, it uses the wind to pull it forward rather than to push it, as it does when running or reaching. This is done by letting the sail act as an airfoil, or as if an aircraft wing were mounted vertically on the sailboat (see FLIGHT, PRINCIPLES OF). The sail is angled almost parallel to the direction of the wind but with its trailing edge slightly forward. The fabric of the sail is tensioned so that it can form a slight curve, called a camber, from front to back. Because of the angle of the sail, the airflow over the front surface of the sail is slightly faster than the airflow over the rear. As described by Bernoulli's equation (see AERODYNAMICS), the difference in airflow speeds results in the pressure in front of the sail being lower than that behind the sail. This pressure difference holds the camber in shape and sucks the sailboat forward.

In principle, only a direct head wind (at zero degrees to the centerline of the ship) would be incapable of providing any forward pull for a beating ship. In practice, however, at shallow angles a sail tends to flap rather than form a stable airfoil, and all forward pull is lost. For this reason, when heading directly into the wind (or at a shallow angle toward it), sailors perform a maneuver called tacking: they sail at 45 degrees to the wind in one direction, after a distance they turn the boat using its rudder until it points at 45 degrees to the wind in the other direction, then they adjust the sails and sail for the same distance in the new direction (see the diagram below). In this manner, the overall heading is into the wind, but the sailboat travels at an effective beating angle almost all the time. There is no drive while the sailboat turns (a maneuver called "coming about") and the sailboat's momentum at the start of the maneuver must be sufficient to complete the turn without stopping.

Designing a sailboat

A good sailboat needs sails that catch the wind effectively under a wide range of conditions. It also needs to have a hull profile that generates the least possible resistance to forward motion, or drag, while providing the maximum possible resistance to sideward motion and the tilting forces caused by side winds during reaching and beating maneuvers.

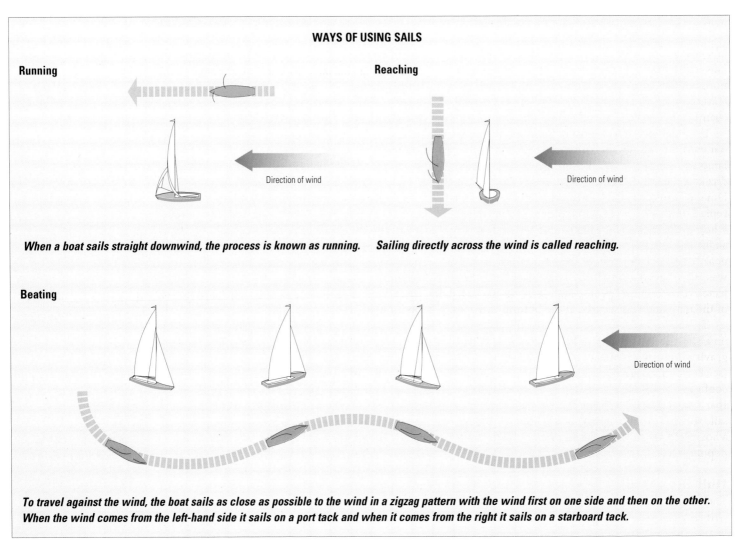

WAYS OF USING SAILS

Running

Reaching

Direction of wind

Direction of wind

When a boat sails straight downwind, the process is known as running.   *Sailing directly across the wind is called reaching.*

Beating

Direction of wind

To travel against the wind, the boat sails as close as possible to the wind in a zigzag pattern with the wind first on one side and then on the other. When the wind comes from the left-hand side it sails on a port tack and when it comes from the right it sails on a starboard tack.

Sail designs

The successful sailing vessels of the past can now be assessed in terms of their performance, particularly when reaching and beating. The ability to hold a correct position against the wind with the early square sail was probably first demonstrated by the success of the phenomenal North Atlantic voyages of the seventh to tenth century Norse longships.

Norse longships, which ranged from 70 to 270 ft (21 to 82 m) in length, had hull profiles that generated very little drag—even by modern standards. Their square sails were rigged (held in place) using cordage (ropes used to keep the sails' stiffened edges, or luffs, taut) and horizontal spars (stout beams from which the sails were suspended). The spars were suspended from a vertical mast. This rigging arrangement ensured that the longships' sails remained in shape even at low wind angles.

Square sails can also be kept in shape at low wind angles by the incorporation of stiff horizontal battens of bamboo, as were used in the early Chinese junk boats. These boats also had low-drag hull profiles and used central rudders centuries before European vessels.

Oceangoing Polynesian sailing canoes of the fifth century used a different type of sail: the lateen sail. Lateen sails, which are triangular, are hung from diagonal spars that hold the leading edge of the sail taut. The sail is held in place by a rope that is attached to the point of the sail opposite the edge that is secured to the spar. This rope is secured at deck level in a position appropriate for the wind angle. Lateen sails were also particularly common in the Southern Europe from the ninth to 13th centuries; they were a feature of the boats used for exploration and merchanting by the Venetians and the Portuguese,

In the 17th century, a modification of the lateen sail was used for Scandinavian *jachts* (yachts) and the famous Massachusetts schooners, which became the direct forerunners of the modern ocean racer. During this development, the lateen sail was replaced by two more manageable sails: the foresail, whose leading edge was kept taut by a forestay—an angled shaft that is fixed between the bow and a point near the top of the mast—and the main sail, which was suspended from a spar, or yardarm, that projected toward the aft (rear) of the vessel from the top of the mast and was secured at the bottom by ropes.

The disadvantage of having a spar mounted high on a ships mast is that it shifts the vessel's center of gravity upward and makes it more likely to capsize (see BOATBUILDING AND SHIPBUILDING). Eventually, the configuration of a rectangular sail suspended from a spar was replaced by an approximately triangular sail, secured at the top of the mast, and held taut by a horizontal boom (shaft) at its base. This is the most popular modern configuration—the Bermuda rig.

Hull designs

The design of a ship's hull determines how much it will resist forward and sideward motion. Basic sailboat designs include a keel—a heavy ridge of wood

Hong Kong harbor is host to numerous sailboats, such as this junk boat.

or metal that runs along the center of a vessel's underside from bow to stern. The weight of the keel helps to keep the vessel upright and maximizes the side profile of the hull, which reduces the vessel's

MODERN SAILING DESIGNS

Developments of sailing vessels in this century are based on many years of experience, together with all the current scientific measuring and deductive techniques. Models of sails and rigging are tested in wind tunnels in the same way as aircraft models are tested: the major measurements taken in these tests are those of drag force, side force, and center of effort (the point where the combined effect of the sails and rigging can be said to propel the boat forward) with varying speed and angle of wind. The forces are measured on the models by devices called dynamometers and are then scaled to predict the actual forces to be exerted on a full-size rig. Similarly, models of hulls are towed to different speeds and forces are scaled to predict actual hull performance.

The many measurements required to predict a potential yacht's performance completely require the skills and instrumental resources of both aerodynamic and hydrodynamic laboratories, and they demand more actual measurements than required for an aircraft and ship together. Such a full program of measurement is rarely carried out for an end product that is essentially recreational. However, with the advent of professionally sponsored racing, research costs for the development of one yacht can be millions of dollars. More usually, yacht development arises from a mixture of limited tests, together with the experience of successful yachts and trial and error with new boats.

As with all types of technology, sailing-boat technology has always advanced as a result of improvements in construction materials. For example, sails need strong, lightweight, fairly stiff, smooth-surfaced, bacteria- and sunshine-resistant fabrics with little or no mechanical fatigue, no stretch, and which do not let the wind through them. Vast improvements in most of these properties have been made by replacing natural fibers with synthetic fibers, particularly Dacron polyester and Kevlar. Rigging needs materials of high tensile strength and density, while spars utilize materials of high intrinsic stiffness, together with high resistance to the damage of corrosion.

Hemp, iron, and galvanized steel have been replaced by stainless steel for the rigging, while anodized aluminum tubes now replace wooden spars. Hulls need corrosion-resistant materials suitable for forming into smooth, lightweight skins of great strength and shock resistance, and wood is being replaced by aluminum alloys and fiber-reinforced plastics.

A CLOSER LOOK

This large three-mast sailing ship was used for transportation in 1850.

tendency to drift sideward under the influence of side winds. Yachts and racing sailboats tend to be made with smooth, light hulls and rely for their resistance to sideward drifting and capsizing on either a retractable centerboard—a vertical fin that can be pulled up when the vessel is in shallow water—or a fixed centerboard that sometimes has an integral rudder for steering (see RUDDER).

Centerboard designs vary enormously and are a major focus of research and development for competitive racers (see the box on page 1149). Racers using radical new designs for prestigious yacht races will often keep their yachts hidden in secure locations until the day of the race as a precaution against espionage by their rivals.

Downwind sailing
Sailing downwind is the least complex aspect of sailing, but potentially the most dangerous. To maximize boat speed, the sail area must also be as large as possible for the given wind conditions. However, very strong winds and gusts can damage sails, the mast, the rigging, or all three if too large a sail area is opened.

A large triangular sail known as a spinnaker can be used for downwind sailing. When the wind is directly behind the yacht, the spinnaker is set symmetrically across the bows of the boat. If the boat turns out of the wind direction and begins reaching, the spinnaker is pulled tighter on the leeward (downwind) side of the boat. At in the same time, the foresail and main sail start to provide more of the

drive. As the boat approaches 90 degrees to the wind, it becomes more difficult to stop the spinnaker flapping. Because it no longer contributes to boat speed, it is withdrawn.

When sailing downwind, a slight change in the wind's or the boat's direction can result in the wind changing sides: in a short time, the windward (upwind) side of the boat can become the leeward (downwind) side and vice versa. This is a potentially hazardous situation, since the pivoted boom at the base of the main sail will swiftly whip from one side of the boat to the other (the boom is normally angled with its rear end slightly leeward). This occurrence is called a jibe. In a very strong wind, this can be extremely dangerous for the crew and puts an enormous strain on the rigging.

R. BROWNLIE

See also: MERCHANT SHIPS; RUDDER; SHIP AND BOAT; SHIP AND BOAT, HISTORY OF.

Further reading:
Crews, D. *Sail Away*. New York: Greenwillow Books, 1995.
Day, G. *Safety at Sea: A Sailor's Complete Guide to Safe Seamanship*. New York: Putnam, 1991.
Driscoll, J. *Learn to Sail in a Weekend*. New York: Alfred A. Knopf, 1991.
Falconer, J. *Sail and Steam: A Century of Maritime Enterprise*. Boston: David R. Godine, 1993.
Harding, R. *The Evolution of the Sailing Navy, 1509–1815*. New York: St. Martin's Press, 1995.

INDEX

Page numbers in **boldface** type refer to main articles and their illustrations. Page numbers in *italic* type refer to additional illustrations or their captions.